WHAT DOES A JEW WANT?

Insurrections: Critical Studies in Religion, Politics, and Culture

INSURRECTIONS: CRITICAL STUDIES IN RELIGION, POLITICS, AND CULTURE

Slavoj Žižek, Clayton Crockett, Creston Davis, Jeffrey W. Robbins, editors

The intersection of religion, politics, and culture is one of the most discussed areas in theory today. It also has the deepest and most wide-ranging impact on the world. Insurrections: Critical Studies in Religion, Politics, and Culture will bring the tools of philosophy and critical theory to the political implications of the religious turn. The series will address a range of religious traditions and political viewpoints in the United States, Europe, and other parts of the world. Without advocating any specific religious or theological stance, the series aims nonetheless to be faithful to the radical emancipatory potential of religion.

WHAT DOES A JEW WANT?

On Binationalism and Other Specters

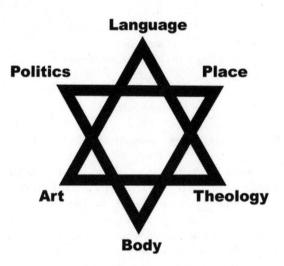

UDI ALONI

CONVERSATIONS AND COMMENTS BY
ALAIN BADIOU, JUDITH BUTLER,
AND SLAVOJ ŽIŽEK

Columbia University Press   New York

Columbia University Press
Publishers Since 1893
New York Chichester, West Sussex

Copyright © 2011 Columbia University Press
All rights reserved

Library of Congress Cataloging-in-Publication Data
Aloni, Udi.
What does a Jew Want? : on binationalism and other specters /
Udi Aloni; edited by Slavoj Žižek ; conversations and comments by
Alain Badiou, Judith Butler, and Slavoj Žižek
p. cm.
Includes bibliographical references.
ISBN 978-0-231-15758-2 (cloth: alk. paper) —
ISBN 978-0-231-15759-9 (pbk.: alk. paper) —
ISBN 978-0-231-52737-8 (e-book)
1. Aloni, Udi. 2. Arab-Israeli conflict—Influence. 3. Israel—Politics and government—21st
century—Philosophy. 4. Motion pictures—Political aspects—Israel. 5. Jews—Identity.
6. Jewish philosophy. I. Žižek , Slavoj. II. Badiou, Alain. III. Butler, Judith, 1956– IV. Title.

DS126.5.A694   2011
956.9405'4—dc22   2010045022

∞

Casebound editions of Columbia University Press books
are printed on permanent and durable acid-free paper.
Printed in the United States of America

c 10 9 8 7 6 5 4 3 2 1
p 10 9 8 7 6 5 4 3 2 1

Don Quixote

TO MY MOTHER, *Shulamit Aloni*

In the bedroom a drawing of Don Quixote.
In the living room a ceramic Don Quixote.
In the yard a sculpture of Don Quixote.
It seems to me you've placed them as an emblem
to remind you of the absurd, or pathetic, aspect of the
    struggle.
In your greatest battles the small demon of doubt was always
    there.
You've acted with the passion of the Man of La Mancha, and
    the doubt
and self-irony of Cervantes. I think it shaped your unique
    voice,
a radical voice
Devoid of self-importance,
fighting for what's right without
self-righteousness.

The questions Freud therefore leaves us with are: can so utterly indeci-sive and so deeply undetermined a history ever be written? In what lan-guage, and with what sort of vocabulary? Can it aspire to the conditions of a politics of diaspora life? Can it ever become the not-so-precarious foundation in the land of Jews and Palestinians of a bi-national state in which Israel and Palestine are parts, rather than antagonists, of each other's history and underlying reality? I myself believe so.

—Edward Said, *Freud and the Non-European*

It is well-known that the Jews were forbidden to look into the future. The Torah and the prayers instructed them, by contrast, in remembrance. This disenchanted those who fell prey to the future, who sought advice from the soothsayers. For that reason the future did not, however, turn into a homogenous and empty time for the Jews. For in it every second was the narrow gate, through which the Messiah could enter.

—Walter Benjamin, "On the Concept of History"

This book is an attempt to think, to act, and to create through these two reflections.

Tel Aviv, 2010

CONTENTS

EPILOGUE

MY VERY SHORT BIBLIOGRAPHY: ONTOLOGY OF EXILE

FOREWORD

JUDITH BUTLER

Udi Aloni's collection renews a theological reflection in the midst of ordinary life, popular culture, contemporary scenes of life and death. His film, *Local Angel,* brings us into visual contact with Walter Benjamin's concept of the "ruin," that animated fragment from the past that drives us in ways that we cannot always know. He moves to the center of violent conflict between Israelis and Palestinians only to find there remnants of a theological relation to the "Temple Mount" that furtively circumscribes the struggle over land, property, ownership, and claims to time and space. In his film *Forgiveness* it is the land and the mental institution built there that acts as the ruin, foreclosing the possibility of a return to the death and displacement of Palestinians who lived in the village of Deir Yassin. The mental institution receives the Jew who emerges from the Nazi genocide as a muselmann—traumatized to the point of losing speech and self-reference. So the muselmann, the Muslim, the Christian, and the Jew are compounded at this multiple and unfathomable site of loss where, on the land where a Palestinian village was destroyed, an Israeli mental institution is built to receive the destroyed lives of Jews from the concentration camps. Madness ensues, but what alternative is there? In his meditation "Jocasta's Dream" Aloni makes clear that there are those humans who are murdered from the start, who live their murdered lives not only in spite of their apparent death but through the endless terms of that deathlike world. Suicide is not simply a tragic conclusion but merely a sign that one has ceased to be able to stop the cycle of violence and the evisceration of those sites that allow for mourning to begin. There is no single loss in this terrain of destroyed villages, destroyed lives, only a question of whether the law that mandates continuing destruction can be openly opposed, whether the sites can be reclaimed for open mourning, and whether a new generation can break the curse that animates the places in their partial memories and constitutive disavowals, whether a wide enough angle can take in the full array of loss, mourning, violence, and inadvertent hope. Since hope, too, emerges in tandem with destruction, only because loss binds us, and binding is the condition for new community.

Aloni lays bare the visual landscape of these ruins, finding theological and mythological resonance in the political and emotional dilemmas they pose. And, in the laying bare, some hope emerges for a life that is not murdered from the start, whose birth is not implicated in the curse of revenge, whose ability to acknowledge an irreparable loss makes way for another future.

EDITOR'S INTRODUCTION

SLAVOJ ŽIŽEK

A short circuit is a condition in which a short electrical path is unintentionally created, causing a power fault—and this is what Udi Aloni does in this book, causing a power fault in the ruling liberal attitude by way of short-circuiting different levels of ideology, art, and thought; rewriting the Oedipus myth and rejecting liberal Zionism. Who but Udi Aloni can combine the tremendous poetic power of creating new myths with the perspicuous mind of a cold theoretician? Who but Udi Aloni can ground his ruthless critique of Zionism into his unconditional fidelity to the Jewish tradition? If anyone needs a proof that political theology is alive and well, here it is!

This book has six vertices—the shape of the Star of David—and is Udi Aloni's take on the *Star of Redemption* by Franz Rosenzweig. Each of the six—Language, Body, Theology, Politics, Art, and Place—has its own separate part but is present in all the other parts as well.

In part 1, "Theology: 'Specters of Binationalism,'" Aloni argues that the Israeli-Palestinian conflict must be reexamined as an act of repression. The two nations quelled a geo-bio-political reality in which they were meant to live bi-nationally, from the dawn of modern time. Following the call of Edward Said, Aloni tried to create a new language that doesn't succumb to a false multiculturalism. His response to Said may exceed the agenda of most Western liberals, but his vision is painted in simple, bright colors.

Through it we realize that this whole conflict is a diversion; it is not the expression of a truth, but the truth of a repression through the violence of social reality itself.

Part 2, "Body," is an attempt to read the body of mythological figures as theological-political texts. The body of Samson is converted to the body of a young dead Israeli soldier; Jacob fights the angel and transforms into the name Israel; and Jocasta, through the slaughter of the innocent, rewrites the story of her son Oedipus.

In part 3, "Place: "Writing from Occupied Territories," Aloni describes life under a state of emergency by drawing out the comic moments—the absurd—from this brutal and violent reality. By unveiling the artificiality of the difference between "here" and "there" in segregation, he reveals the arbitrary iniquities that founded and maintain the ideology of the state.

In part 4, "Politics: Plea to Jewish Artists," Aloni takes off the gloves and exposes a new battle via the written and electronic media. He is transformed from a subtle artist into a ruthless fighter. He does not aim his slings and arrows at those who define themselves as nationalists, but at those who are among the "peace camp," the ones whose rhetoric of "human rights" and "nonviolence" exists on the side of the oppressor. Aloni's incisive writing reveals the duplicity and self-righteousness of an imperious ideology that places the speakers of this so-called liberalism as the loyal soldiers and gatekeepers of the current political system.

In part 5, "Art: Visual Midrash," Aloni puts his new binational language to use. He presents a series of intertextual tributes to Walter Benjamin, Franz Rosenzweig, Jacques Derrida, and Mahmoud Darwish. The image is familiar—but once freed by Aloni from its ideological chains it becomes a means of radical communication, a language redeemed, and an actual expression. A bond is created, connecting Aloni's unique movie *Local Angel* and the angel of history—Benjamin's Angelus Novus—looking back, incapacitated, on the ruins of Mediterranean history. An image captured in Aloni's paraphrase on Benjamin: "He cannot resist the calling of the West, whose voice, like that of the sirens, calls him backward into what we call progress. Meanwhile, the pile of debris before him grows skyward."

Part 6, "Language: Conversations and Comments," unfolds with the famous Jewish tradition of answering a question with a question. Thus, the question "what does a Jew want?" only raises more questions and doubts. Judith Butler, in conversations with Aloni, rethinks "the Jew," using far broader definitions and contexts, but with a greater obligation to ethics. "The Jew" becomes an ethical concept, affecting both the Jewish and non-Jewish alike. Alain Badiou, who visited Palestine with Aloni during the war in Gaza, apprehends Aloni's three movies as an example of the successful creation of art during our troubled times. When Aloni asks, "what does a Jew want?" I am reminded of helpless Freud who, in the early days of psychoanalysis, as he gazed upon Dora, frustrated by futile attempts to understand, cried: "What does a woman want?"

In the same spirit of the Freud-Dora exchange, my modest contribution to this section is an essay titled "The Jew Is Within You, But You, You Are in the Jew." Undoubtedly, we shouldn't believe everything we hear, but Aloni's secular theology is definitely one of the most fascinating innovations of our time. So, if you want to dwell in your blessed secular ignorance, then do not read this book—at your own risk!

ACKNOWLEDGMENTS

Special Thanks

To my daughter Yuli, whose unique view has always inspired me.

To Ofer Neiman for the support, the patience, and the love that he lavished through his translations, through help in moments of crisis, and through suggestions for physical exercise as well as for his endless support of the demonstrations in Sheikh-Jarrah and in Bil'in, where he always induces serenity and security upon those around him.

To Gal Hertz for his great help in thinking and scientific editing, in designing the theoretical structure of the book.

To Dr. Eyal Rozmarin for his invitation and encouragement to write "Samson the Non-European" and for its scientific editing. To Shlomzion Kenan for the devoted editing and for wonderful inventions in an impossible translation into English.

To Tom Yuval, who put the dyslexia in order.

To Columbia University Press and, in particular, Wendy Lochner, Christine Mortlock, and Susan Pensak who helped, labored, advised, organized, improved, and eventually transformed the vision of this book into a reality.

To Sarah Kamens, who helped me with her precision and insightfulness to transfer the spirit of the book as well as the tension between its mixed genres into the English language.

⤎

Jean-Luc Nancy once asked me, when he was preparing for a debate with Jacques Derrida, whether it is correct to claim that in Hebrew the word *beit knesset*, which means "synagogue," is in the plural form, and the word *Knesset,* which refers to the Israeli Parliament, is in the singular form. I thought that the question revolved around Derrida's attempt to describe the tension in Zionist thinking between exile as multiplicity and redemption as oneness. When presented in this form, we find ourselves facing a dichotomy in which each alternative excludes the other—either a concept of oneness, redemption, and negation of Diaspora or a multiplicity, which means Diaspora and relinquishing this fundamental striving for the one. Hence the fascinating aspect of Jewish monotheism of this type is the tension existing between oneness and multiplicity, on the one hand, and the testimony of the community, which tries to maintain this tension within the oneness itself. It is written in the book of Isaiah: "You are my witnesses, said the Lord," and the rabbi from Kutzk said: "If you cease to be my witnesses, I cease to be the Lord."

Apropos contrasting identities coexisting not in harmony but in creativity and prosperity, this is my opportunity to thank those three wonderful people who have been, and are still, guides for an entire generation. I have been honored to call all three my friends and partners on my journey. When people ask me why and how three people, who have such distinct views—Alain Badiou, Judith Butler, and Slavoj Žižek—have influenced my thought, I choose a different metaphor each time. Sometimes I utilize Lacan's four discourses: Master, University, Hysteric, Analyst (and, as any child in Paris knows, truth is revealed only in the transition from one discourse to another). Sometimes I utilize the Jewish *PaRDeS* simile, regarding the four levels of biblical interpretation (this Hebrew word is an acronym for these levels: *Pshat* = literal, *Remez* = parable, *Drasha* = search, *Sod* = mystical). Sometimes I just say that these people fulfill different roles in the psyche of contemporary philosophical discourse: drive, fidelity, and love. But the wisdom and abundance that they have given to the world and to me has no measure. For all this I am thankful to them.

WHAT DOES A JEW WANT?

PROLOGUE

THE VISIT OF THE THREE MAGI
TO THE HOLY LAND

Slavoj Žižek in Ramallah

Back to the Trauma Zone

MERAV YUDILOVITH

The Middle East premiere of Udi Aloni's film, which took place in Ramallah, was attended by theoretician Slavoj Žižek. Two hours before the event, the second Lebanon war began. In spite of some fear, it was decided that the show must go on. As Israel entered Lebanon, the hall in Ramallah was packed with viewers, intellectuals and Palestinian artists and filmmakers. Among them was also Mahmoud Darwish.

QALANDIA CHECKPOINT: WEDNESDAY MORNING

Inside the air-conditioned transit van bearing a German license plate, the blazing sun is less of a nuisance. A long line of cars is crawling slowly. Soldiers, ID cards, the bureaucratic commotion aboveground, can make one forget, for short spells of time, the tensions bubbling underneath: the kidnapped soldiers, the mass draft, shelling, and the dead people in Gaza and on the northern border. The tension between the seemingly obvious reality and the scarred zones is the ground on which filmmaker Udi Aloni's film, *Forgiveness*, takes place. The film's world premiere was held last night in Ramallah.

Ramallah; published by YNET, July 13, 2006.

"People flee from traumatic zones in an attempt to find a new life, only to find out that they are going back to the terror time and again," Aloni wrote in the film's commentary notes, which raises, among other issues, questions about the cost of holding onto life or death and about the place of reason in all this existential chaos. In the film, as in life between Tel Aviv and Ramallah, one moves back and forth between the conscious and the unconscious, between troubled regions of the psyche that threaten to devour one's sanity and the reality that requires one to take action in order to survive.

"Udi Aloni's film has accomplished Eisenstein's old dream about a film as a form of thought," says Slavoj Žižek, who is accompanying the premieres in Ramallah and in West Jerusalem, "He brings different layers together for comparison—the Holocaust and Israel's treatment of the Palestinians, hangmen and victims, the political and the private, reality and dreams—without proposing a direct solution. Aloni forces the viewer to start thinking and to look for possible solutions. The film does not elicit cold appreciation but deep emotional involvement, and the emotional state of compression in many of the scenes is almost unbearable. In spite of being a thoroughly critical piece of work, it also allows the viewer to experience the spirit of Judaism deeply."

Žižek arrived in Ramallah in the midst of a principled, continuous debate between him and the organizers of the global Campaign for an Academic and Cultural Boycott of Israel. In an open letter to Professor Žižek, the campaign organizers asked him not to participate in the Jerusalem Film Festival. "Think of the ethical implications when you consider accepting an invitation from a body which not only benefits from the Israeli establishment's support, but also constitutes a foundation stone in Israel's attempts to portray itself as a part of the civilized world, while exercising malicious colonialist oppression and racism against Palestinians," they write. "We hope you do not legitimize this oppression by participating in the festival, regardless of the significance of the film which you are about to discuss. Do not put a pretty face on an ugly reality." As an act of solidarity with his Palestinian friends, Žižek has informed the organizers of the Jerusalem Film Festival that he would return the money paid for his accommodations. He chose to participate in the discussion of the movie, but only as Aloni's guest.

"A change has to come from within," he explains, "making people listen even to things they are reluctant to hear. This is not an easy decision, but I think that the best solution is to maintain the right of Israelis to try and bring about a change in the minds of other Israelis, through art and various means, while respecting the Palestinian way of struggle."

On the way to Ramallah he says: "The screening of Udi Aloni's film in Ramallah is essential because an internal Israeli dialogue which merely makes you feel good about yourselves does no good. Liberal critique has failed, by presenting a false humanism which gives one that good feeling, but at the same time also enables one to ignore the other in a brutal manner. He regards the screening in Ramallah as a test.

This screening is not just important, it is essential. Without it, the film is a complete political forgery. Not going to Ramallah means taking a subtle form of racist action. This is a test, without which Udi would have become as fake as Oliver Stone's American films about the Vietnam War. Even if these films present a critical point of view, they always focus on the American young man's drama. This is the worst thing about Hollywood movies—even when they try to be honest—the subjective point is that eventually one always comes back to the American hero. They don't really recognize the other. *Forgiveness* goes beyond that. It stays away from the formula and eliminates the borders. Prima facie, it may be perceived as a movie embarking on a journey from the viewpoint of a young Jewish man, but it is not exactly like that. The others in Udi's film are more than a mere backdrop.

At the entrance to Ramallah, Aloni starts getting emotional. Along with cinematographer George Khleifi, playwright Salman Mansour, and Haled Hourani, representative of Artists Without Borders, distinguished Palestinian poet Mahmoud Darwish has also confirmed his participation in the event. Before the screening, Aloni says that "Darwish's poetry has had a great deal of influence on me and on my art. It is a great honor to have him here." On the stairs leading out of the cinemtheque, Darwish praised the film and said, "It is a beautiful and significant film. The key point in the film is the question regarding who has the right to make the victim forget."

From this point onward, Aloni seemed much more relaxed. "It was important for me that the friends in Ramallah, who cannot make it to Jerusalem because of the apartheid policy, watch the film. I hope that the people at the Jerusalem Film Festival realize this, open their hearts, and look around. This movie was born of grace. Law and grace are two very important elements in Jewish religion, and this too should not be forgotten. Now, of all times, when we are in a chaotic state of war, when people are losing their sanity and the guns are firing, being able to sit together in Ramallah and talk to each other through art opens the gates of hope. There is an alternative, and we need the will to follow it."

Alain Badiou in Haifa

Their Entire Particular World

The history of mankind is the instant between two strides taken by a wanderer.

—Franz Kafka, *The Blue Octavo Notebooks*

Alain Badiou landed in Tel Aviv amidst the assault on Gaza. I had been waiting for his coming to Palestine/Israel for a while. He came to support my retrospective at the cinematheque and lecture at the Palestinian Al Quds University and at the University of Nablus (An-Najah). But the war reshuffled all the cards. We couldn't go out in Tel Aviv. The roaming laughter of the city celebrating itself created a shocking dissonance with the sounds of war, broadcast live from Gaza. So we decided to quit the city and travel to the Galilee to visit the Palestinian citizens of Israel and stand shoulder to shoulder with them in vigils against the awful war. We stood with the singer Amal Morcos and held picket signs with actor Salech Bakri and other young Palestinians who wanted to tell Israelis "It is our brothers that you are killing." But Israel is absent from Israel, and no one is there to hear the outcry.

The destruction and death Israel laid on Gaza was heartbreaking and stomach turning; it was difficult to see Palestinian Israelis of the Galilee, time and again, identify the dead of Gaza as their relatives. The wall and Occupation created a complete separation between the Palestinians who live in Gaza and those who are citizens of Israel. The dead Gazans reminded those in the Galilee that once, at least before their unity was split, they had been one people. Badiou gave splendid lectures in public meetings and at the Palestinian universities. I assume these will, sooner or later, be published. But one experience we went through together in Haifa will remain with me forever.

Alain came with his son Oliver, whom he adopted with his ex-wife Cecile, a physician specializing in AIDS medicine. When Oliver's dying mother was expelled back to Africa, she pledged Cecile to take care of her infants. Cecile, apart from being a physician and a leftist activist of Jewish descent, is also a unique woman with the kind of heart that is hard to find in this world. She adopted Oliver, the younger of the sons with Badiou, and his first wife adopted the older son.

When we arrived in Haifa, Oliver was especially excited. It was hard to see in him an eighteen-year-old teenager. Against the background of Haifa, this African French-speaking young man had a uniquely exotic appearance. Suddenly he asked to see the house his mother had visited every summer when she was a girl. Her Jewish grandfather made aliyah and had resided in a charming house on top of Mt. Carmel, and she cherishes numerous memories of those wonderful summer vacations, recollections she has shared with her son Oliver.

We were able to find the house, based on address and memory, and silently stepped out of the car in a search for roots. Oliver approached the doorstep of his great-grandfather's former house and buzzed the doorbell excitedly. No one answered, yet he kept on staring at a tree in the yard as if he had known it for years. Badiou stood on the side—that universalist and rationalist philosopher, that set-theory man—looking lovingly at his grown and beautiful black son, standing in front of the house of a long-deceased little Jewish doctor. He turned to me and said, in his charming French accent, "Udi, look how excited he is, as if he was coming back home; look, look," he said, "he is wiping a tear from his eyes," so that I would not see the tears in his own eyes.

I gazed, an Israeli among Jewish refugees, at the French communist philosopher, the white-haired, tall man, looking at his African refugee son mourning the death of his mother's grandfather, the Jewish refugee who arrived in Haifa and became a beloved dentist.

That very Haifa whose Palestinian refugee stories from '48 we have come to know so well. At that moment I thought to myself that there is nothing that can more lucidly describe the nature of this universalism, which grows from the recognition and love for wandering refugees who carry with them, on their backs, their entire particular world wherever they go.

Judith Butler in Sheikh-Jarrah

"This place which is called Israel"

I went to the airport to pick Judith Butler up last Friday. She had some work to do before the start of her lectures at Birzeit University. My friend Ronnie, who gave up a very bright future in the high-tech industry for scurrying between demonstrations against the Occupation, drove us from the Ben Gurion Airport.

One little smile from Ronnie and the car changed its course—we were on our way to Sheikh-Jarrah's Friday demonstration.

After all, who if not Butler believes in performative repetition as an opening for change in the current ideological structure? And who if not Ronnie, along with the group of anarchists, performs this ceremony by going to Bil'in, Ni'lin, and Sheikh-Jarrah every Friday? A sacred ritual aimed at undermining the stability of everything that we take for granted.

Upon arrival, we were greeted by fierce Jerusalem rain. Since the court ruled that the demonstration is legal, the police have refrained from violence. I walked with Judith on the road, translating the messages on the signs held by the protesters, while everyone called out, "Come on, get back on the sidewalk!" Meanwhile, the rain got heavier. Someone from the queer anarchist community came up, got very emotional when she saw who it is: "You must be . . . hi . . . yes, yes, I heard you lecturing at the

Haaretz, February 12, 2010.

university some time ago!" Within seconds at least ten demonstrators, some of them carrying drumsticks, gathered around little Judith and covered her with love. The rain kept getting heavier, but when I tried to move the group to a roofed venue I was silenced like a nagging Jewish mother. There was something very exciting about this humble, sincere encounter between Judith Butler and her "disciples." Some of them may not have read her complex texts, but they have identified the performative proposal she has offered to the world as a means of change. It was obvious that this encounter was a heartfelt moment for Judith.

The beating of the drums got stronger and stronger . . . as did the rain. It was time to head back and go to grab something to eat. On the way, I got an anxious text message from Ofer, the charming Israeli leftist who runs *Occupation Magazine*. "What do you think Judith meant when she wrote: 'this place which is called Israel' instead of 'the State of Israel'?"

Over a glass of wine I formulated a text message to Ofer: "Dear Ofer, no one was disputing our existence. I'm not sure if that's Judith's intention, however, until everyone in our region has a permanent accepted name and permanent accepted status, and until all the communities have recognized accepted borders under one or two states—there is no justification for one place to have an established, agreed-upon name while the other has barely a temporary one. L'chaim!"

1

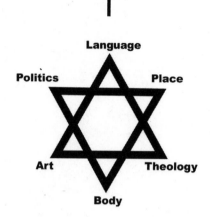

THEOLOGY

"SPECTERS OF BINATIONALISM"

A Manifesto for the Jewish-Palestinian Arabic-Hebrew State

A specter haunts the Middle East, the daunting specter of Palestinian-Jewish binationalism. All the world's powers have joined hands to conduct a holy war to the bitter end, until that specter is defeated. One can read the entire modern history of the region as the history of a violent lasting conflict instigated to deny and expel that specter.

Now, after one hundred years of conflict, with no solution in sight, the time has come to present binationalism in all its glory.

J'accuse.

We are already a decade into the twenty-first century, and still the only visible change in the Middle East is deterioration. The everyday relation between the Jewish and Palestinian nations, the two nations living in this shared land, is a clear and deteriorating relationship of occupier to occupied, dominance to weakness, manifesting exploitation, racism, humiliation, landgrab, and violence. It is true that on the symbolic level relations are much more complex, but the bottom line is that the Jewish nation is sovereign inside territorial contiguity, enjoying democratic, economic, and cultural freedom.

In contrast, the Palestinian nation is divided between five different physical, economic, and cultural provinces that are hermetically separated

A short version of this article was published in *Haaretz Magazine*, July 12, 2009.

in a way that does not allow the existence of a political community. The silence of the Western world, and its massive support for Israel, perpetuate this flagrantly illegal situation. The West is better off letting the Jewish nation guard, in an immoral manner, the immoral wall in the immoral frontier state so as to keep the conflict away from the heart of the empire, where there is still a semblance of the rule of law. Leaders in the Arab world (or the Muslim world, depending on one's point of view) are better off placing the Palestinian people as a human bulwark against the West, while they are free to both conduct commercial relations with the West and maintain an apparent ideological arena through which they criticize the West in the symbolic realm.

In the symbolic realm relations are much more complex: they are not about the balance of power, financial profit, or control of land, water, and natural resources. In this realm one also has to consider overt and covert theological structures. It is about relations of longing, jealousy, and passion, the simultaneous desire for sameness and separateness. Thus, this small piece of land containing the names *Israel* and *Palestine* has become an intense critical mass containing all the tensions between East and West, between North and South, between religions, and between religious and secular thought. The Middle East has become the place where the world brings together all the ideological oppositions, like a testing ground for various ideological explosions. Therefore, one moment before this ancient mythology-infested place implodes into a black hole powerful enough to swallow the whole world, we propose binationalism as the only living alternative.

Binationalism is perhaps the only possibility for a new place, a new beginning and a new language, the only possibility for Israel-Palestine, for the Middle East, and maybe for the entire world.

THE POSSIBILITY OF BINATIONALISM

The binational idea has existed ever since nationalist movements first emerged in the Middle East. Contrary to conventional wisdom, it was not the outcome of some crisis of faith among adherents of conflicting national ambitions who finally concluded that the two-state solution, a cornerstone of their ideologies, could never actually be implemented. In fact, the binational idea is so deeply rooted in the region that the entire Middle East conflict can be interpreted as the history of its rejection. In such a narrative, the earliest fears of binationalism gradually empowered religious and nationalist objectives, which consequently led to the ultimate demise of any underlying humanist ideologies. This is why the binational idea must be reintroduced into the public discourse. We must gain a deeper understanding of why it was rejected outright, if only because it may yet be the last chance we have to avoid the apocalyptic cataclysm now brewing in the feverish ranks of our nationalist and religious fundamentalists.

In order to achieve this, we must first recognize that the goal of binationalism is not simply to tear down the ghetto that we have erected for the indigenous Palestinians with whom we share this land. We must also tear down the golden ghetto walls with which we have encircled ourselves. While many believe that history always repeats itself, this does not necessarily mean that we must repeat the same mistakes or reproduce the same injustices so typical of classical colonialist movements in the last century. Binationalism could well be the ultimate source of resolution for a people that was almost annihilated on the altar of racism and ethnic homogeneity. We can offer no greater good to the world than to build a new society on a foundation of multiple ethnic and religious distinctions.

Binationalism is not a new idea dreamed up by some fringe philosopher or other. It is the reality that we still refuse to recognize. More than one million Palestinians now live *within* (that is, west of) the Green Line, which is the 1949 armistice line, recognized by international law as the border of the state of Israel. The territory east of the Green Line (the West Bank) has been occupied by Israel since 1967. Palestinians living west of the Green Line are also called "1948 Arabs," and they hold Israeli citizenship. In Jerusalem, Haifa, and in many other towns, Jews and Arabs have long lived together. We cannot etch out some boundary line to divide their neighborhoods in Haifa and Jerusalem. We cannot construct a Separation Wall between the Bedouin scattered throughout the Negev and the farms of their Jewish neighbors or between the Arab towns of the Galilee and Jewish outposts, kibbutzim, and development towns. Not only would this be impossible, it would represent Israel's ultimate moral failure— an ethical crisis faced by a society that is willing to take whatever steps deemed necessary to further the cause of racial segregation. With over half a million Jewish settlers now living across the Green Line, Israelis have no right to raise the gauntlet and challenge them: "What does that settlement mean to you—to you, and not to us?" Of course not, because each and every settlement was funded and supported by all the successive governments of the past; each and every settlement received its rubber stamp of approval from the nation's Supreme Court. The current situation is irreversible. The Occupied Territories are an integral part of a single, cohesive state. The same is true of Palestinians on both sides of the Green Line. They have watched as their land was stolen, from Land Day in the Galilee until today in the West Bank. And yet, regardless of where they live—in Israel, Jerusalem, the Occupied Territories, or even in the Palestinian Diaspora—they have emerged as a united people. Today no state in the world has the right to carve them up between two sovereign and distinct entities as part of some permanent solution.

Today no American would dare ask whether it is possible to create a country where blacks and whites are treated equally; the assumption of equality is a given, and the question is now what the necessary preconditions for equality are. The same is true for us. We refuse to accept the possibility that Palestinians will be unequal to Jews throughout the Israeli-Palestinian space. The problems that may result down the road are irrelevant.

We live in a binational reality in which the two-state solution has become little more than an empty cliché intended to preserve the status quo. As such, the time has come to recognize that there is only one realistic option left. This is not some attempt to dodge the many difficult questions posed by a binational solution: Where will the refugees return to? Can one injustice be put right with another? What about the demographic problem? Will the country lose its Western veneer in a sea of Arab culture? We do not ignore these critical questions. We simply reverse the order of things. Our approach places the vision of binationalism squarely at center stage instead of first focusing on all the open-ended questions and concerns that inevitably accompany it. In the long run, the degree to which we disentangle competing narratives—the extent to which we separate and control them—isn't really that important. The fact will always remain that two distinct peoples live in the same land and are as integrated with one another as the warp and woof of some Oriental carpet. There is no way to separate them, but, more importantly, there is no need to separate them either. Instead, what we must do is find a new language, a binational language, as Edward Said, a Palestinian, proposed in tribute to Sigmund Freud, a Jew. It should be an uninfected language, free of racism, which will help to transform the fabric of life into something richer and more beautiful than its constituent parts.

The only solution is radical change to the ideological metastructure of the State of Israel as a Jewish state—or, rather, recognition that this

metastructure has long since breathed its last, but we have been conceal-
ing this from the world. Even though the signs of its decomposing have
overwhelmed us with racist violence.

After all, we know deep inside that the only way to turn off the self-
destructive course that we have chosen for ourselves is to recognize both
Jews and Palestinians as full and equal partners in this region and its
future. (Furthermore, we have already seen how ideologies much more
powerful than our own, such as the Eastern European school of communism or Milton Friedman's school of capitalism, have collapsed like a
house of cards.)

CREDO

The long journey of the binational specter into its realization as a living,
breathing Mediterranean body is a bold odyssey through numerous haz-
ards. And, like Odysseus, who had the wisdom to descend into the underworld, in order to seek the guidance of Tiresias, the blind prophet, so shall
we lend our ears to the spirits of our guides and teachers Walter Benjamin,
Hannah Arendt, Primo Levi, Mahmoud Darwish, and Edward Said. Before
he passed away, Edward Said wrote *Freud and the Non-European*.[1] Through
the reading of Freud, Said demonstrated that an independent identity without other identities contained within it is an impossibility. At the end of his
book, he writes: "The questions Freud therefore leaves us with are: can so
utterly indecisive and so deeply undetermined a history ever be written?
In what language, and with what sort of vocabulary? . . . Can it aspire to
the conditions of a politics of Diaspora life? Can it ever become the not-so-
precarious foundation in the land of Jews and Palestinians of a bi-national
state in which Israel and Palestine are parts, rather than antagonists of each
other's history and underlying reality? I myself believe so." We too believe
so, and therefore we shall seek the language and the vocabulary. We shall do
our best to come up with this vocabulary, striving for it to create, with the
help of our acts and our beliefs, a new place, which will bring together, as a
wonderful warp and woof, our joint and separate pasts. We shall act out of
the belief in and loyalty to the values of equality and solidarity in order to
create a multigendered place with many identities, constantly and dynami-
cally evolving toward an open, invisible future.

1. *Freud and the Non-European* (New York: Verso, 2003).

What is binationalism if not our insistence on being able to gaze out over this beautiful country and see it as it really is, so rich in cultures, identities, and shades of identity? This is the only way we can avoid being held captive by the vile forces of secular and religious nationalism that have flourished in this country. After all, their insistence on ethnic solidarity—on ethnic purity—only serves to remind us of the dark days of the not too distant past.

Only when we reconsider our conceptions of the state, its laws and institutions, its culture and symbols, and adopt this new approach can we truly rid ourselves of ideas and ideologies whose time has long since passed. And in any act, as revolutionary as it is, we shall not forget for a moment our intimate acquaintance with the precariousness of life. Only then will we be able to thrust open the door of all this, our common home, to a new era, to life.

Why We Support Boycott, Divestment, and Sanctions

I find it appropriate that the Israeli public be notified of the emerging movement for Boycott, Divestment, and Sanctions against Israel (BDS), which has been growing at a breathtaking pace. Following bewildered reports published by *Yedioth Aharonot* journalist Sever Plocker, who noticed that BDS has moved from the circles of the radical Western left to the circles of the bourgeois center, I can add that this is now true for Israel-loving Jews as well.

Obviously, this shift is taking place against the backdrop of Israel's war on Gaza, waged one year ago, the publication of the Goldstone report, and the local strain of apartheid policy nurtured by Israel, which differs from the old South African one in some aspects. This policy has local makings and signature. It is not only the Israeli High Court of Justice ruling to evacuate Palestinians living in the East Jerusalem neighborhood of Sheikh-Jarrah from their homes, applying a right-of-return-for-Jews-only rule, while Palestinians, on the other hand, are being denied this right. It is also the denial of Palestinian rights to send Palestinian policemen to carry out the "targeted assassination" of Jewish terrorist Yaacov Teitel (it should be noted that we object to all extrajudicial executions), while the alleged Palestinians murderers of a Jewish rabbi in Samaria can

January 3, 2010.

be extrajudicially executed, with the ballistic weapons examination proving their guilt performed retroactively by the executioners, not by a court of law (the appropriate circumstance should be an international tribunal, since most Palestinians are sure that at least two of the three had nothing to do with the murder).

I am presenting these cases to illustrate the extreme inequality in our joint life, in this land, and to emphasize the reasons behind the emergence of the popular global movement for solidarity with the Palestinian people. And please do not rush to your feet, protesting and chanting: "The whole world is against us, never mind, we shall overcome!" because we shall not overcome.[1]

The aforementioned violations of human rights are precisely the reason why many Jews all over the world have joined the BDS campaign, a key issue for those of us who are trying to prevent violence against Israel while simultaneously countering its arrogant and aggressive policies against the Palestinians living under its rule.

NECESSARY VIOLENCE

In a talk at the New School, Simon Critchley has argued that "violence is never justified even if it is sometimes necessary." This statement lays a heavy burden of guilt on numerous resistance movements all over the world who have been compelled to resort to violence against occupying forces.

When the children in the Palestinian village of Bil'in—whose land is being grabbed by heavily armed Israeli soldiers in broad daylight under the pretext of "lawful conduct"—throw stones at soldiers, the village elders tell them: "Your act of stone throwing is totally justified resistance, but we have chosen nonviolent resistance for this village, and therefore violence is unnecessary here." As part of our support for this type of nonviolent action in places like Bil'in, and following forceful, violent IDF actions against the residents of the village, we, Israeli activists, have formulated our position in favor of BDS.

When the state quells the nonviolent yet effective resistance of a rightless minority with violent unlawful means, then violent resistance to the military forces enforcing this oppression is justified. Indeed, such

---

1. A well-known Israeli song.

resistance may not always be necessary, may not always serve the goals of the struggle, and its shortcomings may outweigh its advantages, but it is still justified in principle.

In comparison, nonviolent resistance in such instances is always justified and also always necessary. Regrettably, such resistance is not always possible.

Therefore, we must try to create the preconditions for nonviolent resistance to emerge in order to render violent resistance unnecessary.

The most proven and effective form of pressure known to us is BDS. Thus BDS actions do not amount to negative, counterproductive moves, as many propagandists try to portray them. On the contrary, BDS actions are a life-saving antidote to violence. These are actions of solidarity, partnership, and joint progress. BDS actions serve to preempt, in a nonviolent manner, justified violent resistance aimed at attaining the same goals of justice, peace, and equality.

If a critical mass of privileged Israeli citizens joins the nonviolent struggle from the inside, standing shoulder to shoulder with the disenfranchised, perhaps outside pressure will no longer be necessary. The three basic principles of BDS are

- an immediate end of the Occupation;
- full equality to all Palestinian citizens of the state of Israel;
- legal and moral recognition of the Palestinian refugees' right of return.

(Obviously, each community's position will be taken into consideration during the desired negotiations.)

No right-wing lobby, not even the messianic-evangelical lobby, can hold back for long the global popular movement that wants to see an end to our local conflict and to see regional peace, according to the principles of international law, for the benefit of both peoples.

The Star of Redemption with a Split א

> You have made me into a single entity in the world, for it is written "Hear O Israel, the Lord is our God, the Lord is one," and I shall make you into a single entity in the world.
>
> —BT Chagiga 3a

ROSENZWEIG AND THE NON-EUROPEAN

Franz Rosenzweig's book, *The Star of Redemption,* might be the last heroic attempt to shape Judaism into a theological-philosophical method of thinking, before the logic of worlds was obliterated in Auschwitz, perhaps permanently. Rosenzweig wrote the book as a sequence of letters, sent to his mother from the front, during his service as an officer in the First World War.

The book, an enigmatic theological text, is composed in the geometric shape of the Star of David, which appears on the cover. The corners of the triangle standing on its base represent the elements of existence, *God* on the upper corner and *Human* and *The World* on the others. The inverted triangle shows the three theological concepts *Creation, Revelation,* and *Redemption* on the bottom, which represent the path between the elements. Rosenzweig's star was an impressive conclusion of the German Jewish school of thought; a beginning never continued; a summary of a culture reaching its peak before being destroyed with unprecedented cruelty.

Although Rosenzweig placed God on top, and maybe because of that, he gave him, simultaneously, a superstatus and a veil. Revelation is the relation between human and God, and creation is the relation between the world and God. Redemption, nonetheless, exists within the relation between humanity and the world. This redemption—a term with an intense theological charge—becomes a human matter, perhaps too human a matter. This new concept of redemption is an opening for radical thought toward Judaism and its perception of humanity and world relations.[1]

From the very first time I read *The Star of Redemption* I was more bewildered than enlightened, even spellbound, by the suspension of God from the traditional role of redeemer. Since then, throughout my attraction to "the Star," I have been reading it not as a scholar but as a man in search of faith and as an artistic creator seeking inspiration. In that position I was troubled by Rosenzweig's attempt to connect to Christianity at all costs, while slandering Islam and removing it from the realm of monotheism. Thus, I, a Sancho Panza of Judaism, embarked on a journey to mend the star of redemption, to make my *tikkun olam* (rectification of the world). The following is my attempt to draw a new star of redemption, removing God from the place at the top. This is the star of *geula* (redemption in Hebrew), without the aleph.

THE SECRET OF EDWARD SAID'S MULTIPLICITY

I have always hoped I would be able to rebuild the star of redemption without God in its top vertex. Between me and myself, I called that star "the star of redemption without aleph" (the Hebrew letter aleph is the first letter in the Hebrew word for God), i.e., the star of redemption without God. However, the more I went on removing the aleph from the triangle, the more I realized things were not so simple, because aleph is not just the aleph of God but also the aleph of the human, being the first letter of the Hebrew word *adam*. And it is also the aleph of language, being the first letter of the Hebrew alphabet, and it is the aleph of oneness, representing the number 1, and it is the gap between truth (*emet*) and dead (*met*), for, if we remove aleph, the first letter from the former, we will end up with the lifeless latter, and that is how the golem was killed. And aleph even makes the difference

---

1. After many years of aristocratic German rule over Jewish studies, headed by Professor Gershom Scholem, came a diligent plebeian from Romania—Professor Moshe Idel—to take his place. Idel, of whom I was an informal student, revealed to me a Judaism of magic and theurgy, more impulsive and demonic and less mystical and obsequious. Idel's ideas helped me conceive the star of redemption without the aleph of *Elohim*, without God.

between redemption (*geula*) and Diaspora (*gola*), for if we remove the second letter from the former, we will end up with the latter, etc., etc. In fact, all we have to do is take a look at this letter aleph and realize that the same letter that symbolizes oneness (and, of course, the Hebrew word *ahad* begins with an aleph) is the same word by which we define God as one in the most sacred prayer of all Judaism: "Hear O Israel, the Lord is our God, the Lord is one," the same words every martyred Jew died uttering as his last. And, indeed, when we look at this aleph we find out that the letter which is supposed to symbolize the oneness of God is a split letter. If we fully understand the secret of the split within oneness, we may understand the secret of monotheism and the secret of Edward Said's multiplicity and the binationalist language, and we will be able to pass from exalted worlds to the everyday sacredness of a place that is a gate to life.

SERPENT = MESSIAH

is the famous story from the Babylonian Talmud (Baba Mezi'a 59b) regarding a debate between scholars revolving around Aknai's stove.[2] The rabbis' debate seems to be about the rules of impurity, but during the argument a different question arises: what is God's authority against man's authority? The answer given in the story is radical—God has no authority to intervene in a community debate. The rule is "follow a majority decision," and the decision lies "not with heaven" but in the hands of human beings. Many of this story's interpreters emphasized this idea as an expression of the pluralistic and democratic nature of Judaism. Few addressed the rest of the story, in which the rabbis destroy one another in the name of such democracy and pluralism. These interpretations disregard a crucial point—on which we shall focus our attention. The story is about the stove of Aknai—"serpent" in Aramaic—and it is brought up while debating something different: deception of matters, i.e., the discourse of truth.

Aknai represents the primal serpent, and *serpent* means *messiah* (in Hebrew numerology and esoteric studies).[3] It represents the ancient

2. In Hebrew numerology the sum of the letters in the word *serpent* (*nachash* נחש), equals the sum of the word *messiah* (*mashiach* משיח), which is 358. There is an additional comparison, as described.

3. In those days, in the Middle East, there was a gnostic cult, the Serpantians or Ophites, who believed the serpent was the source of knowledge and salvation.

secret of the Tree of Knowledge (gnosis): knowledge as language—the language of humans—given to Adam and Eve by the snake.

The question discussed by the scholars in the story is whether Aknai's stove is, in its essence, *one,* and thus potentially impure because it functions as a whole, or actually a *multiplicity,* because it is compiled of bricks with sand in between each piece. God attempted to intervene in the discussion and was silenced by the scholars. It was said that the decision is part of the community discourse, and God has no right to intervene, let alone veto. Judaism has transferred the concept of revelation and authority into the language not only ethically but also ontologically, while God is brought into the language—the discourse of the community. God turns from transcendental to immanent in a language that is now turning transcendental. God lies within language itself, and this may be the reason that the word *Messiah* in Hebrew, *mashiach,* comes from the word *siach,*[4] which means "discourse." A messiah is the one who conducts the discourse, not just originating from, but creating divinity.

This implies that there is no knowledge untouched by the serpent, no whole divinity, different from Aknai's stove, for purity itself is unrepresentable and thus destructive. The primal serpent is the one who made the basis of the language possible, sustaining the tension between purity and impurity. The desire for one is the desire for purity, but only one is destructive. In the story, after the unconcluded discussion, a third of the grain was burned, storms raged, ships sunk, and rabbis met their end. The tale of Aknai's stove teaches us that the tension of multiplicity inside one or the striving for the singular within the multiple is the ability to prevent impurity and to preserve life, the same life with which Rosenzweig ends *Star of Redemption.* God is the borderline of language, creating it while simultaneously being created by it. Divinity exists in the tension between what is immanent in the language and what transcends it, between one and infinity. In our words, God may be described partially by a speech act. Idel, in his book *The Golem,* pointed in a similar direction when he argued that creating the golem is not copying God's actions but creating God with language.[5] Thus, in the new star of redemption, the

---

4. Messiah is משיח in Hebrew, and discourse is שיח. The two words differ by only a single letter.

5. See Moshe Idel, *Golem: Jewish Magical and Mystical Traditions on the Artificial Anthropoid* (Albany, NY: SUNY, 1990).

vectors of creation and revelation are bidirectional. This is revealed to that and that creates this in mutual relations, which produce a divinity that is both immanent and transcendental. In this star of redemption, God and human are not self-sustaining but a product of the discourse maintained by the six new vertices.

A NEW STAR WAS BORN

According to the new star of redemption, God is not revealed to man and God does not create a world. Instead, creation and revelation are bidirectional. One reveals itself to the other, and the other creates the one, in a relation of reciprocity, which yields a divinity that is immanent and transcendent at the same time. Therefore, according to our star of redemption, divinity and God are a product of the discourse generated by the six new vertices. Language is located in the top vertex, and the body is located underneath it, in the opposite vertex. The body strives for unification with language, to form a one that is by no means a Platonic structure of up and down, but, as the Israeli children's song goes, "Seesaw seesaw, go up go down, go down go up, who is down and who on top, just you and I, I and you," alternating toward the moment of unification, which is also the moment of the big bang. The star of redemption is composed of six forces operating as an enormous tension protected by the Star of David, which aspires for oneness and infinity simultaneously. Here lies the essence of true monotheism, which is a world created from the tension of multiplicity within oneness. The monotheistic world acknowledges this tension and accepts it as the only possibility for the one to exist. Members of the community, as separate yet coexistent individuals, testify, of their common free will: "Hear O Israel, the Lord is our God, the Lord is one," or "La ilaha ilallah,"[6] they create that divine entity. In this context God's name in the Torah appears as plural (*Elohim* in Hebrew, with the *-im* plural). When man was created, it was said, "Let us make man in our image, after our likeness" (Genesis 1:26).[7] We may continue along the lines of Jewish theology and demonstrate the folly in reducing the concept of monotheism

6. "There is no God but God."

7. Rosenzweig interprets plurality as a majestic plural, used in Europe. The expression does not exist in Hebrew.

to the literal one, without aspiring for the tension between one and multiplicity and its constant recreation. Monotheism is, therefore, the striving for a one, and it assigns the role of creators to a community of believers. It is written in the Talmud: "You have made me into a single entity in the world, for it is written 'Hear O Israel, the Lord is our God, the Lord is one,' and I shall make you into a single entity in the world" (BT Chagiga: 3a). Therefore God's oneness is recreated by the community with the use of language. The community must repeatedly create God's oneness within its own multiplicity by means of language—with the most important prayer, Shema Yisrael.

The prayer is not a testament to God's oneness, it is a theurgy: it creates God as one. From this act the community emerges as a single entity whose existence is not predetermined, but conditional and dialectic.[8]

For me, Edward Said's book *Freud and the Non-European* is a book of revelation and also a book of study. My star spouts from Said's writings, and as I was reading I felt a revelation of humanism. I had a similar experience when I read *If This Is a Man* by Primo Levi, a book that left a notable mark on my movie *Forgiveness* (מחילות). I felt the same feeling once more when attending Jacques Derrida's second seminar on forgiveness in Avital Ronell's course at New York University. The dust and stench of smoke from the World Trade Center devastation lingered over the campus and crept into the auditorium. Derrida was very sick and weak then. He spoke slowly, his back bent, while leaning on the podium. I was filled with sadness and love for this man, who appeared to me as Benjamin's Angelus Novus, powerless against the ruins of the world, nothing left for him but to say his prayer over Yankelevich and the German student, who are playing the piano together, and seek a forgiveness that cannot be spoken. This experience was the initial spark for the film *Local Angel,* but I am beginning to wander off to other regions of revelation among people, and we are here to discuss the

8. A few notes are in order here. Judith Butler has written seminal texts, which have undoubtedly influenced my thought, in her book *Gender Trouble* (New York: Routledge, 1990), and in her ensuing discourse about the relations between body, language, culture, and nature as well as the way in which language relates to the body. Alain Badiou, in his book *Logics of Worlds,* trans. Alberto Toscano (New York: Continuum, 2009), writes that there are only bodies and languages, except that there are truths. The truths, according to Badiou, lie outside the binary structure containing bodies and languages, the same binary structure Butler attempts to dismantle.

redemption of the star and a political theology from Rosenzweig to Said, mediated by Freud.

Freud and the Non-European, in a sentence, is Said's reading of *Moses and Monotheism* by Sigmund Freud. However, those familiar with Jewish notions would know that "in a sentence" turns into an endless tale and journey far exceeding the initial sentence, sometimes losing sight of the point, but always keeping it at heart. My reading of Said reading Freud invites you, the reader, to join a constant, continuous motion toward a new language of binationalism. Indeed multiplicity in one. Following Freud, Said deals with Moses the man, the Jew who is always someone else as well. This is the inner identity of a Jew: to be Egyptian, or Austrian, or Palestinian, never to be only oneself. Said focused on the part of Moses the man in order to create an image of a Jew with whom he can compile the binationalist sphere.

This appears in the second part of the title of Freud's book. The structure of monotheistic religion is identical to the portrait of Moses and Freud drawn by Said. This is the essence of the monotheistic God.

Perhaps Freud and Said considered it gnostic and not the heart of monotheistic thinking, and maybe they just did not know they knew. In any case, it was not just Moses the man who was a multiplicity in one, but the "One God" is not the God in whose name the West went on destroying everything different. This is the reason why the concept of the other loses its otherness, as the concept of one is understood in its deep, complex meaning. Perhaps that is a way for the concept of the other to withdraw its Levinasian rage. (An important note: this is not an attempt to appease the polytheistic or monotheistic world. This is a far more radical explanation of how monotheism functions within itself, what it denies and what it could have found in itself if Freud had put it on the couch beside Moses.)

What we are dealing with is a rereading. The Hebrew word for "reading," *kria'a,*[9] has two meanings: "reading" and "calling." The double meaning in our context refers to both reading Said's text and answering the call of this Palestinian in exile to create a new language for the place where both Jews and Palestinians live and both cultures, Hebrew and Arabic, abide. Reading Freud's Moses, Said teaches us about the impossibility of a separate, isolated identity. There can never be only one identity, because each of us is compiled from a rich collection of different identities,

---

9. Kria'a =קריאה.

coexisting, sometimes even in relative harmony. Thus, during one of humanity's darkest hours, Freud writes his book, his will, in fact, leaving us his wish for us to have multiple identities.

Freud describes the way desire for purity and unity causes the people to murder Moses, who is also Egyptian, in the same way that Freud is also Austrian. Their multiple identities symbolize their people. Actually, all those who seek ethnic purity and a single identity end up murdering their source of vitality, their prophet. Using multiple-identity Moses, Freud allows us to reread his monotheism not as static, united, and whole but as a back-and-forth motion between one and multiplicity. Freud, the atheist scientist, shows an unconscious relation with kabbalistic tradition and its fundamental book, *The Book of Creation.* In this book, as in the story of Aknai's stove, divinity is described as the tension between the one and the ten, in a back-and forth dynamic. This is the early description from which the famous ten emanations (the tree of *sefirot*) grew, generations later. After the introduction of the tree, one cannot ignore the multiplicity of the one.

Jean-Luc Nancy asked me once, while he was getting ready for a debate with Derrida, if the Hebrew word for synagogue, *beit knesset,* is really in the plural form while the word used for the local parliament, *Knesset,* is in the singular form.[10] I thought the question was about the tension that Derrida tried to describe between Diaspora as a multiplicity and redemption as oneness in Zionist thought. In this fashion we are in a dichotomy where every possibility excludes the other—either a perception of unity, redemption, and the denial of the Diaspora or a multiplicity of the Diaspora and the forfeiture of the fundamental aspiration for the one. The truly fascinating aspect here is the tension between the two, against the testimony of the community that maintains them both. But, as we know, two is never enough.

It is said in Isaiah: "Ye are my witnesses so speak the God" and the Kotzker rabbi said, "ye cease to be my witnesses, I cease to be God." This is a tension not just between one and multiplicity, but between them and the void itself. Therefore we have a triangle that always has to be maintained, a triangle of relations between the one, the void, and the multiplicity. This triangle exists within the individual, within God, and within the community, and it is sustained by the mutual testimony among them. However, Zionism has brought upon the absolute, a narcissistic one of

10. Beit knesset = בית כנסת , Knesset = כנסת.

vacuuming ethnic purity that does not acknowledge multiplicity or nothingness. It does not matter whether it is nonreligious nationalism, Sephardic traditionalism, Ashkenazi orthodoxy, raging capitalism, or Russian secularism. All falls into the purity of the one Jewish ethnicity that everyone serves. Its most notorious curse is the blunt contrast between the fact that Jews are granted the right of return and Palestinians who once resided in Israel are denied this right of return.

At this moment Palestinian families are being driven away from their homes of fifty years, in the neighborhood of Sheikh-Jarrah, in Jerusalem, and in other areas under Israeli control, and people of Jewish ethnicity are moving in to take their place on the sole basis of racial discrimination and under the approval of the Supreme Court of this Jewish state, Israel. At this time of great despair, I cling to Said's call, a call answering Freud's call, which comes from the other side of great despair. I hope to find in it a beacon of light and a lifeline for creating a new language with which we may create possibilities of unity and multiplicity, of Diaspora and redemption, of room for partnership instead of destruction. Instead of asking "who is a Jew?" We ask "what does a Jew want?" We accept the Jew as a heterogenic being with various identities, each of them arising from different wishes, occasionally contradicting one another.

AV-RAM AV-RA-HAM (ABRAM ABRAHAM)

While reading Freud, I thought of a more ancient forefather, Abraham. His original name was Av-ram, "archfather" in Hebrew. It was he who sent both his sons to their death: the first to die of thirst with his mother in the desert, the second whom he attempted to sacrifice and, according to some interpretations (for which the Hebrew term is *midrashim*), in fact succeeded. A murderous father is the archfather, Avram, and only by the hand of God were Ishmael and Isaac spared. God split his name in two and inserted the divine letter *he* (ה), father, and on the other, gracious Avraham, with his mercy and generous hospitality.[11] Perhaps this is the reason why, when he was about to sacrifice his son, God called to him twice: Avraham-Avraham, as if his name was no longer Avraham, but Avraham-

---

11. The letter He ה in Hebrew is the middle letter in the word *God*, אלוהים, and thus Avram became Avraham—Abraham.

Avraham. From then on, when faced with his kneeling and submissive son as a sacrificial lamb, he will always be the split father, the murderous and the beneficent. After Avraham was dead and buried, Ishmael and Isaac visited his grave together—it is called *tikkun Avraham*.

While we constantly look upon the rule of the cruel father, Ishmael and Isaac, hand in hand, went to Hebron. One who can hear God and one who can laugh God's laugh (the meaning of their names in Hebrew) went together, and in the Cave of the Patriarchs, the cave of Machpelah, they began the binationalist language—

BROTHERLY LOVE

Nevertheless, the rule of the father and the darkness of the cave,
the horror of the blade and the fear of the desert still haunts their nights,
and so they shut themselves in, seeking racial purity and the name of the
father, silencing the voices of laughter and viewing a brother as an enemy
and so we ask, with sadness in our voice,

When will the two brothers walk together fearless out of
the dark Cave of Machpelah
to the sunny light of
Israel-Palestine,
to life?

2

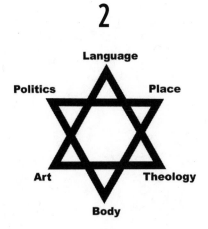

Language

Politics

Place

Art

Theology

Body

BODY

Samson the Non-European

APRIL 1956

PROLOGUE: THE GATES OF GAZA WERE TOO HEAVY TO BEAR

On the April 29, 1956, a security force from Kibbutz Nahal Oz noticed a group of Arabs from Gaza that had crossed the border and were working the kibbutz's fields. Roee, the force's young commander, rode his horse toward them, waving a stick in an effort to chase them away. Unfortunately, the young master was captured by the natives and taken back into the Gaza Strip. The UN returned his body a few days later, his eyes gouged out. At his funeral the following day, Moshe Dayan, then the chief of staff of the Israeli army, delivered a eulogy. He said:

> Let us not cast blame on the murderers today. What claim do we have against their hatred of us? They have been living for eight years in the refugee camps of Gaza, watching us making their and their fathers' land and villages our own settlement.
>
> It is not from the Arabs of Gaza but in our own midst that we must seek understanding of Roee's sacrifice. How we shut our eyes to

An abbreviated version of this essay appeared in *Studies in Gender and Sexuality* 12 (2011): 124–133.

our fate and refused to recognize the destiny of our generation in all its cruelty. Have we forgotten that this group of young men living in Nahal Oz carries on its shoulders the heavy weight of Gaza's gates?

Roee, this tender, blond boy who left Tel Aviv to make his home by the gates of Gaza to be a wall for all of us, the light in his heart blinded his eyes and he failed to see the flash of the butcher's knife. The yearning for peace deafened his ears, and he did not hear the sound of murder lurking. The Gates of Gaza came down heavy upon him and defeated him.

Who was it that raised Samson's specter, thinking that he could control it? Was it the Palestinian refugees who put Roee's eyes out, just as the Philistines did to Samson, that planted the idea of Samson who called "Avenge but one of my two eyes!" in Dayan's mind? Did Dayan really believe that the young man chasing farmers from land that was robbed from them was blinded by a "yearning for peace," just as Samson was blinded by love? Could he not have imagined that it was the arrogance of mastery that led this young Israeli to prod the natives with his stick and blind his eyes? Perhaps if he could see what we can see now, everything would have been different. But Dayan, who was himself a symbol of the masculine, Zionist ethos of mastery so typical of the era, thought of Samson as a blond European. This is what made him see Roee as a sensitive young man, crushed under the burden of the gates of Gaza. But Samson carried the gates of the Philistine Empire to mock its pretensions of power. Unlike the young Roee who came from Tel Aviv to build new gates in Gaza and a wall around its refugee camps.

DECEMBER 2008, TEL AVIV

BEFORE THE MUSES GROW SILENT

A while ago I was asked to write an article about Samson. I stacked a few books on my desk, hoping to enter into dialogue with them, and called on the Muses. The truth is, I had come, to paraphrase Antonius in his famous eulogy for Julius Caesar, "to bury Samson, not to praise him." In the end, just like Balaam, where his donkey opened its mouth and spoke god words, "I also came to curse Samson, and left praising him." Thinking that I would pick up one book and that it would eventually lead me to the others, I started with David Grossman's *Lion's Honey: The Myth of Samson* because I was asked to address this book specifically. But the dialogue I hoped to pursue turned into a confrontation. A confrontation ensued.

David Grossman is incontestably an important author, but his book and what it articulates made me angry. As I read it I kept asking myself, how could I argue with a father who has lost a child to war? I can still feel my throat clenching reading the eulogy he wrote for his son. I remember the sense of mourning and loss that welled up inside me, but also the protest. In his eulogy Grossman writes: "I remember you telling me about your checkpoint policy, because, of course, you spent a lot of time at the checkpoints. You said that if there was a child in the car you stopped, you always started by trying to calm him down and make him laugh. And you always reminded yourself that the child was about Ruthie's age and that he was very afraid of you. And how much he hates you, and that he has reasons to hate, but in spite of that you would do everything in your power to make that terrible experience easier for him, while doing your job without compromising." I thought to myself: Surely Grossman knows that a soldier's smile is the nightmare of the Palestinian forced to stop at a checkpoint. "Please don't let him smile at me!" I can hear my friend Leila from Ramallah saying, "Please don't let him think that he is not a part of the crime machine!" I wanted to explain to Leila that the smile is a genuine expression of tenderness, but I can hear her response: "I know that, and I know that he is caught in a war that isn't his, but I am too tired to understand. I feel too much anger, too much desperation."

Reading Grossman's eulogy, I grew furious at the Zionist left. Why did they not call out to its children "Do not serve in the forces of Occupation!"? On the first day of the war we gathered in the city square and protested: "Don't send your children to fight this unnecessary, unjust battle!" Why did they not lie before the tanks as they set off? Why did they not block the doors of their homes and give the command "Refuse orders, son!" Why did they not at least grab at their uniforms, begging: "This is *not* your war, son. You are not Samson, and they are not the Philistines." But they, the humanists of the Zionist left, saw themselves as Odysseus and dreaded our cries as though they were the alluring song of the sirens. So they tied themselves to the mast of the Israeli warship and plugged their ears with wax. In the end they came to see themselves as the stewards of war. "We have a just war now!" said A. B. Yehoshua, and Amos Oz followed.

Grossman was with them at the press conference. He may not have felt comfortable there, perhaps he did not even want to be there, but he *was* there. I read their presence there as though they were in fact saying: "We are with you, our beloved flock of readers. We will not abandon you as you march off to the moral abyss. We will beat the war drums for you, but we will beat them softly, gently, as befitting humanists like us. And yet we are determined." And we, the few bitter protesters, stood stubbornly outside and continued to demand: "Lay not thine hands upon the lad, neither send him to lay his hands upon other lads, neither to kill nor to be killed, neither to conquer nor to smile." For when he returns home, he will not come bearing the lion's honey but the blood of others, some of them innocent. But they simply stuffed their ears with more wax. Then tragedy struck. Grossman lost his beloved son. We all lost his beloved son, and many other beloved sons, and our neighbors lost their beloved sons too. Yet, despite all the pain and anguish, we must remember that a soldier, armed from head to toe, who smiles kindly at a checkpoint—his heroism is not that of a lion, his smile is not as sweet as honey.

Samson's Greek twin may be Herakles, but, back in the days when I used to flip through the illustrated pages of the *Iliad* and *Odyssey* for children, he seemed to my young mind better paired with Achilles. How beautifully Homer depicts Achilles' rage in his opening verses: "Sing, O Goddess, the consuming rage of Achilles son of Peleus, that brought countless ills upon the Achaeans. Many a brave soul did it send hurrying down to Hades, and many a hero did it yield a prey to dogs and vultures." This is the Achilles who killed my beloved Hector and did not rescue my beloved Iphigenia. How angry I was with him as a boy. He stood there, swaddled in the armor his mother had given him. When I grew up I understood his anguish, the anguish of someone who is not quite human, of someone who wants to be struck in the heel because that would make him an ordinary man. But what if Achilles' anguish, rather than his rage, is the key to crack the mystery of Samson's anguish, of the loneliness and longing for a woman's love that he experiences by virtue of not being like any other man. "Sing, O holy spirit, the consuming anguish of Samson, that brought countless ills upon the Philistines. Many a brave soul it sent down to Hades, many heroes it struck with the jawbone of an ass, one thousand men." This son of god, admired hero, who longed to be loved, like every other man . . .

By now, as you might have noticed, my desk was growing heavy with the weight of brute masculinity. It threatened to break down. And so I decided to seek stability by adding the feminine. In other words, I called Delilah. The next book I held in my hands was Erich Neumann's *Amor and Psyche*, where he compared Psyche's task retrieving wool from the fleeces of Apollo's golden flocks with Delilah's shearing of Samson's locks.

Particularly insightful, I thought, was Neumann's interpretation of the task that Eros's mother Aphrodite gave Psyche as punishment for wounding her son with love (after all, the mother of Love never imagined that Love himself could fall in love; his love was to be reserved for his mother). Neumann describes the discussion surrounding Psyche as a kind of Platonic dialogue, or a *havruta* such as one might find in the Talmud. He then tells the story of Psyche's task to collect wool from the fleeces of Apollo's flock. No one could touch or even approach Apollo's rams, for they were "as fierce as flame" and would devour anyone who dared trying. Aphrodite was convinced that Psyche would be killed on her mission of love. But Psyche was counseled by her friends to wait until sunset when the sheep had gone to sleep. She would then be able to gather their wool off the briers. At this point, one of Neumann's friends suggests the following parallel with Samson: the emasculation of the masculine solar power occurs during the feminine night. Indeed, Apollo is the sun god and Samson is the diminutive form of the Hebrew word for *sun*. Psyche gathers the wool only after the sun sets, and Delilah shears Samson's locks at night while he sleeps. But, then again, isn't highlighting the feminine aspect of the story but another way of introducing man's terror of castration and his fear of women's wiles? The masculine bore down even heavier on my desk, which was about to collapse.

Just then what appeared before me (as it appeared in my youth) was a collection of poems entitled *From Time Immemorial: Ancient Figures* by the Hebrew poet Anda Pinkerfeld. There is in the book a poem about Delilah. It is a very small book, it had been lying next to all the other little books in my parents' living room for almost sixty years. The book was given to my mother by her beloved Mordechai before he died in the 1948 war. It has an inscription from Shimon Peres to "Motke," as everyone knew Mordechai.[1] This was the same Motke who rode a horse and lived in a tree with my mother, two young fighters in the Palmach,[2] so full of lion's honey. Mordechai was also the name of my mother's brother, killed in his youth under mysterious circumstances by diving into an empty swimming pool, perhaps an accident, perhaps suicide. Finally, Mordechai is also my brother Nimrod's middle name, given to him to keep this name, which continues

1. A veteran Israeli politician, defense minister, prime minister, and now the president of Israel.
2. The underground proto-army of the Jewish settlement in Palestine before Israel was founded—acronym for "strike forces."

to haunt my family. Then again, my family does not believe in ghosts—or even in gods for that matter—and perhaps it is better this way. Still, the god Nimrod keeps the god Marduk in my brother's name. Two ancient gods that have become the ghosts of our Zionist, secular, humanist family. And I, the youngest son, see these ghosts, but I remain silent. Perhaps they will never burst out; perhaps they will only occasionally stir beneath the surface, resulting in some involuntary movement of no consequence.

I'm finally ready to begin writing about Samson. I put the books aside and call on the spirits and muses to assist me. I think that, perhaps, through Samson, I could tell the story of my family, the story of the generation that founded the State of Israel and the generation of their scarred children.

But at that very moment the Israeli Air Force launches an attack on Gaza, and the indiscriminate killing by those "Made in USA" angels of Hades begins. The muses are suddenly silenced: "Why write about Samson, when there is so much death everywhere?" they ask me. I dress quickly and run out to the streets to demonstrate, as if I had the power to put an end to the destruction and killing and vengeance. Very few people gather to protest. All the rest swoon at the swoosh of the jets overhead as they soar to do battle for the many against the few, for the strong against the weak, for the occupiers against the occupied. The children of Israel mutter Samson's own words, "Avenge but one of my two eyes!" but we cannot be the blind Samson when we have night vision goggles and virtual reality goggles and can see from a distance and in the dark. And the jetfighter pilot does not say "Let me die with the Philistines!" but "Let the Palestinians be killed by my smart bomb so that I can get back home in time to catch a show at the national theater." On the hills of Ashkelon, the children of Israel look down on Gaza burning and rejoice.

Outside the museum, where we went to demonstrate, there were so few of us that no passersby needed to put wax in their ears; no one needed to tie himself to the mast. The roars of victory are loud enough to silence even the best of us. Gaza, *Azza* (the Hebrew name for Gaza). The meaning is so clear, yet no one notices how it reverberates with our actions. *Azza*, in Hebrew, means "feminine strength." We use the word *azza* in the popular idiom "Love *is stronger* than death." Yet we fail to understand that Gaza has not been defeated. In his day Samson carried off the iron gates of Gaza in order to humiliate the city. Now the city is fenced in yet again, its gates are sealed; no one can come or go. A modern Samson would be a Palestinian resistance fighter struggling to open the gates along the borders that suffocate Gaza turning it into the world's largest prison. In my mind's eye I see myself sitting next to a Palestinian child who is digging a tunnel, a child who will never have a childhood. He is digging the tunnel underneath the border in order to bring food and arms to his besieged city. I tell him that a long time ago a giant man simply carried the gates of Gaza off on his shoulders.

JANUARY 2009, RAMALLAH

THE STRUGGLE

Day after day Israel continues to bomb Gaza. I am on the road, I can't help but join the demonstrations against the war, write articles condemning the war, express my outrage in the face of this evil. I have a hard time looking into the eyes of those who support the war. I don't want to see the joy of victory in the presence of dismembered bodies and, worse, the teary eyes of the sensitive among them, who say "How terrible" and carry on. Soon there will be a cease-fire; soon they will count the bodies. The propaganda machine will describe some fundamentalist monster that must be destroyed. Today it is in Gaza; tomorrow it will be in Kashmir or in any other place where the West decides to draw a line against the barbarians. I imagine that a short time from now a handful of poets will pen their regrets and a few liberal artists will receive a handout from the state so that they can publicly atone for our sins. I'm sure that there will be fundraising events on behalf of the innocent children of such a ruthless enemy.

I am also certain that there is some soldier in Gaza who is planning his next film, and a very sensitive, humane film it will be. The gentle soul of this handsome soldier will be shattered to pieces at the sight of a little girl clutching a doll outside the ruins of her home, which was wiped off the earth by some especially smart missile. That girl's doleful expression will reflect the deep pain felt by that soldier, but then, in painfully slow motion, or perhaps deprived of all emotion because he is so shell-shocked (it all depends on the actor's performance and the cinematographer's disposition), he will hand the girl some medicine or a bar of Toblerone. We will all realize that he is the light in all this darkness and that redemption is possible for us. The film will condemn the masters of that war and the cruelty of the Occupation. To some degree it will even condemn itself (because everyone is a little bit guilty). The soldier will punish himself in the film and be unable to have sex with his boyfriend or his girlfriend or both. The film will be screened at all the festivals and pick up prizes at most of them, and everyone who sees it will say, "How sensitive!" In a revealing interview with the press, the filmmaker will explain how, after undergoing psychotherapy, he can now connect with his feminine side and that, as a result, he can finally get an erection again. Most definitely, there will be no one who stands up in the middle of the theater, tosses his popcorn at the screen, and screams, "We've seen this film before." Just as in some shamanic ritual, everyone has a place and a role to play. In this production even we have a role as artists—preserving all the pleasantries of life between the fences that have been erected around the wild, poor, brutal world out there, the fences that have become our own prison.

So here's a thought: perhaps film cannot be more than what it is allocated in the cultural sphere. Yet, every so often, in moments of kindness, we might be able to find a breach in the fence and cross to the other side. Then it might be possible *not* to describe the other with great pity and sympathy from the vantage point of a watchtower that looms over the walls of Western democracy. Instead, we might be able to climb through the breach and reappear on the other side, gazing back at where we once stood—transforming our gaze from something that creates otherness to something that challenges its very creation.

FEBRUARY 2009, JERUSALEM

"ANNA O. IS BERTHA PAPPENHEIM": A SYMPOSIUM

It has been a long time since I participated in an apolitical intellectual event in Israel. Since returning from New York to live in Tel Aviv, I tumbled into the realm of the real, I could not keep a symbolic distance for very long. It is true that every so often I managed to get out for a few brief moments and inhale the fresh mountain air, but almost as soon as I escaped I crumpled and fell back into the refuse. The people of Israel had their say. On Election Day, after the Gaza massacre, the vast majority of Jews voted for what were essentially racist parties (only about 3 percent voted differently), but even before the elections were held the vast majority of Jews in Parliament voted to deny the Arabs of Israel the right to be elected. Just a few days later we saw a defense ministry document that was leaked to the media. In it the ministry expressly admitted that the state had robbed people of their lands solely on the basis of their ethnic identity and that it had distributed these lands to people of Jewish origin only. He who has not seen the rejoicing of Israel when faced with the death and destruction brought about by low-flying jets against homemade rockets has never seen rejoicing in all his days. My life was overwhelmed with this psychotic feeling that every minute that I failed to do something, anything, on behalf of Palestine, was as if I had destroyed a world and all its wonders. Apart from a few quick trips overseas, it was, paradoxically, only in Ramallah that I felt relief from the chest constrictions that plagued me. Yet here I was on my way to Jerusalem to attend a symposium about Anna O. I would finally be able to devote myself to my one true passion—to that realm of wisdom made up of shards of theology and psychoanalysis that are scattered around our world like the divine sparks of light that were let loose in the mystical "breaking of the primordial vessel." In that realm the act of learning was the means of restoring those sparks to their historical, hysterical place. Who better than Anna O. could serve as a starting point for my archeological expedition, especially as she was to be described by Professor Daniel Boyarin and that short-termed Knesset member Zvia Greenfield, two Jews with impeccable credentials as Orthodox and radicals?

Before we report on what Jews argue about in the sacred harlot that is Jerusalem, we should say a few words about Anna O., whose real name was Bertha Pappenheim. It was under the latter name that she became the subject of activity in the real world, rather than simply some research object for Breuer and Freud to ponder over.[3] Of course, one might argue that even as an object she functioned as a subject by establishing speech as a form of therapy, but that is out of the bounds of our topic. After the scandal in which she claimed that her therapist, Breuer, had gotten her pregnant (she was never in therapy with Freud), she moved to Frankfurt, where she worked on behalf of Jewish girls forced into prostitution by pimps who operated from within the sanctuary of the synagogue. It is worth noting that the percentage of women who worked in prostitution was higher among the Jewish community than among their Christian peers, though this is never taught in history class.

Beginning her talk with "I am Anna O.," Zvia Greenfield spoke about how Bertha Pappenheim had never experienced sex with a man. Her

---

3. Joseph Breuer and Sigmund Freud, *Studies in Hysteria* (New York: Basic Books, 2000).

return to the Orthodox world was, according to Greenfield, a kind of perversion, a pathological act. It was a return to a place where the Jewish male failed in fulfilling his classic role, which demanded three things of him: that he protects his family; that he supports his family; and that he fathers children. Greenfield argued that in the early years of the last century the ultra-Orthodox Jewish male in the Diaspora was unable to protect his family, depending as he did entirely on the kindness of the Gentiles. The yeshiva was obviously the center of his life, but this meant that he was not the breadwinner either, and that role was taken over by women. The only way that a man could prove his masculinity and control women was by fathering as many children as possible. Each child that he fathered proved to the tribe that his masculine potency was indeed intact. Zvia Greenfield's provocative statement struck at the tender underbelly of the secular-Jew-who-fantasizes-about-the-ultra-Orthodox-Jew-as-scholar type. Audience protests were summed up in a question by one flabbergasted secular woman who mustered up all her emotion to argue: "But you know that the Jewish male studies Torah. That's why he sends his wife out to work!" Greenfield, herself an ultra-Orthodox Jew, answered very frostily: "So he studies Torah. Big deal!" Obviously, what she meant was that a woman could study Torah no less well than a man—that the only thing a woman could not do was to have sex with another woman in order to conceive a child.

Daniel Boyarin agreed with the woman in the audience that studying Torah was a "big deal" and fought desperately against Greenfield's assertion that Bertha Pappenheim's return to the ultra-Orthodox world was a pathological act. Instead he argued that it was a place of healing or, at least, her natural environment. Certainly, he added, she did not have a relapse of the illness itself.

While all of this was going on, I began to realize that although I had actually attempted to win a brief respite from politics by coming here to Jerusalem, I found myself caught up in an intense debate between my two learned friends over the essence of Zionism and Jewish masculinity. The word *Zionism* need never have been said. It was obvious to Boyarin that Zvia Greenfield believes Zionism to be a remedy for the desiccated Jewish masculinity of the Diaspora, and that she even went so far as to see it as a stage in the feminist revolution underway in the ultra-Orthodox community. In contrast, Boyarin believes that the Jewish masculinity of the Diaspora is the remedy for masculine Zionist aggression. Zionism cannot be a milestone in Jewish feminism if it is so absorbed in its quest for the ultimate Samsonic masculinity, so disdainful of femininity or learning or gentleness or even weakness or hysteria. In fact, it replaces the latter with some manic vision of pure masculinity to serve as a hegemonic psychosis.

I began to think of male homosexuality in Israel. It may have achieved considerable progress in its struggle for emancipation, including almost complete acceptance by secular Israeli society. But the price that gay men paid for this was the loss of their queer identity. By serving in the army, most gay men had become an intrinsic part of the mechanism of Occupation. While it is true that by exhibiting loyalty to the state they had come to realize their dream, they did so at the expense of another persecuted minority. Perhaps, I thought, that was the fate of all minorities who struggle for their rights. As part of their struggle with the predominant social norms of their respective societies, they find themselves exhibiting loyalty to the meta-ideologies of those societies. This results in the formation of the gay Zionist-nationalist in much the same way that Bertha Pappenheim was compelled to reassert her loyalty to her native Orthodox society (Greenfield is right about this). On the other hand, based on this reasoning, Greenfield should exhibit loyalty to Zionist society (Boyarin is right about this), whereas for Boyarin to be right about the Diaspora Jewish male he must first castrate him—or emasculate him at the very least (Greenfield is right about this).

The next session was given by psychoanalysts and chaired by Dr. Jose Brunner of Tel Aviv University. They also spoke about Anna O., but when Boyarin heard them relate to what he said as a condemnation of psychoanalysis, he thought that he had been misunderstood and wanted to clarify his position. As chair of the session, Brunner rudely silenced him, thus preventing the conference from attaining what every true academic conference strives for: the interplay of content and emergence of dialogue between two distinct sessions at the very same event. Brunner's rudeness pervaded the auditorium, reminding us all not of how right Boyarin was in his description of the Zionist male but rather of how difficult it is to hide from Jerusalem in Jerusalem.

And so I abandoned this conflict between two friends and set out in search of some alternative masculinity. Rather than seeking to find the ideal man in literature or traditional sources and to use that paradigm to construct a new approach to masculinity, I decided to return to Samson. He was, after all, "the ultimate male," and it remained for me to provide his character with new meaning. Guiding me along this quest would be Anda Pinkerfeld's

From Time Immemorial: Ancient Figures, that same little collection of poems that I found among all the other little books in my parents' living room.

MARCH 2009, NEW YORK

EVERYMAN/A MAN AMONG MEN

Back to Anda Pinkerfeld's *From Time Immemorial: Ancient Figures*, and her poem about Delilah. In Judges it is written:

> . . . If they bind me with seven green withes that were never dried, then shall I be weak and as everyman.
> . . . If they bind me fast with new ropes that were never occupied, then shall I be weak and be like everyman.
> . . . If thou weavest the seven locks of my head with the web.
> And she said unto him, How canst thou say, I love thee, when thine heart is not with me? thou mocked me these three times, and hast not told me wherein thy great strength lieth. And it came to pass, when she pressed him daily with her words, and urged him, so that his soul was vexed unto death; That he told her all his heart, and said unto her, There hath not come a razor upon my head; for I have been a Nazarite unto God from my mother's womb: if I be shaven, then my strength will go from me, and I shall become weak, and be like a man among men.
>
> (Judges 16)

Three times Delilah asked Samson for the secret of his strength; and three times Samson mocked her. But the third time she asked him in the name of Love, and when things are done in the name of Love one cannot break one's vow with a lie, and so he revealed his secret. Was Samson's soul "vexed unto death" because he could not withstand the pain of betrayal, or did he believe that no woman would ever name Love in vain? Had he become addicted to the game of bondage, only to learn firsthand that the game works only when each session is more intense, all the way to death itself?

When I think of Samson and Gaza, these verses from the Song of Songs reverberate within me: "for love is strong [*azza*] as death; jealousy is cruel as the grave; the coals thereof are coals of fire, which hath a most vehement flame. Many waters cannot quench love, neither can the floods drown it: if a man would give all the substance of his house for love, it would utterly be contemned" (Song of Songs 8, King James Bible). The relationship between Samson and Gaza can be interpreted as a power struggle between masculine and feminine forces. As I have already noted, the word *azza* is the feminine declension of the word strong or valorous. The name *Samson* consists of the Hebrew word for *sun* followed by the diminutive, which in my reading could be taken to mean "the son of the sun," a reference to male power. In this reading, Samson stealing the gates of Gaza in the middle of the night could represent his robbing his feminine nemesis of her virginity. All Samson's relations with the Philistines are represented in his relationship with Delilah, which is one of betrayed love in its various forms: the innocent lover betrayed, the honorable lover deceived by woman's treachery, the narcissistic lover in love with someone just like him. This is the kind of killing Oscar Wilde wrote about in *The Ballad of Reading Gaol*: "Yet each man kills the thing he loves" or, even more poignantly, Kafka in the *Blue Octavo Notebooks*. "Celibacy and suicide are on similar levels of understanding, suicide and martyr's death not so by any means, perhaps marriage and martyr's death."[4]

The enemy as a manipulative feminine force that deceives and seduces a shimmering-sunlike masculine avatar reappears across many cultures and finds its grotesque apogee in Nazism. And yet the opposite, in which the feminine is depicted as the revolutionary force of the disempowered, also appears frequently, for example in the biblical stories of Esther, the Jewish queen who changed the entire destiny of her nation from within the royal court, and of Yael, who killed the enemy's warlord Sisera: "He asked water, and she gave him milk; she brought forth butter in a lordly dish. She put her hand to the nail, and her right hand to the workmen's hammer; and with the hammer she smote Sisera, she smote off his head, when she had pierced and stricken through his temples. At her feet he bowed, he fell, he lay down: at her feet he bowed, he fell: where he bowed, there he fell down dead" (Judges 5, King James Bible). This is how Anda Pinkerfeld ends her poem about Delilah:

And I loved you like a man among men,
But you are not like
Everyman.

---

4. Franz Kafka, *The Blue Octavo Notebooks* (Exact Change, 1991), p. 26.

The Delilah of the poem is in love with Samson as the perfect embodiment of masculine power; she accepts the archetypal notion of admiration for the perfect, divine man. This is the only way she can and will love him. When Samson, acting in the name of Love, reveals his secret to her, she is disdainful of him for acting as a man among men and not like a god. In fact, the poem describes Delilah's search for Samson's body. Once he has used his divine powers in a suicidal fit of violence to topple down the house and take down Delilah's people, she searches the ruins of the demolished sanctuary. Only from the wreckage of this devastation could Delilah, a "refugee" of sorts, gain some understanding of the kind of love that was offered to her by Samson. Only then is she able to love him as a man among men rather than as her god, tragically, at the very moment in which his divinity most manifests and his appearance as a man comes to an end. Only then is he the subject of love rather than the bearer of some divine hammer or *Mjöllnir*. This could only have been deduced retroactively, posthumously, once such "possible" love is deemed impossible. Or, in Kafka's famous dictum, "The Messiah will come only . . . on the day after his arrival"[5] Delilah now understands that Samson offered to be "a man among men" to her and her alone. Yes, he would still be unique and extraordinary, but he would be a man, not a superman, not the Child of the Sun or the Son of God, but a man, human, all too human, because that is the only way love can survive. A similar theme can be found in Wim Wenders's film *Wings of Desire* in which an angel who falls in love with a human woman must forfeit his angelic nature and become a fallen angel—a man—because that is the only way he can truly learn what love is. "Love *is* stronger than death," because without death there can be no love. That is why Samson reveals his secret, his weakness, the clue to his mortality to Delilah and only to Delilah. For her part, she failed to understand the potency of the gift he granted to her when it was first given—or even that it was given out of love. Rather than believe she had betrayed him, having mistook admiration for love, she felt her own deification of him betrayed by his weakness. How dare Samson appear before her in all his weakness! After all, this was Samson, who had never been defeated, more god than man, who showed himself to be a man after all.

A precise reading of the biblical text shows that there is a difference between the two phrases that appear throughout the story: *a man among men* and *everyman*. Ostensibly, the two turns of phrase are practically

5. Ibid., p. 28.

identical, but in my interpretation there is a world of difference between them. The King James Version of the Bible recognizes the difference by distinguishing between *another* and *any other*. In Hebrew the distinction is more apparent. Although the two terms are often interchangeable, they employ diametrically opposed prefixes: one denoting the one, the other: the all or the generic. I chose to translate what literately read "as all men" as everyman and "as one of the men" as "a man among men."[6]

Whereas the difference between *all* and *one* remains obvious, the text uses expressions that are nonetheless seemingly synonymous. The meaning seems identical in both cases: without his divine powers, Samson is just like any other man. But the difference between these two expressions is by no means coincidental. Rather, it distinguishes between a mob that obliterates singularity (*everyman*) and a unique individual among the community of men (*a man among men*). If my interpretation is correct, should Delilah accept his token of love, Samson will become *a man among men*, an individual in the community of men, but, at the same time, a unique and extraordinary specimen of his gender. By being *a man among men*, he will be unique in his love for her, subject *to* (and not simply the subject *of*) her love. Should she cherish his gift of vulnerability, she will facilitate his apotheosis as a man among men. Yet, having fallen short in acknowledging his gift—the strength of a lover's weakness—she sentences him to a fate of *everymanness*. His only leeway out of such a generic legacy is a resort to the most violent display of love—the gift of death—which, in Samson's case, is death for all.

The lesson in this for us is that the power that resides in life is the recognition of its inherent weakness, or *fragility,* to borrow Judith Butler's term. But, just as Delilah was not yet ready to appreciate Samson's gift, Samson was unable to comprehend her error. That is why he chooses to sanctify his rejected love with blood and becomes a bloodied groom. He recognizes the power of death and rejects the weakness of life. As a metaphor for this story, we might use the Islamic term *shahid*, which means both *martyr* and *witness*. By dying as a martyr, he not only testifies as to God's existence but also as to his love for God.[7] Samson becomes a *shahid*

6. The distinction is not universally recognized in English translations of the Bible and is absent in many modern translations. For instance, *The New Oxford Annotated Bible* (New York: Oxford, 2001) does not distinguish between them.

7. After all, the lover and the martyr act in the selfsame way. As Slavoj Žižek has explained: the *shahid* is not the greatest believer but the greatest doubter, and it is only through his death that he can release his heart of doubt and prove his faith.

of love in the sense of him becoming a martyr, while Delilah becomes a *shahid* of love in the sense of her becoming a witness. Delilah and Gaza can only love Samson as a hero who destroys everyone, including himself. She remains alive as a witness to the devastation only so that she can finally understand she was actually witness to the great moment of truth but did not realize it then. Only against the backdrop of Samson's heroic death and the utter destruction of Gaza, only against absolute, divinely ordained violence, could she finally understand the love of a man in his moment of weakness. Maybe she survived to tell us that destruction is the consequence of failing to recognize the gift of a lover who wants to build a relationship based on the fragility of life rather than on violence and the certainty of identity. In other words, as *a man among men*; in other words, as *death*.

Samson is not some blind *shahid* who sees beyond the physical world. His very existence is, after all, so very physical, yet he is trapped between roadblocks and shackled in chains! Nor is he the Israeli Zionist youth who goes out to gather the lion's honey, who smiles at roadblocks and kills from jets without even realizing that he is like that. Perhaps he does it because, in the end, he is like *everyman* or perhaps he does it to win the admiration of his loving parents. Samson and Delilah command us to love, but they also command us to embrace weakness and fragility as the sources of life's great power. They teach that the superman is *a man among men* but unlike *everyman*. Perhaps they were intended to represent the last great orgy of destruction rather than some orgy of destruction that repeats itself again and again. In other words, as *man and woman among men and women*; in other words as *life*.

APRIL 2009, TEL AVIV

EPILOGUE: SAMSON'S TIKKUN (BIG REPAIR)

Maybe that is Samson's repair: he established the principle of an idea that is liberated from itself, masculinity that breaks free of the need to endlessly represent divine violence without coming apart. I am almost tempted to say that in his otherness and his weakness Samson the Hero becomes Samson the Queero, at one with the object of his love and, through Delilah's insights (and because of her), able to maintain his power. In some mythical-political sense this may even be the same kind of love that is possible between the Palestinian and the Jew. Maybe Samson and Delilah are the first Palestinians and Jews. It is through that exemplary identity rooted in revolution, in otherness, and in a desire for love that they learn to be as *a man and a woman among men and women* rather than like some superman or woman or *all other men and women*. They are the ones who maintain their differences out of unity and recognize the power that lies in nonviolence. Such a figure may only be able to exist on the margins of local politics, but from there its actions can reverberate like a shot heard around the world.

Shortly before he died, Edward Said wrote the essay *Freud and the Non-European*.[8] In it he offered us what may be his greatest gift of all: being a Jewish Palestinian. Through his reading of Freud, Said shows us that there can be no independent identity that does not encompass other, radical identities and that this is the reason why harmony remains so elusive and unobtainable. He writes that we can contend with the past "not through dispensing palliatives such as tolerance and compassion but, rather, by attending to it as a troubling, disabling, destabilizing, secular wound— the essence of the cosmopolitan, from which there can be no recovery, no state of resolved or Stoic calm" (54). At the end of that article he writes:

> The questions Freud therefore leaves us with are: can so utterly indecisive and so deeply undetermined a history ever be written? In what language, and with what sort of vocabulary?
>
> Can it aspire to the conditions of a politics of diaspora life? Can it ever become the not-so-precarious foundation in the land of Jews and Palestinians of a bi-national state in which Israel and Palestine are parts, rather than antagonists of each other's history and under- lying reality? I myself believe so. (55)

That is what I wanted to say about Samson, a Judge in Israel but also a Stranger to Israel, who incorporates other identities within himself, just as they incorporate him. He is part of the universal other, yet despite that, and because of that, he is what he is. But Samson did not have the vocabu- lary with which to preserve the other identities that were encompassed by his own identity, so that, when he said, "Let me die with the Philistines," it was as if he was trying to say "Let the Philistine within me die." And

8. Edward Said, *Freud and the Non-European* (New York: Verso, 2003). See also "A Man- ifesto for the Jewish-Palestinian Arab-Hebrew State" in part 1, this volume.

yet, within his heart of hearts, he knew that without those other identities within him there could be no life, and when he killed the Philistine within him it was obvious to him that he would die along with it. In the same way, according to Freud, when the children of Israel killed Moses the Egyptian what they actually eliminated was the true essence of Israel, an essence that can neither be complete nor at ease without some penetrating understanding of the other identities included within it. Likewise, we can also say that when we bombed Gaza we killed not only the Palestinian but also the Jew. Or, just as Avot Yeshurun wrote: "The Holocaust of the Arabs of Palestine and the Holocaust of the Jews of Europe are both Holocausts of the Jews, staring at us straight in the face."

Now we live in the Land of Israel, which is also the Land of Palestine, but rather than fixing what Samson started, we have only made things worse. We may have compared ourselves to gods, but we were like all other men. Only if we walk hand in hand with Samson and Delilah and learn, together with them, the language of love with which to communicate with the other identities encompassed within us will we realize that the love of Israel and the love of Palestine are one and the same. Only then can we strive to be like a human among humans, inimitable, unique, and yet nonetheless a human.

Pnay El (Face of God)

The Place of Radical Encounter

HE HAS HIDDEN HIS FACE IN HIS HIDDENNESS

While preparing to release my recent book in Israel, my publisher suggested an editor whom I had never worked with before. I was feeling particularly vulnerable about publishing in Hebrew after twelve years in "exile." In order to calm me down, he sent me a text that he had recently translated. Surprisingly enough, it was *Precarious Life* by Judith Butler. Since her work has influenced a lot of my thinking, I was already familiar with the English text, but, in a mysterious way, it was a real pleasure, almost natural, to read it in Hebrew. So, dear Judith, it somehow makes perfect sense to me that I'm sitting with you here, at Jewish Book Week, trying to think together through your book *Precarious Life,* which gave me so much.

In order to help me put my thoughts together, I brought different books and notes with me. You see that among them is the Bible, so whenever I lose track I can always go back to it and start from the beginning.

As you all know, today is Purim, and we should do this talk with wine in our hands. Yet, if they give us water, we'll perform a miracle and turn it into wine. Because this is the essence of Purim, or, to be more eloquent, Purim is

Edited from a talk with Judith Butler for Jewish Book Week, March 2007.

a radical change in destiny. Purim is the mask; Purim is the joy, and Purim is about Esther. Whoever knows the name Esther knows that it means "hidden." But if we go to the origin of the name, we find that it appears in the Bible for the first time when God says: "va-Anochi haster asteer panay." "I am hiding my face" (Deut. 31:18). But *haster asteer panay:* it's not only *haster panim*—it's double. He has hidden his face in his hiddenness.

Therefore God hides his face not only from us but from himself as well. So our responsibility is to reveal his face to himself: first, to put a mirror in front of God's face.

BUT WHAT IS OR ARE THE FACE(S) OF GOD? AND WHY IS IT FOR US TO REVEAL IT?

In the last chapter of *Precarious Life* Butler deals with the face, referring to Emmanuel Levinas's writings on the face of the other. She writes, "Since what the face 'says' is 'Thou shalt not kill,' it would appear that it is through this primary commandment that speaking first comes into being, so that speaking first comes into being against the backdrop of this possible murder."[1] Butler also addresses the representation, or the impossibility of representing, humanity through the face. Or, in Butler's words, "For Levinas, then, the human is not represented by the face. Rather, the human is indirectly affirmed in that very disjunction that makes representation impossible, and this disjunction is conveyed in the impossible representation. For representation to convey the human, then, representation must not only fail, but it must show its failure."[2] Through this line of thought, Butler offers us a new way of thinking about the dehumanization that occurs in images found in contemporary media.

The small midrash to follow, in which I will cite *Precarious Life* citing Levinas citing the Bible, is a small gift that I am attempting to give to Judith for all that I have received from her. One might ask: Why, in such a state of emergency, give a midrash rather than use the stage at the Jewish Book Week to preach your political agenda? But you all already know that I stand against the Occupation, and you all already know that my love of Palestine and my love of Israel are one love. So I want to argue that sometimes,

1. Judith Butler, *Precarious Life: The Power of Mourning and Violence* (London: Verso, 2006), p. 138.
2. Ibid, p. 144.

even in times of emergency, we should postpone the concrete political discussion a bit. In times of emergency this is a particularly complex issue. Because during such times it is of course necessary to respond directly to the emergency itself. Yet not only are we blinded to the face of the other by overwhelming images of the state of emergency. We are also deafened to the command: "Thou shalt not kill" by the chaotic noise with which the emergency is surrounded and, in this way, strengthened or empowered.

So I have decided to share a midrash-panim (midrash about the face) in relation to Jacob and Esau. The first midrash that I gave about *panim,* some time ago, was about to two other brothers, Cain and Abel. To be precise, it concerned the first place in the Torah where the concepts of murder and face are encountered together. Unlike what happens between Cain and Abel, in the narrative of Jacob and Esau their face-to-face meeting is perhaps successful in that the potential murder is converted into love or at least into respect.

THE GIVEN NAME OF JACOB: READING THE FACE(S)
WITH *PRECARIOUS LIFE*

Panim, which in English means "face," in Hebrew is plural. The word *panim* is, further, both masculine and feminine. Also, if, in English, *panim* is surface, in Hebrew it's both surface and interior (*pnim*). So *panim* is inside and outside, it's male and female, and it's multiplicity. Let's keep this full notion of panim in mind as we go through the text of Jacob and Esau.

The story begins as Esau is coming toward Jacob accompanied by four hundred people. Jacob is afraid that Esau is coming to kill him, and we know that he has all the reason, because Jacob attempted to steal his birthright. Not only once, but three times. The first attempt, which failed, occurred the moment Jacob was born. The name Jacob, or Yaakov, means "heel" (*akev*) in Hebrew. Jacob tried to hold the heel of Esau in order to be the first to come out from their mother's womb. Jacob made a second, successful attempt at the theft when Esau came back from hunting. Jacob told his brother that if he wanted to eat a bit of lentil soup he would have to sell his birthright, which Esau then sold. The third attempt, with the help of their mother, was for Jacob's reassurance. He disguised himself as his brother and received the blessing of the firstborn, which was intended for Esau, from their father.

Thus Jacob is in a very defensive position as Esau is on his way toward him. In her book Butler cites a beautiful passage in which Levinas quotes

Rashi (the eleventh-century commentator on Old Testament and the Talmud). Rashi comments on a sentence in the Torah describing Jacob's psychological state as his brother approaches (*Precarious Life* 136): "Jacob was greatly afraid and anxious" (Gen. 32:8). Rashi writes that Jacob was greatly afraid that Esau might kill him, and he was anxious, or sorry, that he might have to kill Esau (136). This powerful and inevitable encounter with the other, an encounter Judith deals with in her book, led me to the question: What is it in this moment that forces one to either become a murderer or to be murdered? It's something that I try to deal with in my recent movie, *Forgiveness*. I think that in her book Butler tries to find a third place for this moment. She writes, "the face makes various utterances at once: it bespeaks an agony, an injurability, at the same time that it bespeaks a divine prohibition against killing" (*Precarious Life* 135).

When you meet yourself, the question is "to be or not to be?" But when you meet the other, the question is, "to kill or be killed?" And Jacob discovers the most radical sort of third place, a place in which he simultaneously meets the self and the other. In the story Esau is on his way toward Jacob, who begins to send him many presents. The various English translations of the Bible do not convey how present the face is within the text, so I'll provide you with my own translation from the Hebrew. However, note that the repetition as such does not reveal itself to even Hebrew readers. So the text reads: "I will make his face pardon me with the gift that goes before my face, and afterward I will see his face; perhaps he will accept my face. So the present went over his face" (Gen. 32:21).

Jacob sends the gifts in order to prepare for this face-to-face. We know that Jacob is afraid and anxious, aware of the gravity of the situation even before he encounters his brother. Yet this is Jacob the manipulator, as his name suggests. This is the Jacob who inveigles his brother by sending gifts, the Jacob who is trying to avoid being murdered alongside his whole tribe.

Rashi's beautiful interpretation regarding Jacob's double fear (to kill or to be killed) can be read retroactively as a prophecy, because at this stage in the story Jacob has only the fear of being killed. The narrative is about to reach the encounter between two brothers—or should I say two nations, as the prophecy stated when the twins were in Rebecca's womb: "two nations are in your womb" (Gen. 25:23). But at this moment, at the very apex, the narrative suddenly, aggressively, splits in the middle. Just as Jacob is sending presents and fretting over his future face-to-face with Esau, a new narrative penetrates the text. In this new narrative Jacob struggles with an angel all night long.

The morning after, the angel tells him: "Thy name shall be called no more Jacob, but Israel" (Gen. 32:29). So in that moment he becomes Israel. The angel continues, explaining the name: "Key saritah im Elohim vay anashim, va yacholta" (Gen. 32:29). The word *saritah* in Hebrew has a double meaning, so the statement is translated as both "You have fought with God and humans, and you managed," and "You have been with God and humans, and you managed." Whereas his former name, Jacob, in a way means "manipulator," the name Israel means "fighting with God" and "being with God." In the moment that Jacob becomes Israel he becomes a powerful person.

In the morning, he gives a name to the place in which they were struggling: Pnay El, "the face of God." Thus the face of God becomes the place of the radical and eternal change, the place from which Jacob, or better said, Israel, will go to meet his brother. I'm almost tempted to use Nietzsche's terminology and to say that he changes from the slave morality to the morality of the master. (In the name Israel, we also find the word *sar*, which can mean "high prince" or "master.")

IN GOOD FAITH

Therefore, in the morning, when Jacob continues to send presents to Esau, I read this as the most radical change of the meaning of giving. If Jacob's gift previously came from his position of weakness, now it's his generosity that generates the giving. So, in a way, we can now understand Rashi's interpretation of the sentence "Jacob was greatly afraid and anxious." Before the struggle with the angel, he sends gifts out of his fear of being killed. And now, when he's very powerful physically and spiritually, he sends the gifts so as not to murder.

What we learn is that even though, at first, it seems unclear why the struggle with the angel appears in the middle of the story, it is now obvious that this appearance comes from the most ethical change in the encounter with the other. It is not, as we might first assume, a separate narrative, rather, it is the heart and soul of the story. The narrative shifts point us in the direction of the true meaning of a radical ethical change in one person and his relations with his other. Interestingly enough, whereas in English the word *brother* contains the *other*, in Hebrew, "other" (*acher*) includes the word for "brother" (*ach*), which emphasizes my point that the other is never an absolute other. Or, moreover, as in the case of Jacob and Esau, the other also always has the quality of the twin.

In the morning, as we have said, Jacob is no longer weak; he's no longer the Jacob who tries to pull tricks; he is Israel now. The giving is now an entirely different act, and the gift is an entirely different gift. It's a gift in good faith. It's the gift to the other from an entirely different position.

Then Esau runs toward him, embraces him, and kisses him on his neck. Both brothers are hugging and crying. Jacob tells Esau, "I saw your face as I saw the face of God" (Gen. 33:10). We have to remember that after he struggled with the angel he said, "I have seen God face-to-face" (Gen 32:31). So the face is not the face of a Big Other; when you act in good faith, the face becomes familiar. The face of God and the face of the (br)other and the face of the self are a multiplicity of faces that meet in this act of good faith.

Now one might think that we could end the story here, with this beautiful happy ending. But, in reality, there is another chapter to the story.

What bothers me is this: when I reread this narrative, I realized that there's something so beautiful in it, in the two brothers falling on each other, kissing each other on the neck, etc. So I wondered: if this is the case, why is Esau always portrayed as such a villain in Judaism? There's something so beautiful about Esau here.

So I went to Bereshit Rabbah, a canonized text from the times of the Talmud, around the fifth century. And I found that they turn the text of the Bible upside-down using the similarity of the words "kiss" and "bite" in Hebrew, nashak and nashach. And they write: "He didn't come to kiss him, but to bite him, and Jacob's neck turned into marble. And the teeth of the villain became dull."

This story then comes to explain why they were crying: "One wept about his neck which became marble, and the other was crying about his teeth that became dull."

One might ask: what is the psychological phenomenon that is happening here? We have rabbis who read this text and felt a lot of guilt toward Esau. Guilt toward someone who has been wronged by Israel, by us. Someone who suffered because of our fathers, our ancestors. Yet Esau accepted our kind of generosity. He came to us and hugged and kissed us. Esau felt the radical change in Jacob, and when he realized that his generosity came from good faith he ran to Israel, hugged him, and kissed him. But what Israel the father understood, Israel the nation couldn't handle: the guilt and the shame of facing the narrative of Esau.

So now we can come back to contemporary Israel. There is something in our time that reminds me too much of this psychological behavior. It reminds me so much of the way in which Israelis act toward Palestinian citizens of Israel. We did something wrong in '48. Some are keen to point out that in this regard there are different narratives. But, at the end of these narratives, we have a state, and they have nothing. At the end of the narratives, they lost their villages, and we have our cities. Something wrong happened, such that these two nations didn't end equally as two brothers, as they should be.

Then '67 came: '67 could have been the moment in which, in good faith, we might have approached our brothers. In good faith, we could have asked forgiveness. In good faith, we could have said, "yes, something went wrong in '48, but you know, we also came out of terrible times." Here was the time to make a true offer. But, instead, the guilt of seeing this other— seeing him face to face, seeing how he reminds us that he has nothing and we have everything—this guilt suddenly makes us do the same thing again, rather than come in good faith. This guilt makes us again take the houses of people who lost their houses once already, take again the land of people who lost their land once already.

Therefore, historically, this has been a moment of meeting the other and, instead of really approaching him in good faith, as Jacob finally did, being utterly unable to handle the wrongdoing and thus repeating it over and over again. This is why I am here, why I am going to every Jewish community that is still ready to hear me, and why I am speaking from my deep Jewishness.

I call out of the love of Israel. It's really important. As you probably know, Gershom Scholem wrote to Hannah Arendt accusing her of not having love of Israel. In my own words, her response was, "I don't know what love of Israel is. I know how to love Jody; I know how to love Moshe. I don't know what it means to have love of Israel." And now we know that there is something like love of Israel, and there is a kind of solidarity, and we're all here at a Jewish Book Week. I am not fighting for a return to this individual love. I think it is a different kind of love at work here. Rather, I am trying to understand that in my community my love of Israel can only come out of my love of Palestine and my Palestinian brothers and sisters, among whom we live and who live among us. And maybe that's why I am here. Thank you.

ISRAEL'S LIMP; OR, "DON'T CONCEAL YOUR HEEL, ACHILLES!" (EPILOGUE)

When I came back to Israel from Jewish Book Week in London, I went out for a coffee with my friend Dr. Itamar Barnea, the head psychologist of

National Trauma Victims and the former chief psychologist of the Israeli Air Force. Itamar was a prisoner of war in Syria after his aircraft was shot down in the '73 war, and he himself was fired at during his emergency parachute exit from the plane. Even when he touched ground the shooting didn't stop. He lost his lung, and his leg was crushed.

At the last minute, a Syrian officer prevented his soldier from executing Itamar. At the same time, on the Egyptian front, a friend of Itamar was preventing a famous Israeli officer from executing an Egyptian pilot whose plane had been shot down as well. I think that the uncanny relationship between the two events, which occurred simultaneously on both sides of the state, was a founding moment in Itamar's work on trauma. After eight months in Syrian custody, he returned home and underwent a long period of therapy that was to make him dedicate his life to helping other people, in particular those suffering from posttraumatic syndromes related to the collective trauma.

Over our coffee I told him about my midrash and about my feeling that I ignored an essential part of the story when I first gave the talk. And, by ignoring the important fact that Israel came out of his struggle with the angel with a limp in his leg, a fact that is emphasized in the Bible, I gave up an essential part of the interpretation. Itamar suggested that we think about Israel's limp in relation to Achilles' heel (as aforementioned, the name *Yaakov* came from "heel") and therefore about the fragility of the warrior (the pilot) in relation to the earth. Thinking with Itamar brought to the fore the open wound as well as the power to be able to carry the wound in the open.

Israel comes to meet his brother limping, i.e., humble. He is not trying to show his power, rather, he is ready to concede his weakness. This limp is the sign we should carry with us in order not to forget the moment of the radical change that empowered us. Yet the limp is also the sign that protects us from our vanity. It is the sign that we carry with us, in good faith and humility, to our inevitable meeting with our other, our brother, our twin.

Jocasta's Dream

JOCASTA'S DREAM; OR, THE BIRTH OF LOVE
OUT OF THE MURDER OF THE INFANT

At the center of this text stands the claim that the murder of the son, or
to be more accurate, the murder of the infant, is a founding act of civilization that gives birth to love, war, and religion, the law of the son, the
death drive, and the pleasure principle. As a result, we can learn that the
law of the son is prior to the law of the father and that actually it is the
mother who founds (and is therefore able to control) the narrative. If we
wanted to emphasize "the political," we would call it "Why we are fighting?" The writing itself, or rather the thinking through writing, guides me
into new territories such as delayed suicide as a way of life and repetitive
trauma as an action outside linear time. Hopefully I will be able to touch
all these issues in the next few pages.

The story of Oedipus is the founding story of guilt: therefore, it's the
founding story of civilization. That's the way Freud constructs it, and
against this structure the many argue. So, the story of Oedipus is also
the story of anti-Oedipus. Oedipus is also the story of Antigone. She
who has been born from incest refuses to carry the guilt, but her act of
refusal is through conviction. Antigone declares in the agora, "I am not

Oedipus, I am post-Oedipus, I refuse forever to be the guilt-carrier." Or, maybe, she as well is ready to die for the sake of incest, i.e., for the love for her dead brother.

From Hegel to Judith Butler through Freud to Lacan and many others, Oedipus and his daughter Antigone have played a fundamental role in understanding the primal forces in psychology, gender, and politics. For a while I've been contemplating the Oedipus story, trying to understand whom this story serves, whose guilt is being obscured. Who could invent such an irritating narrative? Who is he, or she, who returns to their trauma zone? Suddenly it all looks so clear to me. It's so obvious I'm sure somebody has already written about it. I finally understood that the story of Oedipus is really his mother's story. So I call this essay "Jocasta's Dream."

OEDIPUS IS ALWAYS ALREADY MURDERED
FROM THE BEGINNING

On the day that Oedipus was born, his parents had already murdered him. As a matter of fact, he had been murdered much earlier. He was murdered at the same moment when his parents heard the prophecy. He was murdered before he was born, before he was even conceived. Oedipus is always already murdered; his name means "swollen feet," signifying that he was born with his foot bound, prepared as a sacrifice. He was born with his own death sentence hanging over his head. The guilt of the mother was unbearable, so she resurrected him immediately as the symbolic son. Not, as Freud thought, that the murder of the father is the primal scene—that's the way Freud read Oedipus, and that's the why he refers in *Totem and Taboo* to a half-mythical story in which the youngest of the tribe murder their father, who doesn't let them touch the women, and, after they kill him, they resurrect him immediately as the symbolic father, the name of the father, the law of the father.

Freud was convinced that, in the murder of the father, he couldn't read the death of Moses without the people of Israel murdering him as well. I think we should read Oedipus differently. The murder of the infant is the primal scene, which founds the guilt of the mother as the primal guilt. She is the one who resurrects him as the symbolic son, the name of the son, the law of the son. Therefore the mother is the one who gives the names and carries the story. In order for our subject to unfold we have to deal delicately with a few concepts that arise from this radical conclusion.

The law of the son is prior to the law of the father.

The law of the son is the basis of slave morality, which empowers the weak one totally over his parents.

The passion of the Christ is an exact ritual repetition of the murder of the original son and his symbolic rebirth as the law of the son, which is called love. (We have to acknowledge Nietzsche, who recognized the relationship between slave morality and Christianity. Maybe what he missed was that Christianity is only a ritual repetition of the original murder of the infant son that founded the rebirth of the symbolic son and the law of the son. This law is equal to slave morality in order for the infant to survive in his dependent years.)

In the beginning the infant has been murdered, and the earth was without form and void, and darkness was on the face of the deep.

The birth of Aphrodite—the story of Uranus and Chronos, the birth of love from the murder of the son and the castration of the father.

The bloody groom, the murder of Moses by God, who desired the blood of the son (contradicting Freud).

God and the Pharaoh killing each other's first-born sons.

Jouissance, which acts from the pleasure principal and the death drive, in which parents sending their own kids to the battlefield is one of the prime reasons for war.

The substitute sacrifice: the hope of the parents that their son will kill the son of the enemy and by that redeem himself from the altar of traumatic repetition.

The return to the primal trauma of being murdered already from the beginning is what initiates the self-sacrifice of the son in the altar of war. The aggression toward the other is the hope of finding a substitute to be sacrificed in his place. Always in the murder of the other there is a self-murdering, different than suicide.

The fear of Isaac. From the moment Isaac has been put on the altar, he is living-dead. From this moment on, according to the Bible, he didn't make any important decisions by himself—others, instead, have always manipulated him. That's why some traditions claim that actually Isaac was sacrificed on the mountain.

The suicide bomber sets off our imagination because he is the manifestation of the fantasy of the real.

Oedipus is always already murdered.

THE DELAY OF SUICIDE: THE STORY OF THE MOTHER

Before we elaborate on some of the points we've raised, we have to simply tell the story of the mother. Then we can try to understand the motivation of each one of the participants in this ongoing drama in which each one changes position endlessly. On the day that Oedipus has been murdered by his parents, his mother lost her mind. She knew that since no man or force could refuse the order of the king, the baby really had been murdered. In order to escape from her psychotic realm, she resurrected Oedipus in her thought as a symbolic son. Lacan claims the Symbolic is what saves man from the psychotic trap of the duality between the Real and the Imaginary. But here we are dealing with the symbolic not as a structure of language but as a structure of narrative. The resurrection of Oedipus is not enough: the son who is resurrected has a mission to repair the primal crime, which is his own murder.

First, he is sent away to a shelter city, which is ruled by the doubles of Laius and Jocasta. However, this king and queen are not infant murderers, they are instead full of love. They are the ones who can love without murdering first. They are the ones who raise him to be powerful so that he can then return to his past to repair or to redeem the mother from her guilt.

Jocasta would like to be the second mother, her double, the mother who didn't have to kill in order to love, the one who could love already from the beginning. Let's call her the big-Other-mother. This mother functions successfully up to the age in which Oedipus becomes an adolescent. While Oedipus is entering his manhood, the demons return, because it's clear that he has to leave the house, and if this separation is not in order to do the repair it will become a second death. Therefore he has to come back to his doomed mother and redeem her from her madness, her guilt, and her grief. So the journey of Oedipus is the journey of the son from the symbolic beloved mother to the real murderer mother. The journey that takes place in the mind of the murderer mother is a redemptive journey in which the real mother will be purified and will become the beloved mother.

The first act now is the murder of the father. A revenge of the mother on the father is obligatory for a few reasons. The first one is that obviously he is the one who should carry the guilt. He is the real murderer, she was only there passively, really crying. So she has to execute the real murderer in order to free herself from the guilt. Second, she doesn't want to share the love of the symbolic son with the father, and she doesn't want the father to be able to murder him again.

After Laius has been murdered, Jocasta hides from Oedipus the fact that he murdered his own father in order to keep him innocent. Therefore he can come to her pure at heart and yet a man who took his just revenge (let's think about Hamlet in this case). The double status of the symbolic son as pure and as a father-killer at the same time is what prepares him to be the ideal husband. The murder of the father makes him a man; not knowing it keeps him pure like a child. Therefore, there is here also a new definition of the role of the husband. As son-husband he is the pure husband. Oedipus fulfills his mission, and the mother gives him her body as a compensation for his own murder and as a prize for the murder of the father.

This is not Oedipus's fantasy; this is the fantasy of the murderer-mother, which changes the guilt into an unconditional love. At the same time, it takes the blame for the murder of the infant and puts it on the dead husband. But she didn't murder her husband in order to be by herself but in order to bring forward the ideal husband as a son-husband. That's how Oedipus got into his mother's bed. She's going to compensate him, because he is the son reborn with the name of love. It will not be necessary to murder the offspring of Jocasta and Oedipus, because since they already bear the guilt, they will also bear the love.

But, as time passes, Jocasta realizes what she has done. The only possible repair of the murder of the son is incest, i.e., to give the maximum possible love. But incest, which arises from the murder of the son and father, by definition, reveals the secret (in Hebrew the word for incest means "revealing the genitals"). Once the mother understood that the son saw her naked, she understood that he didn't see only a woman—he also saw a mother. The process of getting old returns the body to being a body of the mother. Therefore, we have to tear his eyes out because he saw what he shouldn't see, the body of the naked mother. I'm not going to deal here with the question of whether the prohibition of incest is before the guilt or whether it evolves from bearing witness to the body of the murderer.

Yet when her body begins to reveal the secret of motherhood and the secret of aging, Oedipus tears out his eyes because he sees what he doesn't know he knows. The tearing out of the eyes is the revenge of the father. Therefore one of the names of the father is the name that reveals the secret. There is no murderer spirit that will not come back to haunt you in order to take revenge. The name of the father is the return of the father from death to demand what he deserves, the body of the queen, and Jocasta prefers to die rather than to return to the original husband. Therefore, she expels her son and commits suicide, because there is no other solution but suicide. She has a deep understanding that the love was born from murdering her son. So we shouldn't say "each one kills the thing he loves," but instead, "each one loves the thing he kills."

In order not to commit suicide, the mother had had to stop the narrative before the end and give up her voice to the father who came back from the dead driven by his need for revenge, which is more powerful than his guilt. Is the mother able to take back the reins of the narrative without committing suicide? Maybe what Lacan calls the phantasma can help her, i.e., by freezing the story a minute before its tragic end.

Another option for the mother not to commit suicide is by a violent ethical penetration into the founding narrative, saying, "Despite the guilt, it is more important to stop the revenge of the name of the father than to commit suicide." I would like to reflect on this second option. The committing of suicide is inevitable when you meet the real. Many books have been written on the question of suicide, and most of them try to explain why not to. The myth of Sisyphus by Camus is one of the most heroic. The more the text becomes apologetic, the more an appeal to suicide grows stronger as the only option.

But here I would like to open a way that does not reject suicide as an ethical act but rather asserts instead a delay—the delay of suicide. At first reading, I will try to claim that the delay should hold until the victory over the name of the father is pronounced, a victory over the one that took upon himself the position of the name-giver, using the weakness of the guilty mother who seeks to die, i.e., the delay is not a delay of pleasure, instead it's the delay of the death drive.

It's not only the drive of the murdered son who tries to repeat his own experience of being murdered; it's also the ethical drive of the mother. In other words, as a reaction to the return of the son (as husband-son) in the role of the redeemer, the mother thinks that she can get over the guilt, but really, in the return of the son, she's bringing back the vengeful father and the memory of the crime. Thus she has no choice but to commit suicide, unless she decides to delay it.

If we can pause for a moment at this point of delay, we will recognize that this space opens us to different opportunities that will compete among themselves. One of them, and a very interesting one, is to believe that the act of the delayed self can be the subversive force against the law of the father and the law of the son, because the law needs verdict, sentence, and punishment. Therefore, maybe, the mother's act of delaying her suicide is the act that renders fragile the law itself.

But we have to consider that maybe the delay itself is not enough. Maybe the father and the son perceive the delay as the passive stance of the mother who gives them meaning through her bearing witness. Even though her act of noncommitting suicide accumulates doubt and paranoia in their minds, it doesn't reach a critical mass, which could destroy them.

Here enter the "yes" of Nietzsche and the "truth-event" of Badiou— but a pure positive force does not constitute this truth-event, as these honorable men want to understand it. Because, as radical as they both are, they are still speaking through the tongues of the father and the son. We have to understand that this truth-event emerges only from the delay of the destruction of the narrative through the mother's suicide, in order to create space for a struggle against the law of the father, which the mother can win only if she truly understands that she is the one who tells the story rather than the listener, as it appears in error. The confusion between the identities of the teller and the listener will create an endless delay of the suicide.

I would like to read Primo Levi in a similar way. I don't think that the only thing Primo Levi tried to achieve was to bear witness. I think he considered his writing also as a theurgic writing—he knew that he could change the narrative and thus change the unconscious of the human being. For the sake of this struggle he delayed his inevitable suicide. The writing that is theurgic is the most difficult, because the older text appears again and again as a metaphysical truth, and the stance of the author should be of having faith in his power to reject this metaphysical force. The moment of suicide can appear as a pure victory or as the understanding that you have nothing to offer in this battle and therefore have to transfer the reins to the next delayer of suicide.

THE SLAVE MORALITY: THE LAW OF THE SON

When the infant is born, it is abandoned immediately. It is in the way of the two, it disturbs the natural order of life. It is demanding and doesn't give anything in return. Therefore, the first murder is not a real murder, but abandonment. The abandonment needs justification, even before the resurrection of the symbolic son. This justification exists in the terms *sacrifice* and *prophecy*. Sacrifice gives meaning to the abandonment by converting the abandonment to a murder. The murder allows the creation of guilt, and the guilt allows the creation of the symbolic son (the law of the son). Only the law of the son can keep the continuity of kin-ship, because it's the only law that justifies the taking care of the helpless, which is equal to the slave morality that Nietzsche speaks about.

Nietzsche equates it with Christianity, maybe missing the point that both of them, Christianity and slave morality, were cultivated on the same furrow, namely, the original murder of the son. Christianity is only the allegory of the first act, and therefore it was so tempting to so many people. Slave morality is the result of this act. So when the mother res-urrects her own infant, she comes to hug and kiss it for the first time. The infant receives, simultaneously, the pleasure principle and the death drive, because it is the hug of the loving/murdering mother.

Those two drives are prior to the infant's language, having been born from the mother tongue. Maybe already in its womb it knew that it had been murdered. I have no idea what a mother can deliver to her unborn child, but it might explain the aggression of the baby toward the breast that Melanie Klein speaks of.

WAR, A REPETITIVE RITUAL OF THE SACRIFICE OF THE SON: THE LAW OF THE FATHER

If we support the argument that the murder of the son is the founding act of civilization, and the founding of the law of the son, which is love, we also agree that it founds the repetitive ritual of the murder by giv-ing a meaning to the abandonment. This meaning grounds the desire for incest and its taboo. This whole process is the basis for the worst of all, which is the act of parents sending their children to die in war as a repetition of the murder of the infant. They sacrifice their son with the jouissance motivated by the pleasure principle and death drive as one split force.

The parents dress their son with the most beautiful uniform, decorat-ing him like a peacock, and send him to die in the name of love, patrio-tism, Deus, or a woman. The son collaborates out of his need to return to the place where he has been murdered already. He goes to battle in the name of love, because only by killing others and being ready to be sacrificed can he regain the love of his parents, because he knows that only by being sacrificed by them can they love him. Only his own murder can give birth to love. He knows that only by dying in war will he gain eternal love.

GENDER TROUBLE

There are some questions about gender that we must raise here. Is the sacrifice of the son a male sacrifice or a pregender sacrifice? Is the love of the mother different in essence from the love of the father? And is the mother, as the storyteller, founding civilization? Is it really the mother as the storyteller who founds civilization and therefore also responsible for the remurdering of the son? She would thus be the one who had the key to change destiny. Or is it the story of the parents—a pregender situation? These questions are critical, and we have to deal with them later, as well as bring in stories like the sacrifice of Iphigenia as the creator of the wind, which sent the ship that started the biggest war for love ever.

THE BIRTH OF LOVE FROM THE CASTRATION OF THE FATHER AND THE MURDER OF THE SON

The father and the mother have seen the fetus as their mutual enemy. He is the excess of their desire. Therefore they have to get rid of him immediately. On the day of conception, the father is more assertive. He knows that an enemy has been born. He already tried to kill him when he was in the womb, with his phallus. But when he penetrated the pregnant mother he understood that the fetus castrates him from within. This is the story of Uranus when he was sleeping with Gaia and trying to avoid the birth of Chronos. Chronos cut off his father's penis and threw it into the ocean. The mix of the father's castrated phallus and the oceanic feeling of divine chaos is what manifests Aphrodite, who is love. It also allows the birth of Chronos, who is time or history. He, in turn, is going to swallow his own children.

Thus the father murders the fetus in the womb and immediately resurrects him as the law of the castrating son. The symbolic castration of the father and the meeting of the phallus, as an organ without body, with the real, the ocean, which might be a body without organs, is what originated the first love.

Are Chronos's story and Oedipus's story complementary? If they are, when Oedipus is born and changes from a fetus to an infant, the love toward him is subsequently changed to a jealousy and revenge for the castration as well as a fear of the endlessly demanding baby. The mother collaborates with her husband to protect their passion. If we continue in this direction, after he castrated his father, while still a fetus (via the prophecy), and after his father attempted to murder him in the womb, the father is waiting in front of the vagina in order to murder him while the mother gives birth. The repetition of the murder of the son is inevitable (in the symbolic realm there's no difference between an act and its attempt). As we have shown before, the murder of the father will not prevent him from coming back after death to murder the son a third time.

I want to emphasize that even though my attempt was to construct the murder of the son as the founding act, I see this act as double-edged. The fundamental mistake lies in a linear concept of time that says the first trauma has to happen in the infant's mind. Instead, I think the law of the son and the law of the father happen simultaneously in a meeting of double castration that happens in the woman's body. The father cannot experience his castration as a baby without being castrated by his own son as an adult, and the son cannot experience his own castration without castrating his own father.

The double castration that takes place in the feminine realm creates concepts that are only partially accurate, but these concepts castrate the woman from her true active force, i.e., the woman's body is conceived as the arena of the father-son battle, therefore the maternal body defines the limits of the discourse and her bearing witness gives it a meaning. So the function of the woman became a physical arena and place of testimony. Because of these two visible characteristics, we forget that she is actually the storyteller.

Jocasta's dream can be the unconscious realm of a woman, and by activating it through postponing guilt she can change the dominant narrative in a radical way. We should not forget that the resurrections of the son and the father, as well as their respective laws, do not only take place in the symbolic realm of the mother but are created by it.

STABAT MATER DE DELAROSA: FROM JOCASTA'S DREAM TO VIRGIN MARY

Is the passion of Jesus Christ Mary's delirium? Is Mary the one who tells the story? Certainly, the story of Jesus is the most accurate one from the point of view of trauma, as Lacan suggests, but not for the same reasons. Rather, because it repeats the murder of the son—the void of the trauma as a black hole is the three days in the grave, and the resurrection is the law of the son, which is called love. The problem is that Lacan, Hegel, Badiou, and many others see Saint Paul as the real storyteller of the event and therefore see the law of the father dying on the cross, i.e., the law or death of God is what we see in the theater of the crucifixion, while the resurrection is only a promise of love, which we have to leave between the two or as a truth-event, according to Badiou.

But if Mary is the one who tells the story, her son was dying on the cross and God died in the resurrection. The passion is her suffering for her guilt because how much more can she suffer seeing her own son suffer without being able to help? She enhances the suffering in order to enhance her own guilt and punishment. To try to connect this narrative to the Jehovah narrative, we identify Paul as the beginning of the founding of the law of the father pretending to be the law of the son, probably including it as well within this marginalization that is called Pauline Christianity. No wonder the gospel of Mary of Magdalene and the gospel of Thomas were excluded. Magdalene is the Virgin Mary as a lover by splitting the subject to mother and lover, spirit and body, etc., in order to avoid Jocasta's destiny. We should remember that Jocasta's split was murderer mother/loving mother. There is much to say about the two Marys and the two Jesuses (his twin Thomas), but it will be kept for another time and with it we will postpone discussion about Moses, about Yitzhak, and others.

3

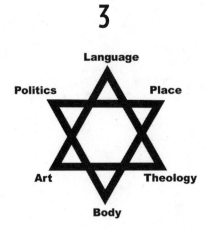

PLACE

WRITINGS FROM OCCUPIED TERRITORIES

The Specters of a Borrowed Village

He is despised and rejected of men; a man of sorrows, and acquainted
with grief: and we hid as it were our faces from him; he was despised, and
we esteemed him not. . . . Surely he hath borne our griefs, and carried our
sorrows: yet we did esteem him stricken, smitten of God, and afflicted.

—Isaiah 53:3–4

The epigraph to this chapter from the book of Isaiah is carved on a panel
bearing the names of donors to the Kfar Shaul Mental Health Hospital,
to which Deputy Minister of Health Yaacov Litzman decided to pay a surprise visit on the January 20. The sanitary conditions observed by the
deputy minister (who is the acting minister of health) were appalling, and
the place appears to be in a dilapidated state.

The donors to the hospital have been giving their money to an institute
established on the houses of the Palestinian village of Deir Yassin, and the
inmates now reside in the homes of the murdered and deported locals. On
April 9, 1948, a Jewish militia entered the village and killed more than one
hundred of its inhabitants. Survivors of the massacre were expelled, and,
according to the Haganah's reports, some victims were also paraded in
the Jewish neighborhoods of Jerusalem. A short time later, the hospital
was opened. Legend has it that, even nowadays, the Holocaust survivors
hospitalized in Kfar Shaul communicate with the ghosts of the murdered
inhabitants of the village.

Watching Deputy Minister Litzman's visit this week, and the harsh living conditions to which he was witness, the painful preliminary research

Haaretz, February 1, 2010.

I had done for my film *Forgiveness*, which takes place at the hospital, came to mind. I wondered then, and I wonder now, how it is that the State of Israel manages time and again to create a reality that exceeds the most surreal symbolism of Latin American literature (it was only natural for Israeli-Arab Knesset member Dr. Ahmad Tibi to quote Gabriel García Márquez when describing the ongoing robbery of Palestinian land by the government of Israel). The hospital's name, Kfar Shaul, literally means "a borrowed village," and indeed one day we shall return it to its rightful owners.

Poor Rabbi Litzman: he sees the patients, but he does not know that on the symbolic level they are being punished for a sin they have not committed, the ancient sin of "Have you not murdered a man and seized his property?" committed by the perpetrators of the massacre who acted in the name of Zionism. After all, what does an ultra-Orthodox rabbi like Litzman have to do with Zionist history. . . . He may also be oblivious to the increased likelihood of renewed demands that the Israeli government be accountable to the original owners of the place if he decides to close down the hospital.

Every reasonable person should realize that those "people of pain," as described by the prophet, or "loonies," according to vulgar language, or "inmates," in standard language, are not there to be punished for crimes committed in our name in 1948 but to serve as custodians of the theft, like the man who accommodates his handicapped relative at a key-money apartment in order to maintain his right to the asset. And since the welfare of the patients is not the state's highest concern, as we are informed by the deputy minister's visit, perhaps one day the Israel Land Administration will decide to close down the place and sell the land to a rich Jewish millionaire from abroad. And this will probably be deemed a Zionist act.

In the meantime, until the day of reckoning, survivors of the Holocaust, those "people of sorrow" from the times of "God's hiding of the face" (*hester panim* in Hebrew) sit there idly. They can tell the ghosts of Deir Yassin how they are maintaining their sheikh's tomb and horrors they experienced in Europe, of hatred toward Jews and the greatest murder of them all. The ghosts of the villagers, in turn, can tell the Holocaust survivors of the olive trees, of the numerous wells that had to be dug because of water shortages, of the budding village industry, and of neighborly cooperation with the Jews who were living nearby.

And maybe at this time, as we are waiting for the Israeli High Court of Justice to explain its puzzling and racist decision to expel Palestinian residents of Sheikh-Jarrah, in East Jerusalem, from their homes and implement the right of return for Jews only, maybe now something will change. Perhaps Deputy Minister Litzman, who is not a part of the Zionist establishment, will close down the malfunctioning institution in Kfar Shaul, transfer the patients to an institution that will take good care of them, and return the borrowed village to its owners. What a wonderful start this could be: the beginning of the healing of an entire people from a wound that seems prima facie incurable.

For Palestine Is Missing from Palestine

Soon we will have another present
if you look behind you will only see an exile

—Mahmoud Darwish, "We Lacked a Present"

In *The Time That Remains,* his third feature film, Elia Suleiman takes on a challenging task: narrating the history of the ethnic definition of "Israeli Arabs" through the story of his own family. He focuses on his parents, who remained in Nazareth following its capitulation to the IDF in July 1948, when it became a kind of regional capital from which Israeli Zionists ruled over Israeli Arabs. As in his earlier films, here, too, Suleiman presents his story through a series of tiny peepholes, granting privilege to the poetic quality of each scene over the formulation of direct political statements.

—Meir Schnitzer, film critic

FRAGMENTS OF REMEMBERING AND FORGETTING

There is no way of writing cohesively about Suleiman's films and remain faithful to them. All one can write are fragments about an attempt to create a chronicle out of fragmented memories, the memories of a family that lives in exile in its own home.

FAILURE

Suleiman's failure to transform his life story into a unified and positive narrative, which shapes a definitive identity, is his triumph. As a director of fragments, of movement and image, he considers sound more important than the meaning of the pronounced words. And so, engaging in a cinematic dance, Suleiman creates an aesthetic of the present-absent subject. Until this present absentee is once again fully present, the place called Israel will remain irremediable and bereft of a permanent name.

THE JOURNEY TO CREATE A VOCABULARY OF THE DIASPORA

What Edward Said teaches us in *Freud and the Non-European* is this: there is nothing further from being a Jew than being only a Jew. Together with Said, I set out on a mission to search for a vocabulary for this new place, which is suffused with a threateningly ancient history. Said alluded to the key that would enable me to exist in Palestine without guilt, as the inhabitant of a place that is a shared home.

Coming upon Suleiman's cinema as I set out on this simultaneously private and public journey, I realized someone had already charted the path, supplying provisions in the form of a visual vocabulary that I could rely on to produce "the politics of exile," which alone can produce "the politics of home." More than anyone else, Elia Suleiman has understood Edward Said's call. As a filmmaker, moreover, he creates an entirely different mood than one a philosopher is capable of creating.

A VOID AND SILENCE

The title of his first film, *Chronicle of a Disappearance,* already makes clear that the space produced by Suleiman is a void of silence, one that leads the viewer to feel like filling the void and shouting to break the silence. Suleiman enacts his chronicle of disappearance on screen, constraining us to fill the empty void, the remaining time. One may describe Suleiman's films as expressing a sense of melancholy, "mourning for a world that will never be his." For Palestine is missing from Palestine (a paraphrase on the Israeli-Jewish poet Haviva Pedaya's "Israel Is Missing from Israel").

THE LEAP OF MELANCHOLY

Ever since Freud published his text on mourning and melancholy, we perceive melancholy as a space of death. The space of a terminal illness, of the person who has given up on the process of mourning that is supposed to enable her to gently return to the world of the living. Many have written about Suleiman's melancholy. The journalist and left-wing activist Gideon Levy, who also has a small role in the film, attributes this mood to a kind of acceptance of reality. Yet I would argue that Suleiman's melancholy could actually be read as a form of protest against reality. Or as the point of departure for the bold leap made by the melancholic. There is a difference between Freud's perception of melancholy and the performative kind of melancholy that can produce a form of revolutionary awareness.

When the process of mourning is impossible, when death repeats itself constantly, only a revolutionary type of leap can catapult the Israeli Arab out of the immanent melancholy of his state. I always thought about the self-proclaimed messiah Shabtai Tzvi, whose name in Hebrew means Saturn, the planet of melancholy. There is no cure for the Shabatean, saturnine state of being other than choosing to take the messianic leap that will liberate you from the trap of nonlife in which you are caught.

Sometimes mourning does not have the power to free you from the shackles that tie you to Hades.

The film critic Meir Schnitzer has written: "Elia Suleiman's *The Time That Remains: Chronicle of a Present Absentee,* was created by a Palestinian native of Nazareth. It presents in detail, in the course of two hours, the political history of the wondrous hybrid known here as 'Israeli Arabs': those seen as having long ago abandoned their rifles in favor of fishing rods, as having exchanged their battle uniforms for pajamas, and as having given up the ardent struggle in favor of leisurely visits to coffee houses."

Yet just as the protagonist is filled with courage and a renewed lust for life, fragments of memory from his revolutionary period come together to produce a last courageous leap. He uses this leap to save a Jewish soldier from being killed by explosives and gives viewers much satisfaction. He is the opposite of a suicide bomber—a suicide savior. One wonders what was going through his mind, what was going through viewers' minds. In Suleiman's films every scene is a gesture that creates a language of the diaspora, a language of alienation—not only between cultures that identify one another through their self-created symbols but also between local Arab culture and itself.

FIREWORKS

At the end of the film, Suleiman's elderly yet still beautiful mother turns her head away from a show of fireworks. We understand that these are fireworks celebrating Israel's Independence Day, which is a Palestinian day of mourning. Who else can understand the fireworks and their meaning? Who else can understand this maternal aversion of the gaze on this day of mourning, as her son looks at her, slumped and expressionless? How much pain the son is in watching his mother avert her gaze from the fireworks? Their hollow exuberance is the exuberance of the occupying victor, who cannot but remind her of the endless pain of being in exile in her own home.

BERLIN: THE INTERNATIONAL FILM FESTIVAL 2010

I have never seen Berlin so white. The city is enveloped in snow. I am sitting in a coffee shop with a melancholic gaze in my eyes. How I long to momentarily be a Berlin Jew in that moment before the beginning of the end. I think of Paul Celan writing: "Once, when death attracted the masses, / you sought shelter inside me."

How strange that I am looking for a place of refuge in the city from which the death machine was run. I summon the Jewish ghosts to drink coffee with me in the Al-Hamra Café, which belongs to my friends Zuzu and Mahar from Ramallah. Their brother Fadi is supposed to be arriving with a draft of the invitation to the prize ceremony organized for Mohammed Bakri. Scandar Copti, the director of *Ajami,* should also be arriving any minute. Together we will be presenting Bakri with the Berlin festival's FREE Speech Award. Scandar, Mohammed, and the others are all "Israeli Arabs," whom we now call "Palestinian citizens of Israel." Perhaps this definition can do something to alleviate the pain, to provide a sense of belonging to something greater than the alienated, detached, decontextualized fragment represented by the term *Israeli Arab.* Why Israeli? What is the connection between these individuals and the name of the country that transformed their people into fragments detached from themselves? Take Bakri, a noble actor. What didn't he do for the Jews to accept him as a brother? But when they invaded Jenin he made a film (*Jenin, Jenin*) meant to call his Jewish brothers to order. And they, instead of listening, decided to persecute him to the bitter end. Scandar Copti, who created the wonderful film *Ajami* together with Jewish codirector, Yaron Shani, also thought he could strike a chord in his Jewish brothers' hearts, and for a moment this even seemed possible; yet, while he chose to speak as an equal, Copti's brother, who also appears in the film, was arrested by Israeli police.

Suleiman continued to direct his movie at a measured pace and invited Bakri's son, Salah, to play the lead role. Elia seems to be saying: Forget it, nobody can understand the innermost thoughts of this fantastic hybrid called the Israeli Arab. All he had to do was use the name Palestinian.

In contrast to the drama and expressiveness characteristic of the first generation of artists such as Bakri, Suleiman chose to focus on the inconspicuous and humorous aspects of what cannot be otherwise. The same humor once referred to as Jewish humor. Strangely, I remember that when Primo Levi wrote that each people has its Jews and that the Palestinians were Israel's Jews, I thought he was referring to Israel's racism against the Palestinians. Not for a moment did I think he was referring to Elia Suleiman's humor.

THE NAME

The name Israel, the name Palestine,
The name Jewish, the name Palestinian,
The name Israeli, the name Hebrew.
The name Arab of 1948,
The name Israeli Arab,
The name Palestinian citizen of Israel,
The name Palestinian Jew,

I attempt to flee my Israeli identity and don't know to where to flee, and so I will call this place Palestine-Land-of-Israel (until everyone can officially call their country what they choose, I cannot call it Israel). Yet, if I don't say "Israel," what can I say in place of "Israeli"? For a moment I hoped I could call myself a Palestinian Jew. Yet that, too, is not really happening. Now, however, it seems to me that Suleiman is the Jewish Palestinian. Jewish in the sense referred to by Edward Said or perhaps in the sense intended by Charlie Chaplin. But this, too, is a name that cannot exist in peace and that will be misinterpreted in a negative, not a positive light.

JUXTAPOSITION

Suleiman's film contains a scene in which an Israeli tank enters Ramallah. The tank comes to a standstill. A man exits his house to throw out the garbage. The tank gun follows him, constantly aiming at his head. The man throws out the garbage. Who knows, it might explode. In Suleiman's previous film, he throws a plum pit out a car window and an Israeli tank explodes. Yet here nothing explodes. The man crosses the road and the turret turns around with a squeak. The tank continues to follow the man's head. Before he enters his house, his cell phone rings. He walks back and forth, ignoring the tank that follows his head, and discusses a party he is planning to attend. The conversation ends. He enters his house. Nobody explodes, nothing has happened. Except for one massive tank following the head of a Palestinian discussing a trance party on his cell phone.

The Israeli film *Lebanon* (directed by Samuel Maoz) won numerous international awards. It is terribly expressive. Its protagonists are Israeli soldiers in a tank during the First Lebanon War in 1982. They are really suffering, these soldiers, breaking down and crying one after the other. The tank itself does not fire a single shot throughout the entire film. It makes you wonder who destroyed Lebanon if this bunch of tormented Israeli soldiers did not fire a single shot. Schnitzer argues that the entire film is actually about the Israeli man's fear of sexual impotence: He looks at naked girls, remembers the teacher who helped him masturbate when his father died, yet in spite of all this the big tank does not fire a single shot.

I thought, with my friend Tahel Frosh, of creating a short YouTube film in which the soldiers sitting in the Israeli tank are all crying hysterically and trying to shoot, filled with fear, while everything is crowded and heavy and hot and sweaty, just like Goliath in his armor on a hot summer day. And outside is Prince David, a young Palestinian, holding the cell phone like a lyre or a slingshot, indifferent to the moral drama of the deliberating soldiers in the tank. The cuts in this film would be quick, the music would alternate between circus tunes and a war drama. The abyss between the hysterical master (soldiers) and the serene Palestinian individual subjected to his rule would continue to grow. All that would remain would be the relationship between the ruler experiencing himself as a victim (he just can't stand himself anymore) and the power of the powerless individual who suddenly learns how to fall in love with himself and realizes he is constructing a world for himself.

WHY DOESN'T ISRAELI CINEMA GO TO NAZARETH TO MAKE COFFEE FOR ELIA SULEIMAN AND HIS FRIENDS?

One day Israeli filmmakers will ask Elia Suleiman how to be sincere.

And Elia will then say to the Israeli cinema: get rid of your uniform and put on some pajamas and pound your rifles and cameras into fishing rods. And, mostly, just disappear for a while. Walk humbly with your God, serve me an Arab coffee you just made yourself at my coffee shop in Nazareth. And then, only when you feel you are truly ready, you can make your first film.

The Fish Who Became a Shahid

One cannot write about the Ramallah Biennale in the same way in which one would write about the Venice Biennale, not even in the same way that one would write about the Biennale in Herzliya or any other Israeli city. The word *Biennale* includes within it a promise of continuity and normality; it suggests something permanent that will repeat itself once every two years. But in Ramallah there is nothing normal—and certainly nothing permanent. Who knows: maybe in two years Hamas will take over the city's streets or, even worse, the army will crush the fragments of normalcy that remain intact. On the other hand, there is something optimistic in the word pair *Ramallah Biennale*. Like a promise for a safe, bright future.

Two years ago, I tried to live between Ramallah and Tel Aviv for a while. Between two cities full of passion for life yet rife with existential melancholia. Two cities in two nations whose destinies are bound together. My destiny is bound to both of them with love and despair. In the meantime, the two cities were torn apart from each other at the speed of light. Tel Aviv looks toward the West with a narcissistic gaze, like a man who looks into a convex mirror, garnering pleasure from his grotesque reflection.

Published in *Time Out, Tel Aviv,* October 24, 2007.

This infamous self-indulgence gave Tel Aviv an international reputation. Ramallah, on the other hand, is encaged by physical and mental walls that multiply both around and inside of it. The Palestinians who live in Ramallah feel crushed from within and from without; they struggle to create and maintain a space of sanity. Only those who live between the two cities understand how much they need each other. The day they merge, the Messiah will come, and the Middle East will become "a light unto the nations." But what then would happen to merchants of weapons and death, the real estate contractors, the uprooters of olive trees, the ultrareligious preachers, the secular paranoids? They have, meanwhile, joined together to build a cement wall to prevent the Messiah from coming.

Until his majesty arrives (and since it takes light years to travel the fifty-minute drive between the two cities), I insist on crossing the wall and, at minimum, keeping in touch with the Hourani family.

THE HOURANIS

Hassan Hourani was a dear friend in New York, an amazing painter and storyteller who drowned in the sea of Jaffa because he refused to accept the artificial separation between Ramallah and the Mediterranean. Borders, in his eyes, were highly archaic. The idea of a one-state solution was, to Hassan, not only a political resolution but the inevitable conclusion of all those who envision life without racism—all those who, with a little bit of healthy common sense, consider all humans to be equal. After Hassan drowned in the sea, they created, in his honor, the Hassan Hourani Award for Young Artist of the Year, the winner of which will be announced during the Biennale. Hassan Hourani had twenty brothers and sisters. Three of them became dear friends to me. Two of them, Khaled and Wafa, are artists, and the third, Ahmad, calls himself Madosophy, i.e., mad Sufi man, or the one who has the knowledge of madness. A month ago, we celebrated Ahmad and Rita's wedding in Ramallah, but this is a story for another time.

This time, I was the guest of Wafa, the youngest brother (who looks a little bit too much like Hassan). Wafa is an artist who, not long ago, finished an exciting and humorous project about Qalandia checkpoint, or, more accurately, about the history of the future. The project, a model of the checkpoint, the wall, and the Qalandia refugee camp in the year 2047, has already been shown in Athens, Greece. This week he received the Delfina Foundation Award, with which he will travel to the UK in order to build the history of the future of London. In the meantime, until he's able to support himself with his art, Wafa works in advertising, a family business. In the morning, when he left for the office, he recommended that I join Riwaq's tour of the villages, one of the Biennale's events. Riwaq, which derives its name from Islamic architecture, is the Palestinian Centre for Architectural Conversation and the organizer of the Biennale.

CHARLES ESCHE

Only after I stepped onto Riwaq's bus did it become clear to me that the bus tour is the Biennale itself. It was a good opportunity to interview Charles Esche, the curator of the Ramallah Biennale and former curator of the Istanbul Biennale.

Me: "Slowly but surely, I'm beginning to understand that the Ramallah Biennale is not exactly what we have in mind when we think about a Biennale for art."

Esche: "That's exactly the point. When I was invited to curate the exhibition, I was quite excited. But very soon I realized that it doesn't make sense to try to create an atmosphere of normality in a place that's under occupation. A place that has been denied independence and, further, has been fragmented in an unbearable way. Therefore, we thought that the term Biennale will not refer to a biannual event or a celebration but rather to a two-year journey that will begin just this week. We brought two artists and ten writers who will try to understand this place, its problems, its sensations, in the hope that they will create works that respond to this place. In a way, the Biennale is constructed from four elements: architecture, art, planning, and heritage conservation. The tours that we are conducting in the villages are focused on two of these elements, heritage conservation and architecture. But our tours are much more than visiting sites of architectural conservation. We thought that in order to understand the Palestinian situation we first have to understand Palestinian space and time. Therefore the Biennale is taking place between Hebron and Jenin. In every location there is an exhibition, a workshop, a conservation site, or a think tank group. During the voyage from one place to another, one must pass through checkpoints, thus addressing the impossibility of arriving, or the possibility of arriving only via the detours and extremely difficult roads that are under the control of the arbitrariness of the Occupation. The second Riwaq Biennale is really about experimenting with the time and space of Palestine. It's about creating dialogue between Palestinian and international artists and about creating a space for these artists to think together about possible forms of expression in the context of critical geopolitics. How can you experience, both intellectually and emotionally, the place that will one day become Palestine?"

We passed a checkpoint. Then we passed a settlement. Then we passed a sign in Arabic, Hebrew, and English that reads, to the right, Nablus, and, to the left, Halamish (a settlement)—implying these two places are of equal significance and size. Then we passed a Palestinian village that Israeli citizens are barred from entering. The village, which lies next to a settlement, will be on curfew most of the time: whenever the settlers are at risk and whenever the settlers are the ones creating the risk.

RUBA SALEEM

We entered the village of Salfeet. In the heart of the village lies one of the historic buildings that Riwaq is conserving; when the renovations are complete it will become a cultural center. That's what Riwaq tries to achieve: the protection and maintenance of classical Palestinian architecture. They restore the buildings precisely and with love. Exactly in the same way that they try to restore Bauhaus structures from the twenties in Tel Aviv. Our guide is Ruba Saleem, a young architect from Ramallah who has dedicated her time to these carefully chosen sites.

Me: "Ruba, what attracted you to this project? Why is conservation of old buildings so important for you?"

Ruba: "Look at these pictures of the buildings before renovation. No one in the village knew how beautiful this house—right in the village center—used to be. Houses are abandoned for various reasons. And the villages forget how incredible they were in the past. Who has the time, in an era of occupation, to think about conserving traditional architecture? The poor people don't build, and the rich build like the rich. I want the people of the village to see how we renovate, I want them to get jealous of the beauty that we restored to the building, and I want them to try to imitate us or to ask for our advice. From my point of view, this is also a method of resisting the Occupation, like the tsumood."[1]

Another visitor on the tour: "Exactly. And we're going to maintain, preserve, and renovate fifty village centers that will become places from which the villages can redesign themselves. The same way in which farmers remain loyal to their land and their olive trees, the villagers should

1. Farmers who refuse to leave their land.

say: 'We will never abandon this village.' The conservation is really a statement about the future, not about the past."

SWEETS AND VIDEOS

After we came back to the city, I jumped from the bus in order to see a video installation curated by Samar Martha. The gallery was directly across from Arafat Sweets, offering the best *knafeh* in Ramallah. Even though the concept of the absence of exhibitions sounds fascinating to me, the desire to see art is still very basic. And what, for someone like me who wanders between visual art and cinema, is better than seeing a video art exhibition? The *knafeh* was unbelievably delicious, as expected, and so was the exhibition. Unfortunately, the piece by Mona Hatoum didn't work—a technical problem with the projector. But there were, among others, two strikingly beautiful works of art. One, a runway fashion show featuring clothing for crossing Israeli checkpoints, was called *Chic Point*. The beautiful, often revealing, and hole-ridden clothing makes it easier for the soldiers to see that you do not carry an explosive belt. The soldier can gaze at your body and touch your belly without undressing you. This work of Sharif Waked, a Palestinian artist from Haifa, received critical acclaim in many exhibitions around the world.

The other work that impressed me was *The Wall Zone Auction,* a conceptual piece by Khalil Rabah featuring an auction of items from in and around the ecological environment of the separation wall. On one screen you can watch the auction itself, on the other the artifact for sale. A mix of earth, industrial garbage, and mutilated agriculture. They say that almost a million olive trees were destroyed or displaced as a result of the wall.

QALANDIA CHECKPOINT, YEAR 2047

In the meantime, Wafa was preparing the presentation of his project. In the past I spent some wild nights with him in Ramallah, nights in which he created and recreated his wild, intricate stories, which often ended up in his art.

Udi: "Must art in Ramallah be political?"

Wafa: "Not at all. But in the end, it always is. Take yourself for example. The longer you stay here with me, the less we speak about the situation. We just go to bars and parties. But the more you're considered a stranger, the more we want to tell you, and the more you want to hear, about the politics of the place. That is the demand from us as artists. The world demands it from us. We are like animals in a zoo of the liberal West.

I really think that our art, that of the young generation, is no less political, but with less pathos than that of the previous generation. It's more ironic. And while the older artists are very united, always helping each other, we, the youngsters, are more individualistic. Maybe it has something to do with the time that passed between the two intifadas, a time that changed all of us. The first intifada was the most beautiful moment of the Palestinian resistance. The second was the saddest moment in our struggle. That's why, in my architectural model of the Qalandia refugee camp in the year 2047, I created a memorial for the stone, the weapon that symbolized, more than anything else, the uprising of the youth. At that time there were friends who were throwing stones all day long in total ecstasy. I was too young then. But after the Goldstein massacre, when I lived in Hebron, I learned how to throw stones. I was shot in my foot, and I lay down on the ground, my leg hanging there. Here, look at the shoe in the corner. You see the hole? It's from the bullet."[2]

THE FISH WHO BECAME A SHAHID[3]

In the heart of Wafa Hourani's architectural model of Qalandia refugee camp in the year 2047, there is a mausoleum for the martyr-fish. Or, as Wafa relates the tale, once upon a time in the future, in Qalandia, year 2016, "One from the camp missed the sea and the fish so much. He found a way to smuggle salt water from the sea, and he made a pool beside his home. Around the pool, he laid sand, and within the pool he placed a golden fish to live with them. People said Abu Jamil brought the sea. The fish loved the camp. She loved the people visiting her, laying in the sun and having barbeques and parties in her garden."

Years later, in 2033, "The fish died . . . all the camp cried. They said, 'the fish died; the sea died.' They took the water out of the pool and buried the fish. They called it 'the FISH TOMB.' The visits changed from picnics, singing and dancing to a martyr's memorial where silence was kept and flowers were laid for the fish who became a shahid."

---

2. In February 1994 a Jewish settler named Baruch Goldstin massacred twenty-nine Muslims at prayer.
3. *Shahid* in Arabic means "witness" or "martyr."

Jenin and Homeopathy

Journey impressions from Café Bialik in Tel Aviv to the opening of Juliano Mer's Freedom Theatre in the Jenin refugee camp, including a dialogue between Tali Fahima, a Mizrahi Israeli Jew,[1] who served as a human shield to Zakaria Zbeidi and was imprisoned in Israel under solitary confinement for allegedly "aiding and abetting an enemy," and Zakaria himself, who was for a time the number one name on Israel's "wanted terrorist" list and now runs the Freedom Theatre in Jenin. Also, along the journey, assistance from a Russian Jewish immigrant, a homeopathic physician who advocates the establishment of resistance cells.

THE FREEDOM THEATRE

FRIDAY 1/12/07, 15:00, THE OPENING OF THE REMEMBERING LEBANON *EXHIBITION IN JENIN*

We are seated in dense rows of chairs in a packed room. The usher is going around with a huge finjan (coffeepot), pouring coffee into the small plastic cups we are holding, and the excitement is felt in every corner. It is not

1. A Mizrahi Jew is a Sephardic Jew whose family comes from one of the Arab countries.

often these days that one sees a dream come true, against all odds. And it is not often that you see two manly men, who have seen and done a lot, running on stage like two excited boys.

The place is the Freedom Theatre in Jenin, named after Arna Mer-Khamis, and the two boys/men on the stage are Juliano Mer-Khamis[2] and Zakaria Zbeidi.[3] I do not know Zbeidi personally. I only know him from stories told by Tali Fahima or Juliano. In my view, he has always seemed to be a sort of Robin Hood. Maybe he is the best embodiment of the term *friend-foe* I can think of. For me he is still an object of Orientalist fantasizing, and until I can detach Zakaria Zbeidi the human being from Zakaria Zbeidi the symbol, I will not be able to write about him. So now we finally meet and shake hands and exchange polite greetings, but I have nothing to recount yet. Tali says that if I sit down to talk to him I will understand a lot. I will experience the longing for quiet, for a life in which your mother is not murdered by a bullet passing through a window straight into her chest. I will experience the longing for a life in which you are not the hunter/hunted, going around with a Kalashnikov hanging from your shoulder, with the manly pride of a boy who has had no childhood. In Juliano's film *Arna's Children*, Zakaria was one of the children who performed at Arna Mer-Khamis's theater. Now I see him onstage, gently ensuring that all goes well, that Jenin's new children have a theater, that there is not just a struggle for the sake of a struggle, but rather something worth struggling for, namely, culture, namely, life.

I will be glad to sit down with him for a longer time, to learn more, to understand profoundly why he chose the armed struggle and understand the complementary or contradictory role that the Freedom Theatre plays in his life. Understand the dreams, the depressions, the pain of a bullet in the back on a cold winter day. Understand death, which has been around him all this time. Killing, being killed, keeping the faith. I need to see how the Occupation is reified in the life of a hero. Seeing the revolution eating

2. Actor and director, the son of a communist Palestinian father and a communist Jewish mother. His mother Arna established a theater in the Jenin refugee camp; after her death and the Israeli army invasion, Juliano reestablished the Freedom Theatre. The story is wonderfully told in his film *Arna's Children*. Juliano was assassinated in front of his theater in 2011.
3. One of "Arna's children" and the Jenin chief of the Al-Aqsa Martyrs' Brigade. Considered a hero because of his persistent fighting against the Israeli occupation forces during the Jenin invasion. Currently in a truce with Israel, which sees him as a terrorist.

its own children, those who have fought for it. Wanting the enemy to have a human face too, like Tali's, that one can love, because this maintains the possibility of having a future.

I will write about Zakaria some other time. It is Juliano I wish to write about here (and, to some extent, I also wish to write to Juliano here). Juliano, with whom I have emptied more than a few whiskey bottles in our lifetime; Juliano whom I have seen at his best and at his less than best; Juliano whom I have heard saying wise things and not so wise things; Juliano, whose behavior sometimes made me fear that others might associate me with him. "Juliano, my friend," I want to say to him, "the opening of the Freedom Theatre you have established in Jenin is one of the most exciting events I have seen and witnessed in recent years. I promise to stand by you in the future even if I sometimes lose face because of you. I love you and I adore you for all that you have done, and I have many reasons. The main reason, which is close to my heart, is the successful way in which you combine the personal and the public aspects of your being to live a full life. You have reestablished your mother Arna's dream place in Jenin. But this time it is also your own dream, ethically as well as aesthetically."

I am excited to think that Juliano did not settle for his wonderful and touching film *Arna's Children* to close a chapter in his life, but also went out and resurrected the theater that is the film's subject. For me, as a director, it is like a miracle. Charming, captivating, full of faith, bewildering, and full of lust for life and libidinal energy, two things that the Israeli peace and justice camp lost long ago.

We sat there at the Freedom Theatre in Jenin: Palestinians and Israelis; Muslims, Christians, and Jews; children and old folks; fat people and not so fat people; we listened to passionate speeches and good music; we had a decent meal. We roamed through the photo and drawing exhibition, some of which was quite good and some of which was less than that (I would like to recommend photographer Majdi Hadid, whose work impressed me especially). And the computer center, donated by Jewish philanthropist Daniel Abrams, is professional and advanced. It is named after Ahmad el-Khatib, a ten-year-old boy killed by the IDF, whose organs were donated by his father, giving life to seven Israelis, Palestinians and Jews, through his dead son.

When Juliano declared that Pnina Feiler, an Israeli Jewish woman, donated 50,000 NIS to the theater, everyone stood up and gave her an endless standing ovation. For me this was proof that being a little crazy is the only sane choice. And living between the worlds, Jewish and Palestinian, is the only humane option. And the love that Tel Aviveans who came to Jenin received in Jenin—and many came, scores in fact—proves how simple it all is, entirely uncomplicated. As if the complexity was formed just to confuse us and perpetuate evil. But let us put aside these large-scale reflections for a moment. Because Juliano Mer's Freedom Theatre can be demolished in a moment by an Israeli incursion or may be shut down because of internecine fighting between Fateh and Hamas. But whoever was there will make sure it is rebuilt, just like a Japanese shrine that is demolished and rebuilt every few years, rendering it everlasting. The love Juliano received in Jenin proves that Israelis can be given a dream better than the one sold by their government and Israelis can replace the Peace Now movement with determination, replace apology with faith and lust for life and ignore the cynicists and the radicals.[4]

TEL AVIV–JENIN AXIS

CAFÉ BIALIK IN TEL AVIV, FRIDAY 1/12/07, 10:00, FIVE HOURS BEFORE THE OPENING IN JENIN

I am having coffee at Café Bialik, talking to Amir Rotem about the evening for a literary magazine being held at the old municipality building.

This is the point of departure, physically and mentally, for the journey to Jenin. I am thrilled. My daughter, Yuli, will soon join us. Dudi Zilber and I are waiting for her. Yael Lerer is instructing some people on the phone. Anat Even is the driver. Osnat Trabelsi is in a third car, bringing Jul's family. We have to meet in Taybeh, then drive somewhere, and then hop into a Palestinian taxi, leaving our car behind. Where we leave the cars we must also leave someone to guard them, so that we do not fall prey to the stolen vehicle industry, although this industry is an indication of coexistence and joint entrepreneurship.

There is something ceremonial about the preparations for the ride. One can take the high road to Ramallah, but when one goes to Jenin one takes the winding roads. The festivity toward the opening event turns to

---

4. Peace Now is a mainstream Israeli peace organization that is often criticized by the consistent left in Israel for its failure to stand up to the Israeli government.

disgust in the face of apartheid. Jews to the left, Palestinians to the right. We do not stop. We keep on driving. Some of us go into the Occupied Territories to demonstrate, some go there to visit friends. Some of us refuse to accept the enforced separation. Some of us have a loved one there. All sorts of reasons can bring a few good Jews to violate the racial laws applied in the Occupied Territories.

This time we are all going to a celebration. All kinds of Tel Aviveans who have found all sorts of ways and made it to Jenin through the garden of forking paths, as if the prohibition imposed on Tali's entrance to Jenin has made us emissaries of a just cause. And thus, as we switch to the taxis, we take off the Star of David and put on the Kafiyeh, or vice versa, depending on the road we take. Some people bypass checkpoints on foot and some pretend to be settlers and take the roads reserved for the lords of the land.

Finally, when we arrive, Juliano cannot believe how many Tel Aviveans show up in the middle of all that mess in Jenin. It is one thing that Juliano does not believe his eyes, but the residents of the refugee camp do not believe it either. Jenin, a place that in recent years has known only Tali Fahima as the sole Tel Avivean coming there, now sees scores of students and directors and lecturers and ordinary people, young and old, who have come from Tel Aviv to celebrate the opening of an exhibition. And I meet friends from Ramallah who came with the organized transportation to express their support for their little sister Jenin. And I also see Tel Aviveans whom I haven't seen for a long time. Just like an opening event should be. And for a brief moment I understand what things could have been like, and a little smile spreads over my face, but then Sanaa tells me, "I am so sad, when you see the computers I see the image of the boy who was killed, and where you see hope I see memories of the destroyed camp [during Israel's incursion in 2002]." And Anat says, "I am always so tired in Palestine; I think it's the depressing sight of the Occupation." And Dudi, who retains some healthy skepticism throughout all this, admires everything, especially Juliano's production talent. And I see Jul from a distance, somewhat blurred, very adamant, speaking in Arabic, Hebrew, and English to all those people interviewing him. And my daughter is all grown up, sitting with her age group from the refugee camp, enjoying a hookah, and I have no idea what they are talking about. And Jul's little girl playing catch with anyone who wants to play. And Sanaa will keep on fighting for justice and for the release of her husband Walid from the unjust imprisonment imposed on him, and Anat will always take her thirty-minute nap and then go on photographing, and I, with my gaze wandering back to Jul, can see that even though he is tired he looks happy and more adamant than ever.

Jul, I assume that your communist mother did not believe in an afterlife, but, if there are moments in which we are better off believing in an afterlife, yesterday we had such a moment, when I could see Arna looking on you and at you from the other side, her eyes fixed on you, wiping a tear of love, grace, and pride.

REMOVING THE TALINESS FROM TALI

THURSDAY, 1/11/07, 19:00, TWENTY HOURS BEFORE THE OPENING EVENT IN JENIN, CAFÉ YAFA, JAFFA

I meet Tali Fahima at Café Yafe. We met at a legal conference at the university and promised each other to have coffee together. Tali told me lots of things. Some of them had already been published in the numerous articles about her and interviews with her. There is no point in repeating them. Dr. Ruhama Marton, director of Physicians for Human Rights, talked about how similar solitary confinement is to real physical abuse. I thought about those nine months alone in prison. As I was eating a stuffed pepper, she had the house salad. I noticed how gentle Tali is, as if she cannot even make up her mind about a cup of coffee, so different from the public image of Tali Fahima, who comes off in the media as such an assertive person.

I think that for a strong person solitary confinement can bring about enlightenment.

HOMEOPATHY AS A PARABLE

WEDNESDAY, 1/10/07, 15:00, FORTY-EIGHT HOURS BEFORE THE OPENING IN JENIN

I am terribly sick. I call a doctor. Some guy shows up, a Russian fellow, a homeopath. I tell him I do not believe in homeopathy. I read a lot about it and I don't like it. He says: "You don't want to believe? Don't believe, but do you know that water has memory?" "You know," he answers his own question. "So I dilute the medication with water, let's say not until it disappears completely, but until it almost disappears completely. And we call this 'water memory,' OK?" "OK," he replies again to himself. "And then, when you take the medication, it reminds the antibodies of their role and they remember and awake and start acting and combating everything that is bad for the body, OK?" "OK," he replies yet again to himself.

And the medication? "It doesn't have any effect. How can it? It's merely a memory. It only reminds the body of what's good for it, and the body has to set up its own resistance cells to achieve longevity and live in physical and spiritual peace with itself and with its neighbors, and let us all say Amen. Got it?" "Got it," I reply and place twenty drops under my tongue.

A Murder Is a Murder Is a Murder

Between Tel Aviv and Bil'in

I went to Bil'in again yesterday to protest the IDF's late-night arrest of village activists who were involved in the unarmed struggle to get their stolen land back. Hundreds of people ignored the August heat to attend the demonstration and show their solidarity with the villagers, whose struggle is so righteous, so just. Even Dov Khenin, a member of Knesset for the Hadash Party (the only joint Jewish-Arab party in the Knesset) was there. He got hit with tear gas as soon as he arrived, and while he was still trying to figure out what had happened, he called out in shock, "But the demonstration hasn't even started yet!?" Just one day earlier Dov had attended the trial of Muhammad Hatib, a local villager and a leader of the struggle. At the trial he wondered aloud why the IDF is so intent on arresting this man—an internationally acclaimed symbol of nonviolent resistance. "Do they prefer martyrs?" he asked. The sad truth is that apparently they do. Israel prefers the martyrs, the *shahids*. After all, it's good for PR.

One thing should never be forgotten: The people responsible for this brutal theft of Palestinian land and for the murder of Bassam Abu Rahmeh, one of

An abridged version of an article that appeared on Ynet on the August 16, 2009, in the wake of the terrible murders that occurred in the Palestinian village of Bil'in and at the GLBT Youth Center in Tel Aviv.

Bil'in's best and brightest, live right here among us in Tel Aviv, a city now cel-
ebrating its centenary as a city just like any other.

The people directly responsible for this theft visit all the newest exhibitions in our museums and galleries and attend all the latest shows in our
theaters. They share beer with us in our sidewalk restaurants and make
sure to hug us and smile for the cameras at the gala premiere of some
antiwar film or other. They even stand shoulder to shoulder with us in
Rabin Square at demonstrations in support of our gay community. These
are the same people who sent a soldier to shoot Bassam Abu Rahmeh in
the chest while he tried to save a wounded young girl; they are the same
ones who make excuses for that murder in court. They are also the same
people who sent soldiers in the middle of the night to abduct Muhammad
Hatib, a man recognized around the world as a leader of the nonviolent
struggle for justice. And when the Supreme Court, which usually collaborates with them, refused to serve as a rubber stamp this time—when
Chief Justice Beinish realized that even she could find no legal justification for the crimes committed in Bil'in—they scoffed at her and showed
their contempt of the courts. Instead of actually moving the fence that
their own justice system deemed illegal, they waited until the dead of
night to arrest those people fighting to ensure the court's ruling be actually upheld.

If I were a religious man, I'd believe that the young people from Tel
Aviv who show up in Bil'in week after week are a homebred version of the
righteous men and women of Sodom. They are the very reason why some
omnipotent god does not pour down his wrath and destroy Tel Aviv, a city
stoned on its own smell, a city convinced that there is no occupation . . .
or racism . . . or murder . . . even though they are the underpinnings of
its very existence.

After all, it wasn't the settlers who robbed Bil'in of its land. It wasn't
some fanatical group of religious nationalists either. Those lands were stolen by consecutive Israeli governments ("seeking peace") to sate the insa-
tiable greed of corporate shills blinded by their own arrogance. They were
stolen for contractors (Blackwater anyone?) who used the land to build
cheap housing projects for large, impoverished ultra-Orthodox families
who will end up being the targets of hate over the coming generations.

These masters of war, these robber barons of Palestinian land, do
not even bother to hide. We see them everywhere in Tel Aviv, but especially when we look straight in the mirror before going out for a night on
the town. In truth, *they* are all of *us*, though I believe that anyone who

opposes these actions does bear somewhat less guilt and that anyone who opposes these actions vociferously is assured a place among the innocent. That is why I choose to go to Bil'in, whenever desperation threatens to overwhelm the least spark of optimism. Bil'in is more than just some Palestinian village whose inhabitants are struggling to survive. Bil'in is the last great hope for anyone who has just about raised his hands in frustration, despairing of the possibility that there can ever be justice and understanding in the Israeli-Palestinian living space.

A shocking murder was committed two weeks ago at a GLBT youth center in Tel Aviv. In response, some leaders of that community met with Prime Minister Benjamin Netanyahu and organized a rally in Rabin Square. Top government leaders attended, including President Shimon Peres, former Minister of Education Limor Livnat, and current Minister of Education Gideon Sa'ar. Everyone spoke about how shocked they were by the murder, but most of all they spoke about the sacred principle that everyone has the right to be whomever they might chose to be—the right to be different, to identify with the other. Yet, even as they delivered their speeches, IDF soldiers were raiding more homes in Bil'in and other Palestinian villages upon the orders of that same government. It's the sad truth behind our liberal, Western facade. Our GLBT leaders—those celebrities and filmmakers—collaborated with the government on its international PR campaign. They silenced the radical voices in the queer community who struggle against the Occupation under that wonderful slogan, "There is no pride in Occupation!" But there is no pride in Tel Aviv either. It's the only Western city in the world today without an Arab population—a city now involved in expelling the Arab population of Jaffa. But not only did they silence the radical voices in the queer community. They even managed to out a few Israeli artists who refused to attend the rally.

So I turn to my dear friends in Tel Aviv, the city that I love so much, but also the city where it is getting harder and harder to really feel at home. We who drown our sorrows in endless bottles of Jameson and who struggle on behalf of the rights of minorities and other disenfranchised groups—we must refuse to shake hands with Netanyahu or Livnat or Barak. The next time they come to console our community, after some attack or other, we must tell them that in our world blood is blood is blood is blood. The time has come for us to be a virtuous city, and that means that instead of outing artists who choose to keep their sexual preferences private we will pry open the doors of our own stifling closets and take pride in our political convictions. We will scream at the top of our lungs that there is no pride in being part of the Occupation forces. We will call on soldiers to refuse orders and we will refuse to collaborate with the Israeli propaganda machine, whether in this country or around the world. We will refuse to participate in international festivals as representatives of Israel and only appear at those events as representatives of the opposition to the Occupation or, alternately, as artists without a homeland of their own.

And, finally, if and when you are overwhelmed by a sense of existential desperation, or even if it is only by the most basic sense of justice, come and join us in Bil'in. There you will understand how right Shai Carmeli Pollack was to name his film *Bil'in My Love*. After all, it really is true that the struggle for Bil'in is more than just a struggle for justice. It's a struggle that derives from love itself.

4

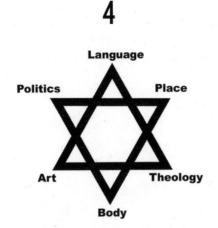

POLITICS

PLEA TO JEWISH ARTISTS

Trust Your Dreams

To Dorit Rabinian

A few years ago my good friend Hassan Hourani from Ramallah drowned in the sea of Jaffa. Upon remembering his passion for life and for liberty, may we all be empowered to survive and see days better than these.

Israeli author Dorit Rabinian's moving letter to her friend Hassan was published by the Israeli newspaper *Haaretz* at the time. Dorit sent it to me, and, in spite of the love manifested in her letter, I also saw through it just how differently we both experience Hassan's death on the personal as well as the political level. That is why I decided to invoke Hassan's specter and invite it to come and listen to the letter I wrote responding to our mutual friend Dorit.

Dear Dorit,

I received your letter, and out of remembrance for the love that existed between you and Hassan I immediately began to read it. Tears filled my eyes as I read, and my heart overflowed with a big love and a big anger. The tears were for the big love and for knowing that I will never see Hassan again. The shivers down my spine were due to your account of the drowning, as if Hassan himself became the protagonist of his story. The anger in my heart was for this haphazard death, for feeling compelled to give some meaning to this terrible drowning, and for the politics of the letter. The love in my heart was due to the fact that you simply flooded me with love: So much love for your beloved, a beloved who first became a friend and then, upon his death, became a beloved again.

It is the politics of the letter as well as the politics in the letter that I would like to write to you about. And perhaps I also wish to write about the politics of love. If you and Hassan had gotten married, Hassan would have brought you proudly to his family, and they would have adopted you as their in-law. They would have thrown a big party, and Jews and Arabs would have been seated there together. If you and Hassan had gotten married, you would not have brought him to your family, they would not have accepted him as their in-law. Some Jewish families even observe seven days of mourning when this happens to them, as if a family member just passed away.

Dorit, the binationalism Hassan talked about is not just a political solution. It was born from a place devoid of any racism, it did not emanate from Hassan the man larger than life, but from Hassan the man who saw the simplicity of life. It did not emanate from the border-transcending romantic, but from human reasoning. It follows from the simplicity in the notion of equality between all human beings. Your letter, all of it, tell us that your heart and your thought and your body know Hassan was right, that binationalism is the simplest, most humane solution. Since you, being an honest person, cannot reject it as a natural idea, you exile it to the realm of the supernatural, messianic, and position yourself as one who settles for very little, just simple peace and not redemption. I think people do not go out to fight for a little dream. People go out to fight only for big dreams, and they are sometimes willing to compromise eventually for little dreams. Hassan was a friend, but I dedicated my first book to him as well because to me he symbolized binationalism. In your ever so sensitive and heart-wrenching observations you have identified the nearly messianic binationalist power that was stored in Hassan, a binationalist approach beyond one political solution or another. Even he said that if a two-state solution can end the bloodshed, then let there be a two-state solution. But in your letter one finds so much fear of the binationalist alternative. Hassan is not the binationalism of the messianic era. Hassan is the binationalism of the feasible, the binationalism of the unity of human beings and the love of human beings. And if Hassan is a human being, flesh and blood, binationalism is possible, but if Hassan is a dream, then binationalism too is a just dream.

Dorit, don't be scared, don't be scared, don't be scared! Listen to your heart!

Listen to the place you and Hassan called home. Don't write about terrorism and occupation as an equation. Write: "Reason: occupation, outcome: terrorism." Don't write that Hassan is a utopian as opposed to you, someone who would settle for little (you have never settled for little). Do write that we are the problem and Hassan is the solution. Don't apologize. Hassan's dream is the only real thing. In New York you experienced binationalism; you experienced love. Love does not lie, and there is more power in it than in all the politics of the world. Follow love, Dorit, and show your readers the way. Dorit, you live in Jaffa now, and Hassan is drowned in the nearby sea. His spirit is wandering in the Palestinian cemetery, looking for a plot of land to lay his dead head on. Eventually he will surely find quiet in one of the Jewish nouveau riche homes of Jaffa, which were once the homes of Palestinians (after all, he was always fond of the good life . . .).

Close your eyes, Dorit, and breathe the air and the scents. Resurrect the spirits, bring the Palestinian back to Jaffa, to the markets and the shops. Hear the street sounds, Hebrew and Arabic blending together, and then tell Hassan: "Yes, this is how I see the Jewish state, which is also the Palestinian state, how beautiful it is, so simple, such a light unto the nations, and I was incredulous, I was nice to the *Haaretz*-reading liberals who thought binationalism is a curse."

But we are ready to go out and fight for peace and brotherhood (and sisterhood) between all the residents of this land (remember that Lincoln thought liberating slaves was good reason for a civil war). We are going out to fight as the few against the many, instilled with the belief that only equality and emancipation of everyone will form the state in which my daughter and son and Hassan's brother can live together. And let me whisper to you again, Dorit, people don't go out to fight for a little dream. Dorit, you told me there is pathos in me. Don't be scared of this pathos in my letter, for it has been meticulously chosen. It aims at bringing some hope into this big despair. There is something Aharon Shabtaiesque about it, something Alain Badiouesque, something that is not willing to give up. Come write binationalism with us, Dorit. Let reality prevail.

Love, Udi

Thus Spoke the Left

An Attack on the Manifesto of the National Left

PREFACE

"The only democracy in the Middle East"[1] mobilized into action to protect the manifesto of the national left, whose selling in Israeli bookstores an ultranationalist group has managed to cancel.

The manifesto was written by former aide to then Prime Minister Ehud Barak and by a playwright. It is an attempt to draw conclusions from the ongoing electoral failure of the so-called Zionist left and to redefine it in a manner that will render it a viable "patriotic" political force with the ability to lead the nation.

Having read the document of the national left, I believe that if it is to be removed from the bookstores it is because of its populist qualities, its clichés, and its ignorance, which borders on slander.

The authors of the manifesto write the following about themselves:

"What will happen if we discovered that our positions are not 'left' and that we are in fact right-wing supporters in the closet?"[2]

Well, after reading the manifesto, it turns out that it was written in order to flank the right from the right with regard to racism and from

---

1. As Israel is often described in the conservative Western media.
2. Likud is the main right-wing party in Israel, currently led by Prime Minister Binyamin Netanyahu.

below with regard to populism. The entire text is written in the language of an aging, nationalist, arrogant Palmach veteran,[3] as if Rehavam Ze'evi's spirit gained control over the authors.[4]

When we focus on a few terms from the text, the ideological world of the national "left" is exposed.[5]

NATIONAL "LEFT"/HUMANISTIC LEFT

In almost any period throughout history when the terms *left* and *national* or *socialism* and *national* merged into one word, a fascist heavy-handed monster arose. This syntax is valid also for the state of Israel, and so we, a group of left activists, have decided to accept the derogatory term *small* (an erroneous spelling of the Hebrew word for "left," hinting also at the English word *small*) and wear it proudly as a badge that separates us from the national "left."

THE UN RESOLUTION: THE ROCK OF OUR EXISTENCE

The authors of the manifesto claim that the Jews accepted the UN's 1947 partition plan and that the Palestinians did not. That's why a war broke out, and the Palestinians goofed up; that's life. That is, the existence of the state of Israel is justified by the UN resolution. Without getting into the historical debate on what exactly happened, there is a consensus that at the end of the war, following the armistice agreement, one state remained—the state of Israel. As the state of Palestine had not been established, the UN adopted resolution 194: the right of the refugees to return.

3. The regular fighting force of the unofficial army of the Jewish community during the British mandate in Palestine; its members later formed the backbone of the IDF high command for many years and were prominent in Israeli politics, literature, and culture.
4. Rehavam Ze'evi: a right-wing Israeli general, politician, and historian who was assassinated in 2001.
5. As we in the radical left do not consider most of the national left or Zionist left to be a true left, we will refer to it in quotation marks and reserve the use of the word without quotation marks for the radical left. As explained, in Israel the national "left" is often alluded to using the normal Hebrew word for left, whereas a derogatory term is used for the radical left.

So, if Israel draws its legitimacy from the UN resolution, the right of return of the refugees is legally intertwined in this legitimacy, and there is no legitimacy for Israel without acknowledging the right of return.

The national "left" denies another truth: it is mainly its spiritual ancestors who are responsible for the refugee problem, for the violation of the UN resolution, and for the main practice of the state of Israel ever since the armistice agreement, which is the expropriation of the indigenous population's lands and their transfer to the hands of the new lords of the land, namely, the Jews of the state of Israel. What started in Iqrit and Kafr Bir'im[6] has never stopped for a moment, and is still taking place in Bil'in, Sheikh-Jarrah, and Ajami.[7] The authors of the manifesto are proud of these actions.

RIGHT AND "LEFT"/LEFT

The authors of the manifesto write:

"Rehavam (Gandhi) Ze'evi's Moledet[8] movement once had a slogan: 'we [shall be] here—they [shall be] there.' Meretz once had the slogan: 'to bid the Territories farewell [*shalom*, the Hebrew word for peace].'[9] Actually, this is the same principle."

As opposed to the national "left," which is more accurately part of the national right and seeks to make the Palestinian vanish on the other side of the wall, for us on the left, the binational reality (which is always already) is not merely compulsory; it is, fundamentally, the realization of a dream for both Jewish and Palestinian emancipation.

6. Christian Palestinian villages whose inhabitants were forced to flee during the 1948 war, having been given a promise they would be allowed to return once the war was over. That promise was never fulfilled, even after a ruling by the Israeli Supreme Court to allow the return.
7. Bil'in has become the symbol of the Palestinian nonviolent struggle against the Occupation after years of weekly demonstrations against the wall. That struggle has recently reached the East Jerusalem neighborhood of Sheikh-Jarrah, whose Palestinian residents are being evicted while Jewish settlers occupy their homes. Ajami is an Arab neighborhood in Jaffa that right-wing religious groups are now trying to take over.
8. *Moledet* is Hebrew for "homeland"; a small right-wing party advocating the notion of a "voluntary" transfer of the Arab population out of the West Bank.
9. Meretz is a left-wing Zionist party.

SETTLERS/LEFTISTS

The national "left" blames the settlers for the entire Occupation, as if the settlers are an external group that is not a part of the state of Israel.

The left, on the other hand, knows that the national "left" is almost solely responsible for the Occupation, and that the settlers are merely the sight hounds. The latter as well as the former serve as an integral part of the occupation's machinery, of its injustices. The national "left" acts as the master who, having sicced his dog on the neighbors' son, claims in his defense: "It's not me, it's him" (pointing at the dog).

LEFT/ULTRA-ORTHODOX

The left asks the Hasidim of Belz to remain in the Shenkin area and live together.[10] The left sympathizes with the ultra-Orthodox because they carry the scent of Diaspora and are still not immersed in militarism.

THE WALL/LIFE IN COMMON (TA'AYUSH)[11]

The national "left" adores the wall, the left loathes it. The wall is not a protective means, but a means for domination and land theft. The wall not only separates Palestinians from Jews but also Palestinians from other Palestinians. It does not cover the entire border, and any young, healthy Palestinian can climb his way across it in many places (it is not the wall, as is widely believed, but complex political circumstances that have caused the number of terror attacks in Israel to decrease). The national "left" has helped crush the Palestinians into five distinct groups, that cannot even intermarry (East Jerusalem, Israel's 1948 borders, the West Bank, Gaza, the Palestinian Diaspora). As long as the five cannot be one, this way or another, there is no equality, there is no justice, and there is no left.

10. Located in the center of the city and offering a diverse assortment of shops, restaurants, cafés, other businesses, and street shows, Shenkin Street is a symbol of the young, open, and liberal culture of Tel Aviv. Secular, religious, and ultra-Orthodox Jews reside in the neighborhood peacefully side by side.
11. *Ta'ayush* is Arabic for "coexistence," or "life in common," and the name of a group formed by Israeli citizens, both Jews and Arabs, that works against the Occupation and the discrimination of Palestinians in Israel and in the West Bank.

The left believes in coexisting in the same place, even when groups are not able to generate common ground, as the only other option is to be the next refugee. Thus on the left you will see a lesbian marching together with a Palestinian woman, both fighting against the separation wall; you will see Menachem Begin's grandson with Ehud Olmert's daughter marching with them, and alongside all these people you will see a secular Muslim shoulder to shoulder with a religious Jew, all against the separation wall.

JABOTINSKY/BEN-GURION/BEGIN/PERES

The authors of the manifesto distort history and write:

"The left believes that you and I will change the world. . . . The right believes that if what exists now continues until the end of eternity we shall all reach salvation."

The manifesto describes Jabotinsky and his disciples as the ones who oppose any change and the Ben-Gurion left as dynamic and revolutionary. Make no mistake. Jabotinsky wrote: "There he shall quench his thirst with plenty and happiness, the son of Arabia, son of Nazareth and my son." It was Begin, Jabotinsky's disciple, who signed the agreement that gave back land,[12] and it was he who opposed the imposition of a military regime in the Galilee and the Triangle,[13] where the Israeli apartheid state was established. Their complete opposite is Shimon Peres, who has managed to sabotage every dialogue for peace and who has founded the Peres Center for Peace on Arab land in Jaffa; a man whose only revolutions were the introduction of nuclear arms to the Middle East (the authors of the manifesto take pride in this dubious achievement) and the creation of the settlement precedent in Qedumim-Sebastia.

YASSER ARAFAT/YITZHAK RABIN

The authors of the manifesto describe Arafat thus:

"A vile scoundrel, a ridiculous clown, an abhorrent murderer who robbed billions donated by the world for the Palestinian people and deposited them in his antipathetic wife's private accounts."

12. As part of the peace treaty with Egypt, signed in 1979, Israel had completely withdrawn from the Sinai Peninsula by 1982.
13. Areas in northern Israel where many Arab citizens of Israel reside. They are the vast majority in the Triangle.

This is clearly a repulsive text that degrades the leader and symbol of the Palestinian people, much like scurrilous antisemitic writings. The manifesto lauds Yitzhak Rabin for his efforts toward peace and his ability to change. Rabin and Arafat got along well and trusted each other in the months that preceded the murder.[14] The left, as opposed to the "left," *does not sympathize* with the two. It never admired them or the Oslo Accords.[15] But the left knew to credit them for the brave move. Only a rare combination of insolence, lies, and racism allows praising Rabin while denouncing Arafat. They did it together, for crying out loud!

Use of claims about Arafat's corruption so as to deprive the Palestinian state of its right to exist repeats itself throughout the manifesto, against the backdrop of our current reality when every day we hear something new about corruption among most of the Israeli leadership.

Yaniv and Hasfari write that "people are judged by their deeds." Well, Arafat signed in Sharm el-Sheikh,[16] and it doesn't matter if it happened only because Mubarak cursed him. For his people, Arafat slept on an iron bed. Ehud Barak jumped ship and did not sign and slept in his luxurious home at Tel Aviv's Akirov Towers.

THE HILLTOP YOUTH/THE IDF

The authors of the manifesto write the following about the hilltop youth:[17]

"Jewish youths who are capable of beating an old Palestinian woman who is trying to harvest the olives in her family's lot, as did her ancestors for hundreds of years, have lost the right to be called Jews. They burn the crop in Palestinian fields, they cut and uproot olive trees, they beat and shoot infants and elderly people. . . . You look at them and your eyes can not believe what they see."

It is true, but half the truth is worse than a lie. It is not hilltop youth who stand at the checkpoints where women about to give birth are greeted with burning contempt, and it is not hilltop youth who sowed terrible death in Gaza. It is not hilltop youth who shoot us in cold blood

14. Prime Minister Yitzhak Rabin was assassinated on November 4, 1995.
15. Declaration of Principles on Interim Self-Government Arrangements, officially signed in Washington, DC on September 13, 1993, in the presence of Arafat, Rabin, and U.S. president Bill Clinton.
16. A post-Oslo agreement toward a two-state solution.
17. A term for Jewish youth who settle in illegal outposts on uninhabited hills in the West Bank.

in Bil'in, and it is not hilltop youth who stand guard with cocked weapons to supervise the apartheid land theft committed by . . . the hilltop youth. It is the IDF that does all that on behalf of most of the Jews in Zion, and thus, according to your principles, it is the Jews in Zion who lose the right to be called Jews!

LEFT (2)

And that small group of *small* leftists whom you mock for their presence in Bil'in against the wall every Friday—on Thursdays they protect Sudanese refugees. And on Wednesdays they can be found at the Akerstein factory in Yeruham aiding exploited workers (Jews, by the way). Not only do they dismantle the terrible wall between Jews and Arabs, they also guard the wall of the morals of the prophets, which are the opposite of the morals of the occupiers.

PROFESSOR LEIBOWITZ IS TURNING OVER IN HIS GRAVE

The authors of the manifesto write, about Professor Leibowitz, "He was probably the smartest Jew in the last century."[17]

The mere comparison, expressed in the manifesto, between obeying the laws of the state and following the religious commandments would horrify Professor Leibowitz. For him the state was but a necessary tool, certainly not the object of love and awe.

Leibowitz would have probably begun his article about the manifesto in the following manner: "I have yet to decide whether the authors of the manifesto are completely ignorant or completely evil."

PIGGISH CAPITALISM/CAPITALISM AS PIGGERY

A whole chapter is dedicated to the capitalist pigs, but they are then led back in through the back door, and God forbid if you dare say socialism. Unfortunately, it is not enough to talk about the capitalist pigs, and

17. Professor Yeshayahu Leibowitz (1903–1994): an Israeli philosopher and biochemist known for his outspoken, often controversial opinions on Judaism, ethics, religion, and politics.

one should also speak of the piggery that is the essence of capitalism. Capitalist pigs change, but the method always remains. And how can attorney Eldad Yaniv who represents the capital-occupation symbiosis (for example, he represents the municipality of Ariel and powerful employers) preach?[18]

THE WOMAN DOES NOT EXIST

The left believes that the two most important struggles in the realm that lies between the (Mediterranean) Sea and the (Jordan) River are liberation and equality for the Palestinian and liberation and equality for the woman. The left believes it is a joint complementary struggle. The woman, in our realm, is traded as a sex slave on Allenby Street,[19] in what is called "an erotic club," and is murdered in Ramle or in Acre, for what is called "family honor," and there is no protector, for the manifesto of the national left is so masculine that the woman has been left out and forgotten . . .

FIXING THE SEWER: PRESENT ABSENTEE

The authors of the manifesto write:

"If you want to talk to them (to the Arabs) about national service,[20] connect their villages to the sewerage."

For historic justice, the only ones to have treated them with that level of dignity, if only for a short period, were Aryeh Deri from the Shas party and Moshe Arens from the Likud.[21] If their counterparts from the national "left" have ever done anything, it was but to win votes. It cannot be helped: "our Arabs" are Palestinians, and when the national "left" sent its glorious army to sow destruction in Gaza, it turned out that many families from the Galilee lost their dear ones and once again realized they are Palestinians. And when Eldad Yaniv called for "killing Gaza without

18. Ariel is one of the largest settlements, located in the central West Bank.
19. Allenby is a major street in Tel Aviv.
20. Exempt from military service—which is compulsory for other ethnicities in Israel—Israeli Arabs are often criticized for not opting for voluntary national service.
21. Shas is an ultra-Orthodox party identified with Sephardic and Mizrahi Jews.

mercy and without batting an eyelid," the Palestinians who are Israeli citizens realized that even if he solved all their sewer problems he would continue to wish for them to be transparent when walking on their land.

The conclusion should be clear. Only when the manifesto of the left is written and signed by both Palestinians and Jews living between the Mediterranean Sea and the Jordan River will it be a true, relevant document of the left. Only then shall we—the *small*—take off our badge and once again proudly call ourselves *left*.

The Betrayal of the Peace Camp

To Achinoam Nini

The Israeli military strike on Gaza (known as operation "Cast Lead") began on December 27, 2008, and lasted for three weeks, claiming the lives of almost fifteen hundred Palestinians and causing vast damage in the Gaza strip. During this war Achinoam Nini, an Israeli singer, wrote an open letter to the inhabitants of Gaza (published on Ynet on January 6, 2009) in which she claimed the Israeli attack was meant to liberate the Palestinians from the dictatorship of Hamas and is therefore an act of love.

I chose to answer you, Achinoam Nini, and not the entire raging right, because I believe that the betrayal of the peace camp, at this of all times, exceeds the damage caused by the right a thousand fold. The ease with which the peace camp gives itself over to the roars of war hinders the creation of a meaningful movement that could put up a true resistance to the Occupation.

You roll your eyes, use your loving words in the service of your conquering people, and call upon the Palestinians to surrender in a tender voice. You bestow upon Israel the role of liberator. Upon Israel—which, for over sixty years, has been occupying and humiliating them. "I know where your heart is! It is just where mine is,

Published on Ynet, January 8, 2009.

with my children, with the earth, with the heavens, with music, with HOPE!!" you write; but, Achinoam, we took their land and imprisoned them in the ghetto called Gaza.

We have covered their skies with fighter jets, soaring like the angels from hell and scattering random death. What hope are you talking about?. We destroyed any chance for moderation and mutual life the moment we plundered their land while sitting with them at the negotiation table. We may have spoken of peace, but we were robbing them blind. They wanted the land given to them by international law, and we spoke in the name of Jehovah.

Who are the secular people of Gaza supposed to turn to, when we trample on international law and when the rest of the enlightened world ignores their cry? When enlightenment fails and moderation is seen as a weakness, religious fanaticism gives a sense of empowerment. Maybe, if you think about the mental situation of the people under siege in Masada, you could get a better sense of what's happening in Gaza.

The secular people in Gaza find it hard to speak against Hamas when their ghetto is being bombarded day and night. You would probably say that "we would not need to shell them if they held their fire," but they fire because they are fighting for more than the right to live in the prison called Gaza. They are fighting for the right to live as free citizens in an independent country—just as we do.

"I know that deep in your hearts YOU WISH for the demise of this beast called Hamas who has terrorized and murdered you, who has turned Gaza into a trash heap of poverty, disease, and misery," you write. But Hamas is not the monster, my dear Achinoam. It is the monster's son.

The Israeli Occupation is the monster. It and only it is responsible for the poverty and the sickness and the horror. We were so frightened of their secular leadership, which undermined our fantasy of the Land of Israel, that we chose to fund and support Hamas, hoping that by a policy of divide and conquer we could go on with the Occupation forever; but, when the tables were turned, you choose to blame the effect instead of the cause.

You write, "I can only wish for you that Israel will do the job we all know needs to be done, and finally RID YOU of this cancer, this virus, this monster called fanaticism, today, called Hamas. And that these killers will find what little compassion may still exist in their hearts and STOP using you and your children as human shields for their cowardice and crimes." It is the same as if your Palestinian sister were to write: "Let us hope that Hamas does the job for you and rids you of the Jewish right."

So maybe, instead of ordering around a people whose every glimmer of hope we have surgically eliminated, you could help your brothers and sisters in Palestine rid themselves of the occupation, oppression, and arrogant colonialism inflicted by your country. Only then can you urge them to fight democratically and return Palestine to the mental state it was in before we pushed it into the corner of the wall that we built.

And if your brethren in Palestine choose Hamas, you have to respect their choice, just as the world's nations respected Israel when it chose the murderous (Ariel) Sharon. Hamas is theirs to fight, just like you fought him. That is what democracy is about. Only then can you and your brethren in both Palestine and Israel share—as equals—the joy of the land, the sky, and the music; only then can we fight for equality together, for every man and woman living in our holy land. Amen.

From Now on Say I Am a Palestinian Jew

To David Grossman

The following article was written in response to the somewhat enthusiastic welcoming of Israeli Prime Minister Netanyahu's "acceptance" of the two-state solution in June 2009 by prominent left-wing figures in Israel. Netanyahu stated that the Palestinians must recognize Israel as the Jewish national state with an undivided Jerusalem. He rejected a right of return for Palestinian refugees and also stated that a complete stop to settlement building in the West Bank would not occur. He did not discuss whether or not the settlements should be part of Israel after peace negotiations, simply saying that the "question will be discussed."

Leading authors of the Israeli left have cleansed the impure with their analysis of Netanyahu's Bar-Ilan speech.[1] They have proven that they too need to change their position.

Israeli Book Week is always a good time for our authors to express protest and place themselves exactly where the Jewish Israeli reader can or wants to accept them. That is, a bit leftist, a bit pessimistic, a bit prophetic, but always "on our side."

---

1. Benjamin Netanyahu's speech at Bar-Ilan University, on June 14, 2009, in which he endorsed the notion, for the first time, of a Palestinian state alongside Israel.

And this begs the question: How long will Israeli intellectuals collaborate with this task that has been assigned to them?

David Grossman and A. B. Yehoshua have interpreted Benjamin Netanyahu's Bar-Ilan speech. Grossman in a somewhat pessimistic article that repeats, in other words, the parable of Samson's foxes whose tails were tied together with a burning torch. This parable describes how he sees our relation to the Palestinians: All of us living here, members of the two peoples, are jointly setting fire to our very own fields, and this cannot be rectified unless America saves us from ourselves.

In comparison, A. B. Yehosua assumes the role of consultant to the king and claims that if Netanyahu only retracted his demand that the Palestinians recognize Israel as a Jewish state all would be solved. As if there is no Occupation, as if the speech is not mere lip service, as if the formerly genuine and sincere two states idea has not become Machiavellian, in the service of those perpetuating the wrongdoings of the Occupation in 1967 and the wrongdoings of the Nakba in 1948. The two-state solution has become a legitimate excuse for denying Palestinians their equal rights, and mainly to deny the right of return, which is well founded in international law.

A. B. Yehoshua wants us to put aside theology and ideology and be practical, but theology and ideology underlie all his arguments. The Zionist left has not allowed even those Palestinians uprooted from Iqrit and Bir'im to return to their homes, in the name of its principle—redemption of the sacred land.[2] In view of all this, how pathetic is Yehoshua's call for egalitarian secular Israeliness. For them, the word *Israeliness* includes only Jews and their culture and excludes Palestinians and their culture.

In other words, secular Israelis may not believe in god, but they are sure that god promised the Holy Land to them alone. And thus, time and again, Israeli Jews feel free to grab lands that do not belong to them and then elect a new leader whose sole task is to manipulate the Gentiles with sweet talking and trickery. By doing this the elected leader buys enough time to delay the resolution until the coming of the Messiah (or the day of judgment) and, at the same time, writers, artists, and intellectuals—maybe in good faith, maybe out of sheer opportunism—imbue him with a dignified, liberal, somewhat Western facade.

2. Iqrit and Bir'im are two Palestinian Christian villages whose inhabitants left in 1948. See p. 111, n. 6.

MINCING WORDS

Grossman and Yehoshua's critical reading of Netanyahu's speech is equivalent to the laundering of illicit merchandise. Our authors whitewash Bibi's words, presenting him as someone who may be mistaken, but who is still legitimate. They purify and legitimize the racist excess, or at least render it tolerable, and they turn us into passive, helpless people. Then they comfort us with all sorts of rituals: the Rabin memorial ceremony (with speakers on the podium), Israeli Book Week (where authors sign their books). The author and readers are actually joining forces: first, horrendous acts are whitewashed with words, and then the words are whitewashed with the words of authors and poets.

Quoting the late great Hanoch Levine, "We are all together, the men of all's OK, with a finger in our ass and a song in our throat, waiting for the Messiah to come, because things are good, stinky and warm." And if the Messiah ends up wanting two states, then he will establish two states, and they will have the state of Palestine, and half a million settlers will leave willfully singing hallelujah, and then the refugees too will be allowed to implement some halfway right of return. But, in the meantime, they seem to be saying, please be seated and keep quiet, sweet Palestinian natives, and let us negotiate your wretched fate among ourselves. Give peace a chance, pleads Grossman, and give peace a chance since, in any case, your life sucks, and for heaven's sake stop bombing and exploding. After all, we are trying to establish a model literary ethnocratic democracy here . . .

So, dear writers, I think the moment of truth has come or, as the famous children's song goes, "We've smashed the vessels, and we're not gonna play anymore." For the sake of Hebrew literature, for the sake of your faithful readers, for the sake of Jews and Palestinians, and for the sake of the entire Middle East—the time has come to cross the lines and change your identity. Adopt the identity of the oppressed, not the identity of the occupier (it will also assist you in your writing). From now on say, "I am a Jewish Palestinian author, their fate is my fate, their despair is my despair, their joy is my joy." Because the truth is that no Bibi or Barak or Livni intends to divide this land, neither in justice nor in grace nor in mercy. And now there is only one state on this land, and this state is racist, cruel, and ethnocratic. So, if we have one state, why struggle to divide the indivisible? All that we have to do is turn it into a democratic Jewish Palestinian state, a binational, multicultural, multigendered, and vital state.

P.S.:

A question to Grossman: If the United States is the only country capable of saving us from ourselves, why don't you call for a comprehensive boycott against the state of Israel, until the last settlement is dismantled, to save us from ourselves? Or, to allude to the late Israeli poet Avot Yeshurun: "Let Hebrew literature go and learn integrity from Iranian football."[3]

3. During the 2009 uprisings against Ahmadinejad, the Iranian football team famously wore green armbands to symbolize the opposition in solidarity with the uprising, which put them at risk of imprisonment.

And Who Shall I Say Is Calling?

A Plea to Leonard Cohen

After the Israeli elections giving rise to an extreme right-wing government and following the Gaza war and the international criticism against it, more and more voices were heard pleading for a cultural boycott against Israel. The concert of Leonard Cohen, scheduled for September 25, 2009, became a test case to all sides in this debate. Cohen, known for his human rights activities and support for the peace process, did not cancel his concert, but suggested giving one in Ramallah as well. The Palestinian resistance committee decided to turn down the performance in Ramallah. Leonard Cohen performed in Tel Aviv and donated some of the proceeds to Israeli-Palestinian peace organizations.

Dear Leonard,

It was two months ago that I had the privilege of seeing you perform in New York. You might say I'd been waiting thirty-five years for it. I remembered the first time I'd heard your music in Israel, and you could tell from my smile "that tonight would be fine." As I arrived outside the show, I met some old friends—partners in the

Published on Ynet, August 3, 2009.

struggle—who were demonstrating across the street: "Leonard, don't play Israel!" After all the kissing and warm embraces, I told them that I really must go in so that I wouldn't miss the opening song. They nodded and slipped a small placard in my hand, then warily asked if I would hold it up during the show: "Leonard, don't play Israel!" Amid those hearts that burn like coal, the sign seared my hands like hot coal too.

I was there with my only daughter. Your wonderful voice had been a soundtrack to my life, and now I wanted to share that with her. I recalled the day, when we were living in New York, that her grandfather died in far-off Beersheba. She lit candles around her bed to the strains of "Hallelujah," and the two of us wept over Grandpa Jukey. Jukey was a wonderful man, who apparently died from a cancer he contracted at the Dimona nuclear reactor, a modern-day temple to the new god that has "become Death, the Destroyer of Worlds." My daughter had never heard "Hallelujah" before, and I hadn't yet told her about the reactor in Dimona, but that's when she first fell in love with your music. Now, in New York, we had come to take advantage of that brief moment of kindness that you so generously shared with us.

Who am I to tell you "Don't play Israel"? Your voice, so mature, so moving, so shattered, could shatter even a heart of stone. And yet that placard still seared my fingers—fingers belonging to an Israeli and a Jew who believes that we are ultimately responsible for the fact that the Palestinian people have lived in exile in their own land for the past sixty years. I was hesitant about raising that sign, but just then you came onstage and sang in your broken, heartrending voice, "Like a bird on the wire, like a drunk in a midnight choir, I have tried in my way to be free." The placard slipped from my hands and the romantic idealism that still fills my soul quivered and shook off years and years of accumulated dust. I sang along as if I was you or you were me. I remembered you well in the Chelsea hotel . . . and it was as if we were there with Janis Joplin herself . . . I never wanted it to end. You knew who I am and you gave me your all. Then, when the concert was finally over, I got up and laid the sign gently on my seat. Maybe someone else would raise it.

I was very excited when I first heard that you would be playing in Ramallah. I said to myself, "It's different with him." I always knew that you are not like Paul McCartney and the others. You are a true symbol of art, who is (still) trying to make this world a better place.

In New York I heard you sing, "I'm your man." It's true: you are my man, indeed. I called my friends in Ramallah and said, "Let's go see Leonard together," and only then did I learn that the Palestinians had decided to cancel your show. It goes without saying that I was quite disappointed. You are someone who listens, who cares. You are different from all the others. Why must they be so stubborn? Why can't they finally reap the fruits of their success: "Leonard Cohen plays in Palestine!" What right do they have to rob their fellow Palestinians of this chance to hear the best that music has to offer? What could they possibly gain from this boycott of the arts? The very idea of mixing art and politics is very problematic, to me at least.

But then my daughter looked me right in the eye and said, in her straightforward way, "Dad, write to Leonard and explain to him why the Palestinians are right to cancel his concert. They don't have the privilege of free access to culture that we have in Tel Aviv or New York. They're tired of all the goodwill gestures and the petty benefits we concede as an alibi for our own dirty consciences. They want justice, and that's why they are asking 'Don't go and amuse our occupiers, and then come to us with a consolation prize.'" Her words were so simple, so wise, that as soon as I heard them I knew I had to write to you.

Well, Leonard, maybe you should only play in Palestine. Maybe you should open your heart to the oppressed and not to their oppressors. If you cancel your show in Israel, no other self-respecting artist will perform here. At first the self-indulgent audience in Tel Aviv will be annoyed at those artists and say that they are all antisemites. Over time, however, they will come to realize that they cannot gain acceptance in some escapist fantasy as long as the Occupation continues. Israelis will not join the struggle against the Occupation as long as the Occupation doesn't hurt them directly. Israelis must be told: "The Occupation is not normal. Nothing here is normal, God dammit!"

The Palestinians can afford to miss your show, not because they don't like you or admire your art, and not because they necessarily believe that art should be political. They simply think that the artist Leonard Cohen should side with the oppressed. So much so, in fact, they are even willing to sacrifice this chance to hear a truly great artist like you so that they too can be like that "bird on the wire," finally free. Leonard, I just want you to know that even if you did play in

Ramallah, you would not be able to give a show in Gaza, because the 1.5 million people living there are trapped in a prison where no one comes or goes. To paraphrase you, "The walls of this prison still surround them, and they cannot break away."

You might ask: Why me? Why Leonard Cohen? What about all the other artists who perform in Israel? All I can say is that yours is the fate of the last of the troubadours—the same fate shared by Moses on Mount Nebo. Take it as a compliment that the Palestinians chose you. Someone there must believe that you represent the human conscience. And if Madonna, Depeche Mode, McCartney, and the rest can play only in Israel and only for Israelis, then you can play only in Ramallah and only for Palestinians.

After endless consideration, I finally realized the question that should be asked is not whether we support or oppose a cultural boycott. It is not even whether the Palestinians were right for canceling your concert in Ramallah. The question is really whether we should comply with the request of those Palestinians who have chosen the path of nonviolent resistance in their struggle against occupation and racism. It may be difficult for me, emotionally, to accept a cultural boycott; I already described how I failed in my attempt to raise that placard during your show in New York. That is why this time I will comply with their wishes. With my actions I will offer those denied self-determination the right to determine their response. By accepting their right to decide, I will empower those who've been disempowered for so long and help to restore the sovereignty they lack. That is what solidarity really means.

Leonard, I truly admire you as a poet. My admiration for you and your work is unconditional and will continue unabated regardless of whether you decide to play Israel or not. I am not boycotting you at all, and I will send all my friends to hear you sing anywhere else in the world that you might play. Here, however, in response to the calls of the Palestinian people, in solidarity with a people denied their basic rights for the past sixty years, as a Jew, and as a citizen of Israel who supports the nonviolent struggle of the Palestinian people for freedom, equality, and justice, I regret that I will not be able to attend this show, this time. This is the one place where I cannot allow the placard to slip from my hands. I cannot be derelict in my duty to help tear down the roadblocks and walls. Because here in Israel-Palestine, only when all the inhabitants who share this very special place can come to see your show, regardless of their race or ethnicity, could I possibly sit back in my seat, close my eyes, and sing with you: "The holy or the broken, Hallelujah!"

With deepest regrets,
Sincerely yours,
Udi Aloni

Come Out of Your Political Closets

To Israeli Filmmakers

After the murder in the LGBT youth club in Tel Aviv (August 1, 2009), Gal Uchovsky and Eitan Fox organized a memorial assembly. They prevented Knesset member Hissam Makhoul of Hadash from speaking in the assembly, claiming "this is no time for politics," and embraced right-wing political leaders. At the same time, they were outing artists who refused to take part in the assembly.

The reason that I choose to criticize you so publicly (even though I still hope to maintain our friendship) is because of your aggressive outing of artists—a tactic that should be reserved "for emergency use only" and not to settle personal accounts (as you did with Benny Ziffer by comparing him to the vile murderer). Even worse, however, is your scandalous criticism of the lesbian community, which refuses to comply with conventional wisdom by kowtowing to facile cultural icons. Instead they prefer to straddle the boundaries of what is "out" and what is "in" here, in our own local culture, and they do it in such an exemplary manner.

Dori Manor is truly one of the cornerstones of Tel Aviv's queer community. Gal and Eitan, you are also very talented and have done so much for the community, but you acted in stark contrast to the approach he laid out in a brilliant, moving piece that appeared in *Haaretz*. You have

Published in *Haaretz*'s online magazine, August 26, 2009.

decided to adopt an outright political agenda, but with this you are transforming the GLBT community into an integral part of the Zionist nationalist consensus.

Yes, there was a once-in-a-lifetime opportunity to forge bonds of solidarity between the GLBT community and the Palestinians of Israel and the Occupied Territories, but you prevented it from happening. As organizers of the event, you refused to allow Knesset member Issam Makhoul to establish the context, which should have been so obvious. Instead, you preferred to invite political leaders to occupy the stage, even though they stand at the head of a racist regime that engages in an endless campaign of war crimes. Rather than show the participants and the nation that Makhoul represents all that should be obvious in a political and human sense—that he represents the struggle against all forms of oppression and violence—he was presented as a political radical, while you claimed that "this is not about politics." You did not want to "stray from the consensus" that the community under your watch is so intent to join, no matter what the cost.

By doing this you indicated unequivocally that the Arab is the political "other"—an outsider—whereas Israeli politicians represent Western values, openness, and "apolitical" tolerance (within the ethnic consensus, of course). With this, however, even more than you represent the gay community, you have become spokesmen for "left-lite," representing continued collaboration between power, wealth, and the arts.

What happened at the rally is reflected in your films too. In them the only way for gay men to win acceptance in Israeli society is by adapting to the myth of the handsome Israeli soldier. By donning a uniform and serving in the army, not only does the gay male enter the mainstream of Israeli society, but the IDF enters the mainstream of European and American culture. You have focused on the Israeli soldier from the perspective of the metrosexual, as an internationally acclaimed icon in the struggle for rights and equality and as an image of beauty and tenderness. But what this effectively creates is a naively enlightened image of the Israeli soldier that provides moral sanction for his actions. In keeping with mainstream Israeli mythology, the Israeli soldiers you depict are handsome, Ashkenazi males pained by the ethical dilemmas they face. In keeping with the mythic storyline, they are always killed by some Arab and thus transformed into tortured martyrs—in *Yossi and Jagger* it was a faceless Arab who did it; in *The Bubble* it was the Palestinian lover who blew himself up. With this, the gay soldier is installed in the national pantheon as an innocent sacrifice who fell victim to war and the consummate expression of Zionist masculinity. Through his death he commands us to seize upon the emotional bond not with the oppressed minority but with the Jewish society of occupiers and its masculine, nationalistic values. It is no wonder that overseas, collaboration between Fuchs-Uchovsky and the foreign ministry has always been so successful.

So my dear friends, Gal and Eitan, instead of outing famous singers, come out of your own political closets! Take a stand alongside the oppressed and don't try to turn the gay community into part of a violent, racist mainstream. An aggressive nation of occupiers can never truly be enlightened and tolerant, even if it looks that way on film. The Israeli soldier of today, regardless of whether he is gay or straight, will always be an occupier and never a martyred saint.

This Time It's Not Funny!

The Toronto film festival 2009 dedicated its City to City project to Tel Aviv. This was a result of fruitful cooperation between the festival and the Israeli ministry of foreign affairs as part of their effort to "brand" Israel as an enlightened and liberal country. A group of artists and intellectuals organized by Naomi Klein published the Toronto Declaration pleading that the festival withdraw from this initiative and that artists protest against the political use of art. After over fifteen hundred artists joined the declaration, among them Ken Loach, John Grayson, Danny Glover, David Byrne, and Jane Fonda. The UJA Federation of Greater Toronto and the Jewish Federation of Greater Los Angeles organized a counterdeclaration, which was signed by Sacha Baron Cohen, Jerry Seinfeld, and others.

Jewish international celebrities, from Jerry Seinfeld to Sasha Baron Cohen, have come out once again, riding the horses of glory, to save Israel from the cruel enemy that is to save Israel from us, those fighting for human rights. They have published a counterdeclaration to the Toronto Declaration. The latter, of which I am a codrafter along with Naomi Klein, John Greyson, and others, protests the cooperation between the Toronto Film Festival and the rebranding of the State of Israel as an enlightened democratic state (instead of an occupying state). Whoever has read our

Published in *Walla* online magazine, September 16, 2009.

declaration should know that we do not boycott any filmmaker and any Israeli film. We have simply protested the festival's choice, intentional or not, of celebrating Tel Aviv as part of the "Brand Israel" campaign. Therefore I was surprised when the aforementioned celebrities, under the baton of the UJA Federation of Greater Toronto and the Jewish Federation of Greater Los Angeles, attacked us on the basis of statements we had never issued ("blacklisting and censorship"). In fact, we have stated the opposite! One wonders in whose interest it is to circulate, all over the world, the mendacious claim that we are calling for a boycott against Israeli cinema. Who wishes to turn Israel (once more) into a victim?

In view of these false claims, I would like to reiterate: we give our blessing to every good piece of work coming from Israel or any other place in the world. All we asked for was that Israeli filmmakers and other artists not cooperate with Israeli embassies in the branding of Israel. My friends and I have appealed to Israeli artists, thinking that they truly oppose the occupying racist regime in Israel and that they are merely being exploited unwillingly by the state and its ministry of foreign affairs. However, it now seems that cooperation between some artists and the Israeli propaganda machine is closer than we thought. Shmulik Maoz did not hesitate to attack Jane Fonda for the boycott that she had allegedly declared against Israeli cinema (although he knows we have stated explicitly that we would not boycott any person), but he did not say a word when Minister of Culture Limor Livnat, known for her right-wing views, called him and his fellow artists, upon his being awarded the Venice Film Festival prize, "the best ambassadors of the State of Israel."

At the exciting moment when he received the Golden Lion Prize in Venice, Shmulik Maoz did not dedicate his film *Lebanon* to the victims of that criminal war, the product of the Israeli government's arrogant and violent brain. Nor did he ask forgiveness for his participation in the war. Nor did he speak of the Palestinians who are still suffering under a terrible occupation at the hands of the same army with which Shmulik had served in Lebanon. He dedicated his film to soldiers all over the world who return from battle with psychological damage and who have not yet recovered even though they have children and families. That stance recalls another ceremony at which Ari Folman, another soldier-director, whose film *Waltz with Bashir* won a Golden Globe (alchemists indeed—Israeli soldier-directors turn the trauma of conquering soldiers into pure gold). As Ari himself testifies in *Waltz with Bashir*, he was a direct or indirect participant in the terrible massacre at Sabra and Shatila. And what did

Ari have to say? He too failed to ask forgiveness from the murder victims. Maybe he "only" sent up flares so that others could commit murder, as he claims. Maybe he stood with a machine gun and prevented people from fleeing the slaughter. Who knows? He does not remember anything, and it did not occur to him for a moment to go and ask the real witnesses: the residents of the camps. For Ari, the real testimony was not that of the witnesses; instead he turned to the Israeli military commentator Ron Ben-Yishai. For that same reason, when Ari stood on the stage before millions of people all over the world at the awards ceremony, he did not call for a halt to the slaughter that was going on in Gaza as he spoke, which, like the nightmare described in his film, recurs like a terrible curse. He did not seek forgiveness from the residents of the camps or even express sympathy with their suffering. Instead, he blessed all the children who were born to the crew while the film was being made. Mazel tov indeed!

Listening to the empty speeches by Shmulik Maoz and Ari Folman, I came to realize that they are not haunted by the ghosts of their dead victims but are rather haunted only by the unpleasant images of war and in their art they seek to create some peace for their soul. They wish the images might go away so that they, not their victims, may finally get a good night's rest. Once more it is all about us. There is no place for the other, it is us and the West that will always be the subject (shooting and crying), while the Arab will continue to participate as nothing but an object. That is why even if the Arab is the slain, even if it is clear that it is he who is the victim, he will remain the object. Not a full person, certainly not sovereign or free.

Open letter to the celebrities who signed the counterdeclaration: many of you have made me laugh countless times, and indeed I love you. Please don't make a fool of yourself. Fight for the right of a Palestinian director to shoot a film in his homeland as a free man and do not go after those who take part in a legitimate protest. We have no guns or warplanes that may kill women and children without distinction. We do have the right to protest. I expect a public apology from you for your part in the system of lies directed at us, the human rights activists in Israel, by the Israeli embassy in Canada. Personally speaking, I am against all forms of boycott against the arts, regardless of the political view they convey, but it is my right to protest against the cynical use of artists, us in Israel and you, the Jewish American artists. If it is real love of Israel that is in your hearts, please help us end the Occupation, advise us on reaching a worldwide audience, correct us if you think we are overdoing it at times, but don't cooperate with the Occupation itself. It has brought about the destruction of the Palestinian people and it will next bring about our own destruction, since there will be no free Israeli Jew as long as the Palestinian is not free, without the same and equal rights.

You, Shmulik Maoz and Ari Folman, two exceptionally talented artists, you and the rest of the Israeli artists, please join our call, "No Celebration Under Occupation." The debate about the part your films play in the Israeli propaganda campaign can be interpreted by your actions and declarations, not just through your films.

To conclude, a call to all the Jewish artists in North America, Israel, and elsewhere. I think we should be asking ourselves not why Israeli directors create films about Lebanon (it makes sense that people will deal with their own scabs) and not even why Israel's government supports these films and uses them for its own aims. The real question is why the image of an Israeli soldier, agonizing and crying, is so appealing to festival curators and audiences of the Western world? When we find the answer to this question, we will be able to comprehend the unreasonable, international sympathy the state of Israel is awarded regardless of its actions, which are perceived by the same West as violent.

Elementary, My Dear Schnabel

Plea to Julian Schnabel

Following the Toronto debate, Julian Schnabel, together with Vanessa Redgrave, published an article criticizing the Toronto Declaration in the *New York Times Book Review*. They argued that this Israeli government is a legitimate government that is responsible for actions no different than in other democratic states. The way to oppose them, in their view, is through art and cinema, rather than boycotting them.

I'm replying only to Schnabel because I believe that the letter against the Toronto Declaration is part of the PR for his new film to come, *Miral*. A film that takes place in Israel-Palestine. Vanessa Redgrave, whom I adore, is one of the cast members of this film.

Dear Julian,

I am replying to your letter, as one of those Israeli residents of Tel Aviv who demonstrated against the massacre in Gaza, the event that you describe with such high admiration, using our act to argue against the Toronto Declaration. I am writing as one of those Israeli residents of Tel Aviv who make critical Israeli cinema, a genre that has also won your admiration. We are both great fans of Daniel Barenboim and the late Edward Said, and if you only read Said you would not be writing a letter taking his name in vain, using the Divan Orchestra (founded by Said and Barenboim) to attack a nonviolent means of struggle to free his own people.

So, because of all the above, it was only natural for me to help initiate the Toronto Declaration, which makes the simple point that there can be no celebration with the Occupation in place. All the points you raise to try and refute the Toronto Declaration should actually go hand in hand with the declaration. Moreover, I feel confident in asserting that the overwhelming majority of those who attended the aforementioned demonstration against the massacre in Gaza (many of them, by the way, were Palestinians citizens of Israel) support the Toronto Declaration, and many of them have signed on as its supporters. In contrast, based on opinion polls, at least 90 percent of Israel's Jewish citizens supported the war on Gaza. All this information provides good reasons to stop turning a blind eye to Israel's policies.

When Palestinians who have chosen the path of nonviolent resistance to the Occupation issue a call to action to us filmmakers, I try to comply.

But you really have the urge to criticize a nonviolent means of resistance on the pages of the New York Times Book Review. For a fair critique, you might have called Naomi Klein first, to make sure you knew all the details. Perhaps then you would have been in a position to deliver fact-based legitimate criticism of our action and propose alternative campaigns to highlight the blatant, almost unilateral wrongdoing inflicted upon Palestinians by Israel.

I was born and raised in Tel Aviv and I do what I do out of love for my city, not hatred. I do not want Tel Aviv to be a liberal facade for a brutal Occupation regime. After all, one of the most distinct manifestations of colonialism is a lively, liberal modern city in the heart of the colony that is defined by the contrast between the natives of the land and "the Barbarians at the gates."

Your comparison of the destruction of Palestinian villages to the destruction of Indian life and culture by white America was certainly not a display of good taste, since in the context of your letter you are implying that we Israelis are also entitled to commit the heinous acts that you Americans committed in previous centuries!

Your letter also exposes a misunderstanding in the relationship between time and event: while Israeli films of the genre admired in the West deal with posttraumatic stress disorder, asking for forgiveness and sympathy from the West (and receiving it), Palestinians are not in a position to deal with posttraumatic symptoms, since they are remain within the traumatic experience itself. Therefore your talk of "reconciliation" is irrelevant at this point. Reconciliation can only take place after the end of the Occupation, when both sides are equal and free in the same point of time to look into their posttraumatic wounds and try to heal them slowly.

But you don't stop there. You let the national liberal narrative speak out of your throat. You write that Israeli governments are elected, and therefore the derogatory term *regime* does not apply to them. Well, four million Palestinians are not allowed to vote in the elections that decide who will seize their land, who will give them (not enough) water, who will (or will not) let them get through the checkpoint to their workplace or to the hospital, who will decide if they can go abroad to meet their dying parent for the last time (or not), and this is not the worst. For the elections also decide who will start a full-scale war against them and bomb them with the most lethal U.S.-Israeli weapons of shock and awe. So, when it comes to the Occupation, *the Israeli regime* is a very precise term according to your own definition of the word *regime*. You see, it is not just some sterile dictionary semantics that assigns a truth value to one's statements. It is also a matter of one's point of view. And, from the Palestinian point of view, it is an apartheid regime par excellence.

It was nice of you to recognize Palestinian suffering caused by lost empires such as Great Britain and the Soviet Union. But isn't it strange that you fail to refer to Palestinian suffering caused by a living empire, the alive and kicking United States of America? So was that a display of patriotic American attitude? Or maybe it was a calculated move, considering the future distribution of your new film *Miral?* It looks like you've got yourself an alibi in Hollywood now . . . or (how shall I put it?) Hollywood loves liberals as long they are romantically human but not freedom fighters for Palestinians, for example.

Let me just state for the nth time that I object to any kind of boycott of movies and works of art! It should be stressed that even the hardliners in the cultural boycott campaign are well aware of the fact that there is no cinema without government support, and they state very clearly that if the money is not given to an artist for propaganda purposes the ensuing work of art should not be boycotted. Again, you could have read all this on the PACBI (Palestinian Campaign for the Academic and Cultural Boycott of Israel) Web site and then made your comments based on facts.

Today state-sponsored crimes against Palestinians are not being committed because of paranoia (or because of Great Britain and the Soviet Union . . .), but for land theft, for religious fundamentalist Jewish sentiments, and for secular ethnic racism. The state of Israel is the only state in the world that views itself as democratic while seizing, in broad daylight, on a daily basis, the land of one ethnic community and transferring it to another ethnic community. This is what going on—the rest are just footnotes. Label it as you wish. But the generic name is apartheid.

I would like to conclude with a fact you know well: even though you made a film about Palestine, your production office was located in Tel Aviv, not in Ramallah, for the simple reason that it is nearly impossible to shoot a film in the Occupied Territories of Palestine. A curfew may be imposed any minute, people out of town may be denied entry, and everything depends on Israeli army permits. Consider a Palestinian filmmaker who wishes to shoot a film in the Occupied Territories. This may be impossible, just like visiting his mother who lives on the other side of the wall built by Israel or driving on a road paved for Jewish settlers only. You know that is the constant reality in the Occupied Territories, regardless of the government in power. Apartheid and settlement expansion have been the legacy of all Israeli governments.

Let us Jewish filmmakers and others around the world embrace the call that every conscientious Jewish filmmaker should embrace. Let Palestinian filmmakers make films in freedom, and let the entire Palestinian people be a free people on their land. It does not matter for now whether this materializes as part of a "one-state solution" or a "two-state solution," as long as all human beings in the Israeli-Palestinian realm enjoy the same rights, regardless of religion, ethnicity, and gender. Elementary, my dear Schnabel.

Sincerely yours,
Udi Aloni

What Do You Mean When You Say "Left"?

An Answer to Professor Nissim Calderon

If one suggests silence for the Israeli left, this silence should be accompanied by clear protest action against wrongdoing committed in our name.

Reading Nissim Calderon's article "And the Left Shall Stay Silent at That Time," I was momentarily filled with hope: Here is a man who has done some soul-searching and, in retrospection, has figured out that something truly awful is happening under our noses. He must be fed up with being a fig leaf for the right wing; maybe he even thinks it is time to let them struggle alone with reality and stop all this nationalist blabbering of the populist sycophant left; maybe the moment has come to apply "A time to do for the Lord; they have made void Your Torah" (Psalm 119). Reading Nissim Calderon, I thought that finally we have found the man who will tell the left "quiet here now!" in the words of Israeli poet Meir Wieseltier, meaning, Dear leftists, the time has come to be silent and stand shoulder to shoulder with the Palestinians whose land is being

Published on Ynet on October 1, 2009. On the September 28, 2009, Professor Nissim Calderon published an article on Ynet—"The Left Shall Stay Silent at That Time"—demanding that the Israeli left go silent. Calderon argued that the Israeli right has accepted the peace process as its policy, and they will now propel it forward: it is the left's obligation to keep quiet and stay out while the right government fulfills this vision.

robbed in broad daylight, their people detained at night, all under legal and military supervision.

I was thinking that now, as the Israeli left lies in tatters and the public all seem to be against us, the role of most self-proclaimed Israeli "leftists" in the Occupation battlefront amounts to merely creating a facade of democratic progress, so that the Western world can find it easier to keep supporting the wrongdoing of Occupation, maybe now it is time to be silent.

Oh, what a thundering silence this could have been: not saying anything, just protecting the oppressed with our bodies, just chaining ourselves to the houses of Palestinians or other poor people whose houses the law has come to demolish. Just sitting still, not letting anyone in, blocking the gates of the racist law that underlies our wretched penal colony, blocking until we are dragged by the locks of our graying hair.

Two things exist in our world, body and language, and at first I inferred from Kalderon that, if the language has failed, we should be silent and act with our bodies. Like in Bil'in, like in Ni'lin, like in East Jerusalem, like in Um el-Fahem: we shall place our bodies at the front line and say nothing, maybe like Women in Black, maybe like Anarchists Against the Wall.

Alas, Calderon turns out to have an utterly different kind of silence in mind. His silence is the silence of doing nothing, the silence of letting life go on as usual. Maybe help some poor members of the ruling Jewish public, but don't let that public think for a moment, god forbid, that we have forsaken them. And to achieve that, according to Calderon, we must stop preventing land theft, we must stop going to the separation fence in the wee hours of the night to dismantle it. We must be obedient, silent, just hoping for the best.

And then I thought that the main question one should ask, paraphrasing a popular Israeli song, is

What do you mean when you say "left"?
Because you say "left" so gracefully,
That it sounds more right than right to me . . .

So, seriously, which left should stay silent? To the right of him, Calderon places Hasfari and Yaniv, authors of the ultranationalist *National Left*, but this abomination of a manifesto has no place among the left in the first place. The manifesto uses the same nationalist, antisemitic language, calling cosmopolitan Jews "kikes," like other nationalists, in other ages, in other places, who called my grandfather a "kike" for the very same reasons.

To the left of him, Calderon places Meron Benvenisti, disqualifying by a single stroke of demagoguery the entire binationalist movement with which the latter is affiliated. He relies on the ethnic cleansing in the former Yugoslavia as proof, but fails to mention that the most horrific acts of massacre in history were committed by nations who regarded ethnic uniformity as a primary value.

I do not intend to start a front for the advancement of binationalism here. Let us assume for a minute that we, the binationalists, are wrong. Nevertheless, Calderon has to admit only binationalism is worth talking about. About the rest we can indeed stay silent, for at the end of the day one must prepare for any possible future, and it is binationalism that is already here, knocking on our door from both sides of the wall.

To be silent or not to be silent? That is not the question. We must stand, placing our bodies shoulder to shoulder, in Bil'in, Ni'lin, Um el-Fahem, and recall that there is one thing we were taught many years ago at the youth movement meetings, a simple truth that can be uttered with our body and with our language: "Jewish-Arab Solidarity."

5

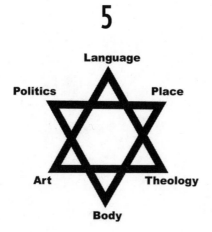

ART

VISUAL MIDRASH

An Angel Under Siege

To Hassan Hourani

With every blink God creates countless new angels, and their only purpose is to sing the Lord's praise, and then vanish. An angel who attempts to escape this bitter fate usually adopts a man and disguises himself as his guardian angel. But his angelic nature will not allow him to withstand the company of the man for long, for his vices are unbearable. From that moment on, the angel's only wish is to sing the Lord's praise and vanish. But the man will not permit the angel to return to his future, because suddenly he feels he has a God all his own—and he loves it. As a matter of fact, he loves it so much he will fight the angel with all his might. He will detain him, first with pleas and then with cunning and finally by force.

Local Angel

To Walter Benjamin

The Moslem cemetery is so quiet.

The tombstones, planted like bushes among the weeds, face the Mediterranean Sea.

Only the plastic bag blowing in the wind reminds us of the living.

Beside it stands the Christian graveyard, well kept and tended.

A stonemason placed an angel in the Palestinian Christian cemetery in Jaffa.

The angel looks as though he is about to move away from something he has been guarding.

This is how one pictures the local angel of history. He faces the East, and his back is turned to the sea. The waves, in constant motion behind him, beckon him to sail westward. Momentarily it appears as if the sea stands still and an easterly wind is propelling him back. Where we perceive a chain of events, which we call the history of Israel-Palestine, he sees one single catastrophe that keeps piling wreckage upon wreckage and hurling it in front of his feet.

The angel would like to stay, awaken the dead, and make whole what has been broken, but the easterly wind blinds his teary eyes, and the sea beckons him to sail into the future.

He cannot resist the calling of the West, whose voice, like that of the sirens, calls him backward into what we call progress. Meanwhile, the pile of debris before him grows skyward.

Holy Language, Holy Place

To Franz Rosenzweig

On a hill in the heart of Jerusalem sits a mosque where Moslems praise the Lord day after day.

The Dome of the Rock has come to symbolize Jerusalem, but we never take pleasure in its splendor. We experience the Al-Aqsa Mosque as the absence of the Temple. We bury our dead on the Mount of Olives facing the dome, hoping for resurrection, hoping to find the dome no more. Though there are those among us who consider themselves secular and are taken with the magnificence of the mosque, they look upon the sweet elusive beauty of the East with an Orientalist gaze and see the bazaar reflected in the dome's golden glow. They spoke Hebrew when they bargained in the markets of the Old City and knew nothing of the terrible prophecy written by Gershom Shalom in his 1926 letter to Franz Rosenzweig.

"Will not the holy language open up like an abyss and swallow us whole? Certain as we are we have turned the Hebrew language into a secular language, one day its hidden religious force will erupt against its speakers, a language composed of names. After evoking these age-old names day in and day out, how can we keep their powers at bay? We have awakened them and they will arise. The revivers of the Hebrew language did not believe in the day of judgment they destined for us with their acts."

Forgiveness

To Jacques Derrida

Some people asked me:

What right do I have to ask Arafat to forgive us?

Who appointed me to ask forgiveness, and who is he to grant it?

And I thought about the Jews unable to forgive the Nazis.

It was always clear to me that the Nazis were pure evil, and the Jews, the ultimate victims. Sheep to the slaughter.

I was seeking forgiveness from another place.

Here the occupier is not pure evil, it's possible to understand him, and his motives. And the victims surely are not sheep led to slaughter.

Still, it seems to me that asking forgiveness from the Palestinians is the place to start a dialogue.

So I chose Arafat because he is the Palestinians' elected leader.

I don't think it is my place to ask forgiveness on behalf of the Israeli people, but I can offer it as an option to start a dialogue.

So I went to try and ask forgiveness. Not so much for Arafat to accept it on behalf of the Palestinians, but as an option to consider in the Israeli discourse.

An Angel I Borrowed

To Mahmoud Darwish

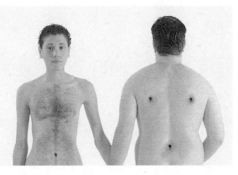

SOLDIERS

So here, in Israel, I began to hear
a voice that arose from me when alone, a voice of myself from
    myself to myself,
not allowing me to sleep.
Who am I at night in a Tel Aviv hotel?
I become a female Jewish singer of Arab origins, graceful and
    beautiful, singing in Arabic and Hebrew.
Unable to fall asleep, I send her,
in my image, in her image, to dream about an angel I borrowed
    from Walter Benjamin.
An angel I borrowed . . .

Stabat Mater

To My Father

The mother endures her pain. Maria endures her pain as she regards Jesus on the cross. I look at the mother looking at her crucified son, crucifying himself, and feel that this scene epitomizes the tragedy of Jerusalem. On one side you have the mother who endures the pain instead of rising in revolt and saying: Enough! And perhaps this is the reason why I cherish the bond between my mother and Hanan Ashrawi, as two mothers who refuse to accept the human sacrifice that Jerusalem has demanded all these years. On the other side, you have the image of the weak God, whom we hardly ever mention.

When my father passed away, he appeared in my dreams, and I tried to hide from him that he's already dead. Then I thought about Adam in the Garden of Eden, trying to hide from God that He's been dead all along. And when I spoke with Haviva,[1] I understood that God hasn't been dead from the beginning, but is dying. So He's a God who doesn't want us to kill for, or in, his name. He is a weak God who needs our help, our compassion. I found that these two images—the mother who, instead of enduring, protests and the concept of a weak and fragile God—these two concepts can be the beginning of a different discourse on Jerusalem.

---

1. Israeli poet and theologian Haviva Pedaya.

6

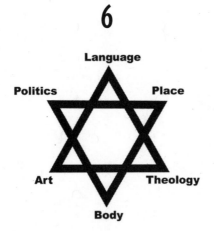

Language

Politics   Place

Art   Theology

Body

LANGUAGE

CONVERSATIONS AND COMMENTS

"The Jew Is Within You, But You, You Are in the Jew"

SLAVOJ ŽIŽEK

Ismail Kadare's *The Palace of Dreams* tells the story of the Tabir Sarrail, the "palace of dreams" in the capital of an unnamed, vast nineteenth-century Balkan empire (modeled on Turkey). In this gigantic building thousands assiduously sift, sort, classify, and interpret the dreams of citizens systematically and continuously assembled from all parts of the empire. Their intense work of bureaucratic interpretation is Kafkaesque: intense yet a meaningless fake. The ultimate goal of their activity is identify the Master-Dream that will provide clues to the destiny of the empire and its sultan. This is why, although supposed to be a place of dark mystery exempted from the daily power struggles, what goes on in the Tabir Sarrail is caught in a violent power struggle—which dream will be selected (or, perhaps, even invented) as the Master-Dream is the outcome of intense dark intrigues.

> "In my opinion," Kurt went on, "it is the only organization in the State where the darker side of its subjects' consciousness enters into direct contact with the State itself."
>
> He looked around at everyone present, as if to assess the effect of his words.
>
> "The masses don't rule, of course," he continued, "but they do possess a mechanism through which they influence all the State's affairs, including its crimes. And that mechanism is the Tabir Sarrail."

"Do you mean to say," asked the cousin, "that the masses are to a certain extent responsible for everything that happens, and so should to a certain extent feel guilty about it?"

"Yes," said Kurt. Then, more firmly: "In a way, yes."[1]

In order to interpret properly these lines, there is no need for any obscurantist themes like the "dark irrational link (or secret solidarity) between the crowd and its rulers." The question to be raised is that of *power (domination) and the unconscious*: how does power work, how do subjects obey it? This brings us to the (misleadingly) so-called erotics of power: subjects obey power not only because of the physical coercion (or its threat) and ideological mystification, but because of their libidinal investment into power. The ultimate "cause" of power is *objet a*, the object-cause of desire, the surplus-enjoyment by means of which the power "bribes" those it holds in its sway. This *object a* is given form in (unconscious) fantasies of the subjects of power, and the function of Kadare's Tabir Sarrail is precisely to discern these fantasies, to learn what kind of (libidinal) objects they are for their subjects. These obscure "feedbacks" of the subjects of power to its bearers regulates the subjects' subordination to power, so if they are disturbed the power edifice can lose its libidinal grip and dissolve. *The Palace of Dreams* is, of course, itself an impossible fantasy: the fantasy of a power that would directly try to deal with its fantasmatic support.

In European societies antisemitism is a key component of this obscure "feedback"; its fantasmatic status is clearly designated by the statement attributed to Hitler: "We have to kill the Jew within us." A. B. Yehoshua provided an adequate comment to this statement: "This devastating portrayal of the Jew as a kind of amorphous entity that can invade the identity of a non-Jew without his being able to detect or control it stems from the feeling that Jewish identity is extremely flexible, precisely because it is structured like a sort of atom whose core is surrounded by virtual electrons in a changing orbit."[2] In this sense Jews are effectively the *objet petit a* of the Gentiles: what is "in Gentiles more than Gentiles themselves," not another subject that I encounter in front of me but an alien, a foreign intruder, *within* me, what Lacan called *lamella*, the amorphous intruder of infinite plasticity, an undead "alien" monster who cannot ever be pinned

---

1   Ismail Kadare, *The Palace of Dreams* (New York: Arcade, 1998), p. 63.

2   A. B. Yehoshua, "An Attempt to Identify the Root Cause of Antisemitism," *Azure* no. 32 (Spring 2008), http://www.azure.org.il/article.php?id=18&page=all.

down to a determinate form. In a sense Hitler's statement tells more than it wants to say: against its intention, it confirms that the Gentiles need the antisemitic figure of the "Jew" in order to maintain their identity. It is thus not only that "the Jew is within us"—what Hitler fatefully forgot to add is that *he, the antisemite, his identity, is also in the Jew*.[3] What does this paradoxical entwinement mean for the destiny of antisemitism?

WHAT GOES ON WHEN NOTHING GOES ON?

It is against this background that one should approach the Middle East imbroglio. One cannot but respect the brutal honesty of the first-generation founders of the State of Israel who in no way obliterated the "founding crime" of establishing a new state: they openly admitted they had no right to the land of Palestina, it is just their force against the force of the Palestinians. On 29 April 1956 a group of Palestinians from Gaza crossed the border to plunder the harvest in the Nahal Oz kibbutz's fields; Roi, a young Jewish member of the kibbutz who patrolled the fields, galloped toward them on his horse brandishing a stick to chase them away; he was seized by the Palestinians and carried back to the Gaza Strip; when the UN returned his body, his eyes had been plucked out. Moshe Dayan, then the chief of staff, delivered the eulogy at his funeral the following day:

"Let us not cast blame on the murderers today. What claim do we have against their mortal hatred of us? They have lived in the refugee camps of Gaza for the past eight years, while right before their eyes we have transformed the land and villages where they and their ancestors once lived into our own inheritance.

It is not among the Arabs of Gaza but in our own midst that we must seek Roi's blood. How have we shut our eyes and refused to look squarely at our fate and see the destiny of our generation in all its brutality? Have we forgotten that this group of young people living in Nahal Oz bears the burden of Gaza's gates on its shoulders?"[4]

3 I am here, of course, paraphrasing Lacan's famous statement: "The picture is in my eye, but me, I am in the picture."

4 Quoted from Udi Aloni's outstanding analysis of this case, "Samson the Non-European" (a revised version of his essay appears in this volume).

Apart from the parallel between Roi and the blinded Samson (which plays a key role in the later mythology of the IDF), what cannot but strike the eye is the apparent non sequitur, the gap, between the first and the second paragraph: in the first paragraph Dayan openly admits that the Palestinians have the full right to hate the Israeli Jews, since they took their land; his conclusion, however, is not the obvious admission of one's own guilt, but to fully accept "the destiny of our generation in all its brutality." i.e., to assume the burden—not of guilt, but—of the war where might will be right, where the stronger will win. The war was not about principles or justice, it was an exercise in "mythic violence"—the insight totally obliterated by the recent Israeli's self-legitimization. As in the case of feminism, which taught us to discover the traces of violence in what appears, in a patriarchal culture, as a natural authority (of a father), we should remember the grounding violence obliterated by today's Zionism—Zionists should simply read Dayan and Ben-Gurion.

The same violence goes on today, but disavowed, masked as multicultural tolerance. On August 2, 2009, after cordoning off part of the Arab neighborhood of Sheikh-Jarrah in East Jerusalem, Israeli police evicted two Palestinian families (more than fifty people) from their homes; permitted Jewish settlers immediately moved into the emptied houses. Although Israeli police cited a ruling by the country's Supreme Court, the evicted Arab families had been living there for more than fifty years. The event, which, rather exceptionally, did attract the attention of the world media, is part of a much larger and mostly ignored ongoing process.

Five months earlier, on March 1, 2009, it was reported that the Israeli government had drafted plans to build more than seventy thousand new housing units in Jewish settlements in the occupied West Bank;[5] if implemented, the plans could increase the number of settlers in the Palestinian territories by about three hundred thousand—a move that would not only severely undermine the chances of a viable Palestinian state but also hamper the everyday life of Palestinians. A government spokesman dismissed the report, arguing that the plans were therefore of limited relevance: the actual construction of new homes in the settlements required the approval of the defense minister and prime minister. However, fifteen thousand of the plans have already been fully approved; plus, almost twenty thousand of the planned units lie in settlements that are far from

5   See Tobias Duck, "Israel Drafts West Bank Expansion Plans," *Financial Times*, March 2, 2009.

the "green line" that separates Israel from the West Bank, i.e., in the areas Israel cannot expect to retain in any future peace deal with the Palestinians. The conclusion is obvious: while paying lip service to the two-state solution, Israel is busy creating the situation on the ground that will render a two-state solution de facto impossible. The dream that underlies this politics is best rendered by the wall that separates a settler's town from the Palestinian town on a nearby hill somewhere in the West Bank. The Israeli side of the wall is painted with the image of the countryside beyond the wall—but without the Palestinian town, depicting just nature, grass, trees . . . is this not ethnic cleansing at its purest, imagining the outside beyond the wall as it should be, empty, virginal, waiting to be settled?

This process is sometimes covered in the guise of cultural gentrification. On October 28, 2008, the Israeli Supreme Court ruled that the Simon Wiesenthal Center can build its long-planned Center for Human Dignity–Museum of Tolerance on a contested site in the middle of Jerusalem. (Who but) Frank Gehry will design the vast complex consisting of a general museum, a children's museum, a theater, conference center, library, gallery and lecture halls, caffeterias, etc. The museum's declared mission will be to promote civility and respect among different segments of the Jewish community and between people of all faiths—the only obstacle (overturned by the Supreme Court's ruling) being that the museum site served as Jerusalem's main Muslim cemetery until 1948 (the Muslim community appealed to the Supreme Court that museum construction would desecrate the cemetery, which allegedly contained the bones of Muslims killed during the Crusades of the twelfth and thirteenth centuries).[6] This dark spot wonderfully enacts the hidden truth of this multiconfessional project: it is a place celebrating tolerance, open to all . . . but protected by the Israeli cupola, which ignores the subterranean victims of intolerance—as if one needs a little bit of intolerance to create the space for true tolerance.

And as if this were not enough, as if one should repeat a gesture to make its message clear, there is another, even vaster similar project going on in Jerusalem: Israel is quietly carrying out a $100 million, multiyear development plan in the so-called holy basin, the site of some of the most significant religious and national heritage sites just outside the walled Old City, as part of an effort to strengthen the status of Jerusalem as its

6   See Tom Tugend, "Israel Supreme Court OKs Museum of Tolerance Jerusalem project," *Observer*, October 29, 2008.

capital.[7] The plan, parts of which have been outsourced to a private group that is simultaneously buying up Palestinian property for Jewish settlement in East Jerusalem, has drawn almost no public or international scrutiny. As part of the plan, garbage dumps and wastelands are being cleared and turned into lush gardens and parks, now already accessible to visitors who can walk along new footpaths and take in the majestic views, along with new signs and displays that point out significant points of Jewish history—and, conveniently, many of the "unauthorized" Palestinian houses have to be erased to create the space for the redevelopment of the area. The "holy basin" is an infinitely complicated landscape dotted with shrines and still hidden treasures of the three major monotheistic religions, so the official argument is that its improvement is for everyone's benefit—Jews, Muslims, and Christians—since it involves restoration that will draw more visitors to an area of exceptional global interest that has long suffered neglect. However, as Hagit Ofran of Peace Now noted, the plan aimed to create "an ideological tourist park that will determine Jewish dominance in the area." Raphael Greenberg of Tel Aviv University put it even more blundly: "The sanctity of the City of David is newly manufactured and is a crude amalgam of history, nationalism and quasi-religious pilgrimage . . . the past is used to disenfranchise and displace people in the present." Another big Religious Venue, a "public" interfaith space under the clear domination and protective cupola of Israel . . .

What does all this mean? To get at the true dimension of news, it is sometimes enough to read two disparate news items together—meaning emerges from their very link, like a spark exploding from an electric short circuit. On the very same day the reports on the government plan to build seventy thousand new housing units hit the media (March 2), Hilary Clinton criticized the rocket fire from Gaza as "cynical," claiming: "There is no doubt that any nation, including Israel, cannot stand idly by while its territory and people are subjected to rocket attacks." But should the Palestinians stand idly while the West Bank land is taken from them day by day? When Israeli peace-loving liberals present their conflict with Palestinians in neutral "symmetrical" terms, admitting that there are extremists on both sides who reject peace, etc., one should ask a simple question: what goes on in the Middle East when *nothing goes on there* at the direct politico-military level (i.e., when there are no tensions, attacks,

7. See Ethan Bronner and Isabel Kershner, "Parks Fortify Israel's Claim to Jerusalem," *New York Times*, May 9, 2009.

negotiations)? What goes on is the incessant slow work of taking the land from the Palestinians on the West Bank: the gradual strangling of the Palestinian economy, the parceling of their land, the building of new settlements, the pressure on Palestinian farmers to make them abandon their land (which goes from crop burning and religious desecration up to individual killings), all this supported by a Kafkaesque network of legal regulations. Saree Makdisi, in *Palestine Inside Out: An Everyday Occupation*,[8] described how, although the Israeli Occupation of the West Bank is ultimately enforced by the armed forces, it is an "occupation by bureaucracy": its primary forms are application forms, title deeds, residency papers, and other permits. It is this micromanagement of daily life that does the job of securing the slow but steadfast Israeli expansion: one has to ask for a permit in order to leave with one's family, to farm one's own land, to dig a well, to go to work, to school, to a hospital . . . One by one, Palestinians born in Jerusalem are thus stripped of the right to live there, prevented from earning a living, denied housing permits, etc. Palestinians often use the problematic cliché of the Gaza strip as "the greatest concentration camp in the world"—however, in the last year this designation has come dangerously close to truth. This is the fundamental reality that makes all abstract "prayers for peace" obscene and hypocritical. The State of Israel is clearly engaged in a slow process, invisible, ignored by the media, a kind of underground digging of the mole, so that, one day, the world will awaken and realize that there is no more Palestinian West Bank, that the land is Palestinian-*frei*, and that we can only accept the fact. The map of the Palestinian West Bank already looks like a fragmented archipelago.

In the last months of 2008, when the attacks of illegal West Bank settlers on Palestinian farmers grew into regular daily events, the State of Israel tried to contain these excesses (the Supreme Court ordered the evacuation of some settlements, etc.), but, as many observers noted, these measures cannot but appear halfhearted, counteracting a politics that, at a deeper level, IS the long-term politics of the State of Israel, which massively violates the international treaties signed by Israel itself. The reply of the illegal settlers to the Israeli authorities basically is: we are doing the same thing as you, just more openly, so what right do you have to condemn us? And the answer of the state basically is: be patient, don't rush too much, we are doing what you want, just in a more

---

8   See Saree Makdisi, in *Palestine Inside Out: An Everyday Occupation* (New York: Norton, 2008).

moderate and acceptable way . . . The same story seems to go on from 1949: while Israel accepts the peace conditions proposed by international community, it counts that the peace plan will not work. The wild settlers sometimes sound like Brunhilde, from the last act of Wagner's *Walküre*, reproaching Wotan that, by counteracting his explicit order and protecting Sigmund, she was only realizing Wotan's own true desire, which he was forced to renounce under external pressure, in the same way that the illegal settlers only realize the state's true desire it was forced to renounce because of the pressure of the international community. While condemning the open violent excesses of "illegal" settlements, the State of Israel promotes new "legal" West Bank settlements, continues to strangle the Palestinian economy, etc. A look at the continuous changes on the map of East Jerusalem, where the Palestinians are gradually encircled and their space sliced, tells it all. The condemnation of extrastatal anti-Palestinian violence obfuscates the true problem of *state* violence; the condemnation of illegal settlements obfuscates the illegality of the legal ones. Therein resides the two-facedness of the much-praised nonbiased "honesty" of the Israeli Supreme Court: by way of occasionally passing a judgment in favor of the dispossessed Palestinians, proclaiming their eviction illegal, it guarantees the legality of the remaining majority of cases.

THE "NAME OF THE JEW"

And, to avoid any kind of misunderstanding, taking all this into account in no way implies an "understanding" for inexcusable terrorist acts. On the contrary, it provides the only ground from which one can condemn the terrorist attacks without hypocrisy. Furthermore, when Western liberal defenders of peace in the Middle East oppose, among Palestinians, the democrats committed to compromise and peace and the Hamas radical fundamentalists, they fail to see the genesis of these two poles: the long and systematic endeavor by Israel and the USA to weaken the Palestinians by way of undermining the leading position of Fateh, an endeavor that, up to five or six years ago, even included the financial support of Hamas. The sad result is that Palestinians are now divided between Hamas fundamentalism and Fateh corruption: the weakened Fateh is no longer the hegemonic force that truly represents the substantial longings of the Palestinians (and is, as such, in a position to conclude peace); it is more and more perceived by the majority of Palestinians for what it is, a crippled puppet supported by the U.S. as the representative of the "democratic" Palestinians. Similarly, while the U.S. worried about Saddam's basically secular authoritarian regime in Iraq, the "talibanization" of their ally Pakistan progressed slowly but inexorably: Taliban's control now already spreads over parts of Karachi, Pakistan's largest city.

There is a shared interest on both sides of the conflict to see "fundamentalists in control" in Gaza: this characterization enables the fundamentalists to monopolize the struggle and the Israelis to gain international sympathies. Consequently, although everyone deplores the rise of fundamentalism, no one really wants secular resistance to Israel among the Palestinians. But is it really true that there is none? What if there are two secrets in the Middle East conflict: secular Palestinians and Zionist fundamentalists—we have Arab fundamentalists arguing in secular terms and Jewish secular Westerners relying on theological reasoning:

The strange thing is that it was secular Zionism that brought god to bear so much on religious ideas. In a way, the true believers in Israel are the nonreligious. This is so because for the religious life of an orthodox Jew god is actually quite marginal. There were times when for a member of the orthodox intellectual elite it was in a way "uncool" to refer too much to god: a sign that he is not devoted enough to the real noble cause of the polemical study of Talmud (the continual movement of expansion of the law and evasion from it). It was only the crude secular Zionist gaze that took god, which was a sort of alibi, so seriously. The sad thing is that now more and more orthodox Jews seem convinced that they indeed believe in god.[9]

The consequence of this unique ideological situation is the paradox of atheists defending Zionist claims in theological terms. Exemplary here is *The Arrogance of the Present*,[10] Milner's exploration of the legacy of 1968, which can also be read as a reply to Badiou's *The Century* as well as to his exploration of the politico-ideological implications of the "name of the Jew." In an implicit, but, for that reason, all the more intense,

9 Noam Yuran, personal communication.

10. Jean-Claude Milner, *L'arrogance du present: Regards sur une decennie: 1965–1975* (Paris: Grasset, 2009). Numbers in brackets refer to the pages of this book.

dialogue with Badiou, Milner proposes a radically different diagnosis of the twentieth century. His starting point is the same as Badiou's: "a name counts only as far as the divisions it induces go." Master-Signifiers that matter are those that clarify their field by simplifying the complex situation into a clear division—yes or no, for or against. Milner goes on: "But here is what happened: one day, it became obvious that names believed to bear a future (glorious or sinister) no longer divide anyone; and names dismissed as thoroughly obsolete began to bring about unbridgeable divisions" (21–22). Names that today no longer divide, generate passionate attachment, but leave us indifferent, are those that traditionally were expected to act as the most mobilizing ("workers," "class struggle"), while those that appeared deprived of their divisive edge violently reemerged in their divisive role—today, the name *Jew* "divides most deeply the speaking beings": "Contrary to what knowledge predicted, the culminating point of the twentieth century did not take the form of social revolution; it took the form of an extermination. Contrary to what the Revolution has been promising, the extermination ignored classes and fixated on a name without any class meaning. Not even an economic one. Not a shadow of an objective meaning" (214).

Milner's conclusion is that "the only true event of the twentieth century was the return of the name Jew" (212)—this return for an ominous surprise also for the Jews themselves. That is to say, with the political emancipation of the Jews in modern Europe, a new figure of the Jew emerged: the "Jew of knowledge" who replaces study (of Talmud, i.e., of his theological roots) with universal (scientific) knowledge. We get Jews who excel in secular sciences, and this is why Marxism was so popular among Jewish intellectuals: it presented itself as "*scientific* socialism," uniting knowledge and revolution (in contrast to Jacobins, who proudly said, apropos Laplace, that "the Republic doesn't need scientists," or millenarists who dismissed knowledge as sinful). With Marxism, inequality/injustice and its overcoming becomes an object of knowledge (201). Enlightenment thus offers European Jews a chance to find a place in the universality of scientific knowledge, ignoring their name, tradition, roots. This dream, however, brutally ended with holocaust: the "Jew of knowledge" couldn't survive Nazi extermination—the trauma was that knowledge allowed it, wasn't able to resist it, was impotent in the face of it. (Traces of this impotence are already discernible in the famous 1929 Davos debate between Ernst Cassirer and Heidegger, where Heidegger treated Cassirer with impolite rudeness, refusing a handshake at the conclusion, etc.)

How did the European left react to this rupture? The core of Milner's book is the close analysis of the Maoist proletarian left (*la Gauche proletarienne*), the main political organization emerging out of May 1968. When it fell apart, some of its members (like Benny Levy) opted for fidelity to the name of the Jew, others chose Christian spirituality. For Milner, the entire activity of the proletarian left was based on a certain disavowal, on a refusal to pronounce a name. Milner proposes a nice Magrittean image: a room with a window in the middle and a painting covering up and obstructing the view through the window; the scene on the painting exactly reproduces the exterior one would have seen through the window. Such is the function of ideological misrecognition: it obfuscates the true dimension of what we see (183). In the case of the proletarian left this unseen dimension was the name of the Jew. That is to say, the proletarian left legitimized its radical opposition to the entire French political establishment as the prolongation of the Resistance against the Fascist occupation: their diagnosis was that the French political life was still dominated by people who stood in direct continuity with the Petainist collaboration. However, although they designated the right enemy, they kept silent on the fact that the main target of the Fascist regime was not the left, but the Jews. In short, they used the event itself to obfuscate its true dimension, similarly to the "Jew of knowledge" who tries to redefine his Jewishness so that he will be able to erase the real core of being a Jew.

Benny Levy's transformation from a Maoist to a Zionist is thus indicative of a wider tendency. The consequence drawn by many from the "obscure disaster" of twentieth-century attempts at universal emancipation is that particular groups no longer accept "sublating" their own emancipation in the universal one ("we—oppressed minorities, women, etc.—can only attain our freedom through universal emancipation," i.e., the Communist revolution): fidelity to the universal cause is replaced by fidelities to particular identities (Jewish, gay, etc.), and the most we can envisage is a "strategic alliance" between particular struggles.

Perhaps, however, the time has come to return to the notion of universal emancipation, and it is here that a critical analysis should begin. When Milner claims that the class struggle, etc. are no longer divisive names, that they are replaced by "Jew" as the truly divisive name, he describes a (partially true) fact, but what does this fact mean? Should it not also be interpreted in terms of the classic Marxist theory of antisemitism, which reads the antisemitic figure of the "Jew" as the metaphoric stand-in for class struggle? The disappearance of the class struggle and the (re)appearance of antisemitism are thus two sides of the same coin, since the *presence* of the antisemitic figure of the "Jew" is only comprehensible against the background of the *absence* of class struggle. Walter Benjamin (to whom Milner himself refers as to an authority, and who stands precisely for a Marxist Jew who remains faithful to the religious dimension of Jewishness and is thus not a "Jew of knowledge") said long ago that every rise of Fascism bears witness to a failed revolution—this thesis not only still holds today but is perhaps more pertinent than ever. Liberals like to point out similarities between left and right "extremisms": Hitler's terror and camps imitated Bolshevik terror, the Leninist party is today alive in Al-Qaeda—yes, but what does all this mean? It can also be read as an indication of how Fascism literally replaces (takes the place of) the leftist revolution: its rise is the left's failure, but simultaneously a proof that there was a revolutionary potential, dissatisfaction, that the left was not able to mobilize.

1 + 1 = 3

How are we to understand this reversal of an emancipatory thrust into fundamentalist populism? It is here that the materialist-dialectic passage from the Two to Three gains all its weight: the axiom of Communist politics is not simply the dualist "class struggle," but, more precisely, the third moment as the subtraction from the Two of the hegemonic politics. That is to say, the hegemonic ideological field imposes on us a field of (ideological) visibility with its own "principal contradiction" (today, it is the opposition of market-freedom-democracy and fundamentalist-terrorist-totalitarianism: "Islamo-Fascism," etc.), and the first thing to do is to reject (to subtract from) this opposition, to perceive it as a false opposition destined to obfuscate the true line of division. As we have already seen, Lacan's formula for this redoubling is 1+1+a: the "official" antagonism (the Two) is always supplemented by an "indivisible remainder" that indicates its foreclosed dimension. In other terms, the *true* antagonism is always reflective, it is the antagonism between the "official" antagonism and what is foreclosed by it (this is why, in Lacan's mathematics, 1 + 1 = 3). Today, for example, the true antagonism is not the one between liberal multiculturalism and fundamentalism, but between the very field of their opposition and the excluded third (radical emancipatory politics).

Badiou already provided the contours of this passage from Two to Three in his reading of the Pauline passage from Law to love.[11] In both cases (in Law and in love) we are dealing with division, with a "divided subject"; however, the modality of the division is thoroughly different. The subject of the Law is "decentered" in the sense that it is caught in the self-destructive vicious cycle of sin and Law in which one pole engenders its opposite; Paul provided the unsurpassable description of this entanglement in Romans 7:

> We know that the law is spiritual; but I am carnal, sold into slavery to sin. What I do, I do not understand. For I do not do what I want, but I do what I hate. Now if I do what I do not want, I concur that the law is good. So now it is no longer I who do it, but sin that dwells in me. For I know that good does not dwell in me, that is, in my flesh. The willing is ready at hand, but doing the good is not. For I do not do the good I want, but I do the evil I do not want. Now if I do what I do not want, it is no longer I who do it, but sin that dwells in me. So, then, I discover the principle that when I want to do right, evil is at hand. For I take delight in the law of God, in my inner self, but I see in my members another principle at war with the law of my mind, taking me captive to the law of sin that dwells in my members. Miserable one that I am!

It is thus not that I am merely torn between the two opposites, Law and sin; the problem is that I cannot even clearly distinguish them: I want to follow the Law and I end up in sin. This vicious cycle is (not so much overcome as) broken, one breaks out of it, with the experience of love, more precisely: with the experience of the radical gap that separates love from the Law. Therein resides the radical difference between the couple Law/sin and the couple Law/love. The gap that separates Law and sin is not a real difference: their truth is their mutual implication or confusion—Law generates sin and feeds on it, etc., one cannot ever draw a clear line of separation between the two. It is only with the couple Law/love that we attain real difference: these two moments are radically separate, they are not "mediated," one is not the form of appearance

---

11   See Alain Badiou, *Saint Paul: The Foundation of Universalism* (Stanford: Stanford University Press, 2003).

of its opposite. In other words, the difference between the two couples (Law/sin and Law/love) is not substantial, but purely formal: we are dealing with the same content in its two modalities. In its indistinction/mediation, the couple is the one of Law/sin; in the radical distinction of the two, it is Law/love. It is therefore wrong to ask the question "Are we then forever condemned to the split between Law and love? What about the synthesis between Law and love?" The split between Law and sin is of a radically different nature than the split between Law and love: instead of the vicious cycle of the mutual reinforcement, we get a clear distinction of two different domains. Once we become fully aware of the dimension of love in its radical difference from the Law, love has, in a way, already won, since this difference is visible only when one already dwells in love, from the standpoint of love.

In authentic Marxism, totality is not an ideal, but a critical notion—to locate a phenomenon in its totality does not mean to see the hidden harmony of the Whole, but to include into a system all its "symptoms," antagonisms, inconsistencies, as its integral parts. Let me take a contemporary example. In this sense, liberalism and fundamentalism form a "totality": the opposition of liberalism and fundamentalism is structured in exactly the same way as the one between Law and sin in Paul, i.e., liberalism itself generates its opposite. So what about the core values of liberalism: freedom, equality, etc.? The paradox is that liberalism itself is not strong enough to save them—i.e., its own core—against the fundamentalist onslaught. Why? The problem with liberalism is that it cannot stand on its own: there is something missing in the liberal edifice; liberalism is in its very notion "parasitic," relying on a presupposed network of communal values that it is itself undermining its own development. Fundamentalism is a reaction—a false, mystifying, reaction, of course—against a real flaw of liberalism, and that is why it is again and again generated by liberalism. Left to itself, liberalism will slowly undermine itself—the only thing that can save its core is a renewed left. Or, to put it in the well-known terms from 1968, in order for its key legacy to survive, liberalism needs the brotherly help of the radical left.

What Does a Jew Want?

On the Film Local Angel

SLAVOJ ŽIŽEK

The reason *Local Angel* fascinated me is that I see it as a process of the self-questioning of Jewish identity. It's totally mistaken to perceive the film as on a simple political scale where on one end we have extreme fundamentalist Zionists who just want to get rid of the Arabs, then Jews who are a little more liberal, then at the other end pro-Palestinian Jews who are for a united secular state, and the final point is, where do you stand? This is because what is going on with Jewish identity today is not such a self-evident question. I don't know how it appears from the Jewish perspective itself, but for me my experience was between two extreme images. One was these kibbutz Jews, fighting to reestablish their homeland but at the level of a new collectivity of labor, an approach to which I'm deeply sympathetic. In quite a naive way, this site of collective labor, which is not limited to manual work but can even be something like an Internet company, can also be a site for intense interaction where you discuss your problems, a place for social redemption. This big legacy of the Jewish tradition is central for me. Then, of course, you get the image of how Jews were trying to cope with the horror of Shoah. How I see the movie is that it's not just a disgusting, patronizing solidarity and compassion with victims, instead I see, to put it in Hegelian

Transcription of a video lecture, Saas-Fee, Switzerland, 2003 terms, a deep awareness of how the truth of relating to an other always involves a self-relation.

Questioning how Israeli Jews relate to Palestinians and what is going on today with the Jewish identity itself are two aspects of the same process. This is where I found the movie the most touching—maybe I'm reading too much of my own utopian dreams in it, but if I were asked where the Hollywood punch line is, I would say that it is in a very profound insight into how, in a naive and serious way, if the tendency of treating the Palestinians the way the Zionist establishment is treating them continues, the ultimate victim will be Jewish identity itself. The ultimate result may be that Israel will become just another ordinary nation and the Jewish exception will be lost. Connected with this is another aspect that fascinates me: the movie forces you to rethink this simplistic opposition between so-called fanatical, hardline Jews, who, as we Gentiles misperceive it, would just like to sacrifice the Arabs to some obscure god, and the good liberal Jews, who have a problem with terror but want to be more open, and so on. Where I really got the closest you can get to an intellectual orgasm was during the interview with the female theologian. This lesson is that, precisely because the stakes are very high for the Jewish identity itself, one of our allies can be one of those involved in the deepest Jewish reflection, among those who might be dismissed as fundamentalist. The lines of political division to be drawn are definitely not secular liberals versus religious fundamentalists. What this movie did to me was to restore my faith in emancipatory potentials of Jewish tradition. Again, the problem today is a new version of the old Freudian question, "What does a woman want?" For me the subtitle of *Local Angel* is "What does a Jew want?" This is where I felt a deep solidarity. The second thing I liked about the movie is that although it's clear where it stands, it does not do what in America is referred to as "objective reporting," which is always a fake, where we say "let's hear both sides and then we'll let the public decide."

Local Angel is clear where it stands, but, at the same time, there is a kind of parallax split: obviously you can see how Udi himself is torn between an attitude of radically liberal Zionism (which I don't want to refer to in a dismissive way, as it has an honesty and consistency of its own and can be sustained heroically), that is, "all the rights for the Palestinians, but not a secular state, that's too risky," and an attitude that would be willing to risk a secular state. From a primitive radical perspective, that's the limitation of the movie, wouldn't it be better to go to the end? I disagree. We can even play cheap pseudo-deep psychoanalytic games and claim that the director of the movie is playing out his oedipal fixations on his mother, he being the more radical one wanting a secular state, his mother being still a liberal Zionist. The truth of the situation is not some kind of a synthesis, "let's have a secular state, but a little later on"; the only truthful thing you can do is to render this constellation as such. The problem here is a real one; I say this as deeply sympathizing with the Palestinians. I'm not playing this liberal distrust of claiming "of course we love Palestinians, but they're sometimes primitive and a little bit violent so it won't work." It's deeper. I think that sometimes, when there truly are tensions between ethnic groups, the first step toward reconciliation is, paradoxically, to establish a space of minimal distance. Sometimes if you force this push toward universality too much it can backfire.

The third thing I liked is what some people find problematic. I'm also a little bit skeptical, but the movie just reports on it, it doesn't commit itself, namely, the emancipatory potentials of this transcultural phenomena of Arab singers singing in Hebrew, Jewish singers in Arabic, and so on. Of course one can argue that this is the worst way of multiculturalist liberal co-opting: you take Palestinian protests and turn it into a hard rock band and it appears radical but is really part of the game, thus every subversive power is neutralized. It's not as simple as that. In the present state of things, many of my liberal Israeli friends are claiming "but we tried everything, now they are throwing bombs, we can't even negotiate." In this situation any and all links or mixtures between the two cultures are worth their weight in gold. It's good simply to know about this.

Here truthful information itself is the best propaganda weapon. For example, I simply didn't know that at the ground level of young people there are still these kinds of intercultural contacts. It's extremely important that people know it, so that we can hopefully generate a positive mechanism of self-fulfilling prophecy. To be quite naive, if we pretend and act as if there is, at the level of rock bands and so on, alot of communication between young Jews and Palestinians, then maybe we will end up with real communication. It is real information, which is not neutral but crucial. It goes one step beyond information in the West, which has been still pretty limited and downplayed, about refuseniks. As a Leninist I like them because they went one step beyond this purely private moral gesture of saying "I refuse" and then withdrawing into private life: it was instead an organized, networked collectivity.

The fourth feature that I appreciate about the movie is its theological dimension. I'm a pure, simple, old-fashioned dialectical materialist. The point is simply to see the emancipatory potentials of a certain logic of social, collective space of thought and action that can function in atheist or religious terms. The idea of a weak god is perhaps the deepest insight in the Judeo-Christian tradition. From my limited perspective, not knowing enough about Judaism, my strange reading of Christianity is precisely that Christianity is caught in the economy of exchange—that Christ's redemption is buying us off from sin—he paid the price. This notion of redemption and grace is catastrophe, because it involves a trick: apparently it's a liberation, but one in which we are forever indebted to Christ. This is for me the ultimate superego nightmare. My point is how to read the core of Christianity outside this perverse argument, precisely along the lines of a weakened God. The way I read Christ's sacrifice is as a kind of desperate existential engagement. To put it in naive theological terms, God created the world, things went wrong, and the only option for God as the creator was to throw himself into it, to fall into his own picture.

This is a formula of such tremendous spiritual revolution: God as an impotent weakness. Ultimately, my twist is that this famous Benjaminian angel to which the title of the movie refers is Christ himself. It's not that he redeemed us—he made a crazy gesture, he failed, and it's up to us to pick up the pieces. It's not "he paid the price, so let's go on and drink and kill and seduce ladies because we have a blank check written by it." If it were possible at the level of an atheist symbolic logic to reconcile Judaism and Christianity, it would be along these lines of the weak God. This has nothing to do with the idea of return to paganism—they also have weak gods, no god is the absolute boss, they counteract each other and behind them there is fate—it has much more to do with something else, with the center of the Judeo-Christian legacy. Only now this came to me; I'm still not satisfied with it: how do I see Jewish iconoclasm? At first I thought of it as a fake: if you want to prohibit it, you still take images too seriously. But another thing came to me, which probably to every Jew is self-evident. I think that it's wrong if we read this invocation of "don't build any images, etc.," along the lines of gnostic-mystic traditions, in the sense that God is not a concrete, ontological being, but this pure ineffable Otherness, which no positive figuration can do justice to. This is gnostic reinscription. The way to read it is along with another Jewish insight, which is that the basic ethical implication of the Jewish tradition is that the only space where you practice your religion is social interaction with other people. There is no shortcut to God, he is actualized in your dealing with other people. This is iconoclasm: don't paint God, because he is here in concrete social space, not up there.

I find *Local Angel* extremely important maybe even more in the West than in Israel itself. It has shocked me again and again how much more open to discussion with Palestinians the Jewish community in Israel is than, for example, the Jewish community in New York. It is vital that all the scenes of asking Arafat for forgiveness, of Jewish singers singing in Arabic, be targeted at a Western audience. If you want to look at how the Middle East crisis is reported in the Western media, what is much more important to consider than simply addressing a factual bias like "do they correctly report the number of deaths?" is something I'm tempted to call the microphysics of the situation: the texture of gestures, of types of persons, everything that gives an abstract item of news the concrete texture of life experience. It's very important to reestablish a balance or a different image at this level. I was told by Udi that at a certain point Hanna Asad and these intellectual Palestinian scholars in the film disappeared from CNN because they were considered atypical, too intellectual; these supposedly fanatical fundamentalists who were much more articulate than the representatives of enlightened liberal Judaism. Let me make for some radical Zionists a much more problematic step. Ehud Barak once stated that if he was a young Palestinian he would have joined the intifada. This was in a way important because it accepted the other as nondemonized, as occupying an understandable human position, not just as some brainwashed, crazy suicide bombers whose only thought, if you listen to the Western media, is to hope to die quickly to get the forty virgins. This is the big lesson of how ideology functions: details like this matter. It's a question of which concrete images are used to schematize this position. What do I mean by this? Let's take the American-Iraq war. This was a perfectly orchestrated operation in which the one person elevated into a heroic symbol was poor Jessica Lynch. You have all these false connotations: a young ordinary girl, a symbol of an open society. We have to accept a struggle at this level of images.

Lastly, my secret hope. The very difficulty of the Middle East crisis is what my good friend Alain Badiou would call the site of the possible event, in the sense of an emancipatory breakthrough. Even if it doesn't take the form of a secular state, the only true solution is again the outbreak of what Badiou calls the dimension of emancipatory universality. Precisely because the situation is so complex, what happens again and again in all these "road maps to peace" is that the situation seems almost resolved and then something fails at the last moment. It is too simplistic to say, "Oh my god, Arafat screwed it up, we were so close." Obviously the problem is much deeper. When I say "universalism," I don't mean it in the naive, secular sense, like "they should all realize that their religion is something specific and that there are bigger universal values" and so on.

My dream as an atheist would be the following one: proclaim the old Jerusalem a kind of sacred space only for religious rituals. The catch is that this should be seen not as both sides giving in and compromising, but that both parties should experience it as by giving something we are all gaining. When someone tells me they are deeply religious, this would be the test of his religion: could he abandon political control, experiencing it not as a difficult, necessary compromise, but seeing it as gaining a sacred space? It would need to be a totally crazy gesture like that. People say that it can't happen, but we know that history is full of miracles.

"I will tremble the underground"
On the Film Forgiveness

SLAVOJ ŽIŽEK

Flectere si nequeo Superos, Acheronta movebo.
[If I cannot bend the Higher Powers, I will tremble the underground.]

—Virgil, as quoted by Freud

A short circuit is a condition in which a short electrical path is unintentionally created, causing a power fault—this is what Udi Aloni does in
both his book (*Forgiveness, or Rolling in the Underworld's Tunnels*) and his
film *Forgiveness*, causing a power fault of the ruling liberal attitude by way
of short-circuiting between different levels of ideology, art, and thought.
Aloni achieves a tremendous poetic power by creating new myths with
the perspicuous mind of a cold theoretician, grounding a ruthless critique
of Zionism in his unconditional fidelity to the Jewish tradition.

In the present world, what we call the normal state of things has
become indistinguishable from the state of emergency. The West is more
and more often evoking some figure of fear and then promising us protection from it. This comes at a very high price, because in such a scenario
the rhetoric of fear and emergency attempts to eclipse the act of thinking. All of this comes at precisely the time when the dignity of theory is
·urgent—not in the service of some kind of theoretical narcissism, but
because we must undermine the ultimate goal of the politics of fear, which
seeks to prevent us from questioning and thus from acting. The very logic
of the emergency state, then, is to prevent us from doing what really
should be done. Today, more than ever, we need a thinking that is not a
simple reflexive response to the state of emergency. I'm not an abstract-
idealist here, I'm a Marxist. My favorite passage from Marx comes in a

letter he wrote to Engels in which he asked in so many words whether the revolution couldn't wait a year or two until he finished writing about the spirit it was meant to obtain, i.e., Das Capital. So in the spirit of this letter, it is precisely in these times that a film like Aloni's *Forgiveness* is so needed. We have to remember that a film shouldn't intend to answer questions; it should advocate the formulation and reformulation of the questions themselves.

Forgiveness is not an avant-garde postmodern film playing with multiple narratives; it is a film that, on the one hand, thinks with emotions and, on the other hand, functions as a simple moral story, the story of a young, perplexed, but essentially honest Jewish boy who eventually learns, and becomes able to say, "I'm a killer." This simple recognition saves him from an ethical catastrophe and acts as an ultimate moment of reconciliation; it opens the possibility of seeking redemption through accountability. And redemption through accountability is the very opposite of that which results from granting forgiveness to oneself as the perpetrator.

Israeli and American films dealing with war in the Oliver Stone style often forge an image of the soldier not as a righteous superhero, but rather as a sensitive individual who acquiesces to his own moral weaknesses. In a dialectic way, because he reveals his moral failure, the soldier then receives moral sympathy from the audience. Not only is a liberal audience ready to forgive him for his war crimes, but the fact that these crimes make him so human is the very impetus for us to embrace him as an errant child. Take, for example, the protagonist (who also happens to be the director) of the Israeli film *Waltz with Bashir*. The director took part in the massacre of Sabra and Shatila, only to, years later, make a documentary about his posttraumatic state journey, the end of which includes a scene where he is redeemed by his shrink, who, in so many words, tells him, "You are good person. It's true you made a mistake, but don't ever forget: you are not a killer." In *Forgiveness*, on the other hand, the soldier arrives, at the end of his journey, at the terrible understanding that he's part of a perpetual killing. The crime he commits is not an individual failure within a healthy ethical structure, but an ethical failure built within the ideological structure itself.

Moreover, the film questions itself on the validity of the standard atheist-ideological argument used to explain terrible experiences such as the Holocaust or the Gulags: "God couldn't possibly have allowed such horror; thus it cannot exist." But, as Habermas admitted, when we are dealing with our era's immense discontent, it becomes too obscene to dismiss these horrors as petty human egotism. Aloni's film exemplifies why we need this excessive dimension, what we call the theological dimension, which works in tandem with the political. If anyone needs a proof that political theology is well and alive, here it is! The film introduces this notion of the ontological openness of the universe, the idea that the reality in which we live is not fully, ontologically constituted. This openness is something terrifying, horrible, but it simultaneously gives us hope.

Aloni plays with three versions of alternate realities: the protagonist, David, commits suicide (martyrdom), or he kills the girl (murderer), and only in a third version does our hero achieve reconciliation. This is something like what you encounter in *Run Lola Run*. In fact, *Forgiveness* could have been subtitled *Run David Run*, even though in *Run Lola Run* the contingency is temporal (alternative endings are determined by the time at which events occur) and in *Forgiveness* it's a psychological contingency (the ending depends on David's awareness of the events). In order to arrive to the right solution, which is reconciliation, you have to enact, to play with all the wrong solutions at a virtual level. It's a little bit like the metaphors one might encounter in quantum physics: when one of the quantum options is realized, when the oscillation is contracted into one reality, the other notions are not simply annihilated. To understand properly what really happens, you have to also understand what might have happened but did not happen. Now, one can say that this is empty speculation; what does it mean in terms of ethical experience? It's a very Benjaminian idea. It's not simply that "what is" is and cancels possibilities, but rather that "what is" is accompanied by the echoes of other possible alternatives that are constitutive of ontological openness. I think that without this ontological openness we live in a closed universe and, to put it in brutal terms, there is no place for morality.

In the last scene of *Forgiveness* we have an ontological openness; it takes place in the underground obscenity, with its motif of underground and comedy. Note that the actor who plays Yaacov, the Muslim, muselmann, is one of the best known Israeli comedians. Comedy is precisely— at its most radical, the comical effect—a comedy of character. Something happens to you that comes from outside, entirely contingent. There is an external accident, catastrophe, but the tragic insight is that the hero realizes it was his own hubris that caused the tragic fault.

Another of my solidarities with the film relates to Aloni's use of the Palestinian-Israeli rappers. I really think that there's some hope here, and this relates to my own personal experience. Here I refer to the terrible war in ex-Yugoslavia. At that time one of the bright moments was the alternative youth culture, which simply ignored the full extent of the nationalist conflict. But what we're talking about here is more radical, and I'm more and more convinced of this: there is a redeeming power of obscenities. When are you really love your neighbor, certainly you don't adhere to a sterile, boring multiculturalism. You open yourself to them, and they to you; you tell each other dirty jokes. Maybe the ultimate meaning of Aloni's film lies in this alternative youth culture that ignores the nationalist efforts—and it ignores it only *because* of its deep understanding of the psychological reasons behind this predesigned conflict. Here we find the actualization of Freud's quotation of Virgil in the *Interpretation of Dreams*: "If I cannot bend the Higher Powers, I will move the underground." Maybe now the arms are talking. Maybe we can't change the events at large. But we can at least move the underground.

In the context of the underground we also find the mechanisms of rules, and I cannot emphasize enough how crucial it is that we examine the relationship between ideology and rules today. When it comes to rules, we have plenty of them: rules of contact, how one can act, what one is allowed to think, the ways in which one can be ordered around or instructed, the ways in which one can be prohibited from acting. But, in a concrete social space, rules are not enough; in order to truly be a member of a certain social space, a community, what one must know are not simply the rules but the metarules, rules that tell you how to treat these rules. On the one hand, we have many rules that basically solicit you secretly; they push you to do what they formally prohibit, like in the naive oedipal example of a father telling his son to fear women, to stay away from them, when what he's really saying is "do it." The parallel in the political space is—in a democracy for example—when you are given freedom of choice precisely on the condition that you do not use it. This apparent freedom conceals a much more powerful order: not only do you have to visit your grandmother, but you have to do it out of your free will. I think this is the best metaphor for our present political constellation. And why am I mentioning this? Because I think at the level of the unwritten, the implicit, this is the underground, these other rules that tell you how to deal with rules, i.e., the metarules. Officially, we are all equal, Jews, Palestinians, etc. But there's this whole set of implicit rules; you are given a right on the condition that you do not exercise it, or you can exercise it but only secretly, and so on and so forth. Paradoxically, this is when we have to move the underground, and sometimes this is much more important than changing the explicit rules. This is what Udi tries to do; he is moving the underground, changing those unwritten obscene rules, like one of his protagonists, the muselmann, who calls himself a "mole."

And this is exactly what Hegel called the work of the mole: this underground work, which is the magic of revolutions. As Hegel put it, all the glitter of the display of power can stay there, but they're not even aware of how the mole works via the underground. And then, at a certain point, you just have to touch them and say, "hey, look down, you are there," and all collapses.

Angel for a New Place

On the Film Local Angel

ALAIN BADIOU

Local Angel is not only a very beautiful and interesting movie, but also a very important one. Naturally we can say it's beautiful and interesting because of its subtle construction composed of very beautiful images of New York, the Palestinian territories, and of men and women from several countries, however, there is a more fundamental reason, which is that the movie occurs at the intersection between a very subjective determination and a very objective situation. The story is certainly not only about the Palestinian situation, but also about the figures of the mother and the exile who is dealing with that distance between New York and Israel which is the fundamental division of his consciousness.

This subjective determination is completely linked with the objective situation, with the question of the Palestinian plight, as well as larger questions of war, violence, and history. In fact, there is a sort of a constructive interplay between the subjective question, which is very profound and difficult, and the objective investigation, which is never too partial or too subjective, of the radicality of the political situation. Despite a very complex construction, the great question of the film is very clear: what are the real conditions of peace for everybody?

First published in *Polemics* (London: Verso, 2006).

This great question is most often absent in movies about political situations, which are not very good due to their lack of universal signification. Immersed in the battle, they are primarily one-sided. You have films that are for the Palestinians, against Israel, against Sharon, and sometimes finally against the Jews, too: since Israel says that it is the Jewish state, moving from hostility toward the state of Israel to hostility toward Jews is an all-too-easy passage. It's the case not only for films about the Palestinian situation but for a great number of activist movies in general: they are on one side.

Naturally, I know perfectly well that Udi is operating from a real and radical point of view that is not at all objective or academic. However, the movie's importance is that in its situation it is searching for a way that is understandable by all the agents of the situation and not merely by one side. The movie believes in the possibility of finding something in the situation that is a symbol of peace for everybody. It is not strictly from the point of view of a militant Palestinian or only from the point of view of a pacifist Jew. It is something more complex—and as such it contains a proposition for peace that results from a subjective engagement.

The conviction of the movie is that if we consider the situation from the real point of view of a subjectivity, which is composed of loyalty, faithfulness, and awareness of the other, we can know that the people who live in Palestine are something like the same as those who live in Israel. Not the same in the particularity of religion and so on—we know perfectly well that they are different. If we see they are the same we can find something in the situation that is neither the victory of one side against the other side nor a sort of discussion or negotiation that would result in something compromised and not radical.

The movie is concerned neither with victory nor defeat—neither with compromise without end nor continuation of war, but with the construction of a new place. As Palestine is not just a local situation but a symbol for all humanity, it is the real destiny of the movie to propose something like a new place to all people on earth. It's my final consideration that the great stories of states, wars, and religion and the small stories of one man, one woman, one Palestinian, one Jew, and so on, can have a sort of common point in the future, which is precisely a new place both spiritual and concrete.

I insist that this movie is really a very sensible, material movie, concerned about the colors of very sensible things, about the sea, women, bodies, and the concrete qualities of speech. While it is not abstract, across its concrete sensibility there is a path toward the possibility to construct a new place. The movie is saying to us that when the situation is horrible, full of death and violence, when it has become impossible for it to become something good for all people, there is always the possibility of seizing the situation in another manner, from the point of view of humanity itself and not from some particular part of humanity. From this point of view it can be seen that all people who live here are all the same, and that a new place can be constructed. As I understand it, *Local Angel* is the angel for a new place.

In the film there is a very important subjective declaration about the reconciliation between the weak god, who is not the god of glory and potency but a weak and suffering god, and the figure of the mother who protests and does not accept. The question for me is the gap between these two determinations. Is it possible to have simultaneously a strong protest and revolt and, on the other hand, a god of weakness, pity, and compassion, something like a Christian god? Udi's vision is precisely on this gap between the two. On one side, the question of the construction of a new place is always a question of weakness, because a new Palestine is something that is the result neither of victory nor defeat. If you want to have a new place, you have to renounce the logic of power. So, on one side, you have a god who is not the god of one people but the god of everybody; on the other side you have to do and to say something, because a searching for a new way in a situation can't be purely passive and compassionate.

In the movie we can see Udi facing Arafat. In politics speaking to somebody is an act, it is not pure passivity. The question is, what is the action adequate to my vision of the construction of a new place? It is not the classical form of action, which in this situation would be fighting and aggression. While Udi is not a pure pacifist, he knows as well as I do that a new political conception about this sort of situation is not on the side of the old conception of fighting, fighting, fighting, and then finally victory or death. Another way must be found. In the movie we can see that the art, the singers and love, are determinations immanent to a real conception of a political transformation of place. The gap between protestation, revolt, and the weak god is also a place for a new means for a new place. This gap is certainly a problem: Udi has no mechanical solution—only the gap itself. So my question, which is not an objection, is about the means of Udi's vision.

Udi's means lies in the gap between four figures of messianism: Walter Benjamin, Gershom Scholem, Shabtai Tzvi, and Saint Paul. I think he is between the messianic conception and something that isn't anti but maybe a nonmessianic conception. In Paul, for example, we have something that is not exactly the messianic conception but instead something like the process of the coming of God himself. In the spiritual tradition of Jews, I think Udi is not in a correct place but in between two correct places, and he has to search for a new way out. I see in his movie a fundamental subjective conception, which is that if we have to create a new place it is also because we have to create a new Jew. I think this is his real project: not the renunciation of Jewish identity today, but the creation of a new one.

The Four Dimensions of Art

On the Film Forgiveness

ALAIN BADIOU

This film presents, as does every film, visible two-dimensional images and audible successions—voices, music, and sounds. These are the evident materials of the film's composition.

Now, I would like to examine a slightly different idea: an idea that proposes this film as a four-dimensional universe. As an object, insofar as you see it and hear it, the film has three dimensions—two in the visible and one in the auditory. But insofar as the film constructs an artistic idea, insofar as it is capable of transforming its spectator, or its voyeur, of modifying our thought, yours or mine, the film in reality has four dimensions.

I name these four dimensions: the historical dimension, the narrative dimension, the psychoanalytic dimension, and the cultural dimension. The objective of the film, as art work, is to unite these four dimensions, to make them hold together. The artistic dimension is thus like a fifth dimension, achieved by knotting together the four others.

I will now examine the four dimensions one by one.

The historical dimension is, evidently, a meditation on Israel and Palestine. Udi Aloni's fundamental idea is that *Palestine* is the name that prevents Israel, as it exists, from becoming the incarnation of a Jewish universality in the eyes of the world. But, just the same, *Israel* is taken as a hateful word of separation, or object of blind violence, and *Israel* is what prevents Palestine from becoming the incarnation of Arab universality in

the eyes of the world. Udi Aloni does not inscribe his film into a prefab-
ricated or abstract vision of the division or conflict between Israelis and
Palestinians. The question of war or of the sharing of territory is not his
main problem. Because my friend Udi thinks that Palestine and the Palestinians are inscribed into the very essence of Israel. The powerful image
expressing this idea is that dead Palestinians, their personal effects, their
debris, constitute the soil upon which a psychiatric hospital was constructed in a village destroyed during the 1947 war. That is to say, from its
origin, what troubles and affects Israel as spirit, as thought, what cannot
be torn from it, is precisely the subterranean—fundamental—presence of
the absolute wrong done to the Palestinians. It is thus impossible to think
the becoming of Israel, just as it is impossible to think what could be left
of the becoming of Palestine, under the rule of separation, entrenchment,
and walls. On the contrary, the final scene, which depicts an attempt to
cure the spiritual malady that Israel, as it exists, has introduced into what
constitutes Jewish being, is a scene of descent into the subterranean, a
scene of purification via avowal of origin, a scene from whence another
history could begin, precisely because at last nothing requires separation
and war anymore. It was said, pronounced, that from its origins the earth
itself could have been shared; that it had to be shared. And thus the knot
of daily life that might unite Palestinians and Israelis had no reasonable
reason to be interminably divided.

I want to insist on the following point: what this film tells us, its Idea,
is in no way a political thesis in the current sense of the term. The truth
is inscribed, here, in art. The truth is an effect of art. The film shows in
the same shot what is, what might have been, and what should be. What
is: separation, war, and violence. What might have been: shared love of
place as powerful universal value, combining heterogeneous elements in
an unprecedented music (music and dance, in Udi Aloni's film, speak from
the interior of what is to attest to what might have been). And finally
what should be: a new declaration that would permit starting over, which
the title of the film, *Forgiveness*, recapitulates. Once spoken within the
movement of what exists, the original sin loses its historic power. There
is no longer a need to repeat the separation created by lies. In combining
their action on an undivided territory, Jewish universality and Arab universality would have a pacifying and creative effect on the world—what
Mao Zedong called "a spiritual atomic bomb."

Let us move on to the narrative dimension. The film, after all, also tells
a story. The story of a young Jew, son of a German Jew, living in the

United States. In revolt against his father's sterile silence, the son enlists in the Israeli army in order to finally confront real enemies instead of historical phantoms. He will kill the child of a woman he loves. He will go insane, become mute, virtually criminal or suicidal, when the possible repetition of the murder he committed looms over the child of another woman he loves. The women in this film always come from elsewhere, from the other apparent world, from the Arab world. The film exposes this frightening logic of repetition of that which has not been spoken. But the film also rejects this by engaging in the process of purification by the return to the origin. The narration accepts ordinary materials in their ordinary order: revolt, violence, and war; love, crime, and madness; suicide attempts and ultimate salvation. We have here all the elements for a melodrama. And, in fact, we have it, this melodrama. Nevertheless, that second dimension, this melodrama, carries with it the first dimension, since each of its terms is also a stage for the inscription of the subject (the young hero) within the historic problem in which he is both situated and transformed. It is here that Udi Aloni takes up the old practice of the coming-of-age novel. And, as always in this kind of novel, individual decisions are also symbols for historical and political choices. Thus the two possible endings that the film virtuosically sets forth. Either the young man, symbolizing Israel, accepts this memory of having been a murderer, and peace and reconciliation become possible, or the young man encloses himself in silence, oblivion, and repetition, thus suiciding. That is to say, continuing in the mode of its contemporary political orientation is the real death threat against Israel—a historic suicide.

The third dimension, the psychoanalytic, draws its connection to the two earlier dimensions by virtue of metaphor. Just as the historic underground of the Israelis', and thus of the Jews', spiritual malady is the hidden Palestine, the son's insanity finds its secret origin in what is obscured and hidden in the father. One of the film's major themes is that the contemporary problem resides, without a doubt, in the recognition of the fathers by the sons, but even more forcefully in the recognition of the sons by the fathers.

In this regard, the essential scene is perhaps the confrontation between the two possible fathers of the hero, who are both, as their tattoos show, survivors of deportation and extermination. On one side we have the real father, the German musician who wants to forget—in America—the historic destiny of the Jews. On the other side we have the true father, the asylum's craziest old man, guardian of the depths of the earth ("Well said, old mole!" says this prophesying Marxist), who knows that denying Palestinian deaths also forbids all active or peace-bringing memory of the camps and of extermination. The choice of obeying one or the other opens onto the son's fundamental decision. A decision that also signifies the following: to continue on the path of separation, of war, of wrongs done to the Palestinians, means to give sinister assurance that the millions of dead Jews in fact and forever died for nothing, no matter how many monuments are dedicated to them. In truth, all that can be dedicated to the dead is the living monument of a reconciled Palestine.

Udi Aloni does not shy away from any allusive complexity. This is the difficult charm of his work. Here, we have at once Oedipus, who must kill his father in order to accomplish his destiny, and Freud, with his famous dream of the son who burns under the impotent eyes of the father, who—the father—is incapable of really understanding what the son really means when he says to him, "Father, don't you see I'm burning?" And is it not true today that, everywhere in the world, our sons are burning under our very eyes, in general incomprehension? But we also have Oedipus at Colonnus, for the dead Palestinian girl is a new Antigone who both haunts the son as the incarnation of his crime and gently leads him toward purification. But the film is also a very contemporary plea for the subjective operations of psychoanalysis against the objective and memoryless doctrine of chemical medication. To cure the young soldier, the old Jewish doctor—played with astonishing naturalness by a great Palestinian actor—opposes as best he can his personal understanding and proximity to the official directives that prescribe a good syringefull of oblivion serum. He yields to prescribing psychiatric medication by weakness, by virtue of an intrigue with the state (this power struggle is symbolized by a scene of trivial sex with a functionary). We see, here, a connection to the first dimension: on this bloody earth, to forget the initial wrong, to use chemicals against thought, amounts to preparing an infinite repetition of separating violence. What would force destiny in the direction of salvation would be neither the father's newfound tenderness toward his son nor the doctor's too-easy sympathy for him, but rather the voice of the unconscious itself—individual and historic—that of the madman or prophet who knows it is underneath the hospital, into the depths of the earth, that one must go to interrupt the fatal destiny of separation and reinstate a chance for love.

The fourth dimension, which I name cultural, is, from the start, more polyphonic. It consists in saturating the narration with what we could call artistic and cultural implants, which come from at least four worlds, and in giving, as figures of the country and, more generally, of the world, to see and hear that the road to salvation passes through this multiplicity itself—and never through warmongering palaver about culture shocks. This is not some soft principle of tolerance or respect for difference. It is about directly valorizing the fact that a contemporary universality can belong to no single heritage. Rather, it is something like a braid of knots, some tight, some less so. And it is expressly because *Israel* or *Palestine* are the names of an exemplary knot, where distinct heritages can nevertheless play together, that here a universal dwelling—wholly new—could and must begin.

The four cultural worlds cited in Udi's film are old European artistic creation, the Arab world's subtle and almost timeless savoir-vivre and love of life, American modernity, and the irreplaceable spirituality of the Jews. Extraordinary scenes show the interpenetration, the collision, the simultaneous giving birth, of these worlds that are all implicated in the Israeli-Palestinian turmoil. Let us cite the song of the Palestinian woman, who interrupts and subjugates Israeli nightclub dancers, or the dance of the soldiers in the synagogue, as though they had been seized—they, the oppressive warriors—by a loving drunkenness destined for the entire earth. Let us also cite the scene that touches me personally in which the hero, accompanying himself on the piano, sings a Schumann lied about forgiveness in love, his face streaming with tears. Because in this respect the essential questions of the film—the father, Germany, the extermination of the Jews, Israel, Palestine, the universality of art and the difficulty of love—merge in a whole so complex that a solitary and disarmed subject cannot endure it without coming apart.

You see to what degree Udi Aloni's film is ramified as each of the elements of its construction is grafted onto others in such a way as to make narrative fiction also become artistic allegory, psychoanalytic interrogation, historical meditation, and spiritual proposition. And that, despite the fact that emotional elements circulate freely in the film, each spectator is called not to separate—as I have done—the ingredients of the film's composition but to receive the impact of a situation figured by a film, by an absorbing melodrama, and thus undergoes an evidence as shared as well as indivisible.

I would like to conclude in saying also that the film is essentially optimistic. As repetitive and despairing as a situation can be, there exists within it, within its very entanglement, the chance for a respite. It is this conviction that is ordered by the film. It belongs to what I have called affirmationism—in the hope of thus proposing a motto for the art to come: the doctrine according to which ideas generated by art do not so much carry a judgment on the world as indicate the point from which the world might be transfigured. Udi's filmic figurations of Israel and Palestine are affirmationist in this sense. They indicate the point where separation could be overcome, they announce the power of Palestisrael, or of Israpalestine, to become the immanent transfiguration of the disaster itself.

Translated from the French by Ariana Reines

Existence on the Boundary

On the Film Kashmir: Journey to Freedom

ALAIN BADIOU

It's not simple for me to speak here today because there is a problem of the relationship between philosophy and war, destruction, terror. And you know philosophy is certainly something that is in relation to the real, and death and destruction are part of the real. But the goal of philosophy is always to go beyond war, beyond destruction, and, when it is possible, beyond death. And this is why I can speak of the film of my friend Udi Aloni: This film has something of a philosophical dimension, because it's not only a film concerning people, a situation, culture, voyage, it's a film concerning the destiny of all that, the becoming of all that, this one possibility of the future. So it's not only a film concerning a terrible situation, a situation where we find in fact destruction, but it's a film that goes beyond all that and says, to all of us, that there is always a possibility in thinking, in acting beyond the negative features of the situation, however terrible they are. This philosophical dimension can be named, it is a dimension of hope, and it's a philosophical task to give everybody courage in this situation, when the situation is practically without hope, without a clear future, without peace. And I can speak of some aspects of Udi Aloni's film because it's a film concerning the possibility of life, and not a film

Transcription of a lecture at the Tel Aviv cinematheque during the assault on Gaza (January 2009).

concerning death and destruction. This film is about the formation of a people that has three characteristics or maybe four:

- First of all, it's a people without a state, and so it's a history of a people when there is no real state corresponding to this people.
- Second, it's a film about a people with a specific culture, and this specific culture constitutes what there is inside the people itself; it's not a limitation, it's not a definition of the people from outside, but it's something like the interiority of the people.
- And, third, it's a film about a people and their occupation by a strong army of strangers, and so it's a people with contradictions between its inside: the culture, the long history, and so on, and its outside—but outside inside: that which comes from outside but is here inside, in the land, and the great signification of occupation: something of the outside that constitutes a part of the inside.

These are three great features of Kashmir, and we know that we can naturally do some comparison with Palestine, but comparisons, as you know, are never strict. But I think the fourth characteristic is the most important: the film is about a people who is on the boundary, a people of boundaries—the boundary between India and Pakistan in this particular case—and when the people without a state are a people on the boundary, the boundary itself is the negation of the existence of the people, because the people are neither on one side nor on the other—they is really on the boundary—and so the Kashmiri people are neither a people of India nor a people of Pakistan; they are the people of the boundary itself, but when we reduce the existence of the people to the existence of the boundary, in fact, we suppress the existence of something like the inside, the interior of the people, we exert the negation of their real existence, and because of all that we can say there is a universality of the people when they are the people of boundaries, and this is a philosophical question: why is there something universal in the people of the boundary? It's because this people exists ONLY as such. They do not exist by their presence in something big, in something that is installed, in something that is strong. There is no state, there is no relationship to a great dimension of culture; there is only a pure existence in the boundary itself. It's the universality of weakness, and it's a very important philosophical idea that, generally, what is universal is on the side not of a strong state, not on the side of potency, not on the side of that which is rich, but on the side of weakness—

weakness as the simple existence of the people, who have no other thing as their proper existence (and when people are on the boundaries this is always the case, and it is the relationship between outside and inside that is the really difficult question), who are reduced to their pure existence. So reduced to what there is inside themselves that they cannot be defined by the outside, and it's the same case, naturally, both for Kashmiris and for the Palestinians. It is a philosophical dimension of the situation here, which is the reduction of the Palestinians to people of the boundary. What sort of boundary? There are two types of boundaries: the ideological and religious boundaries between Jews and Arabs and the boundary between the Western world with its potency and what is not the Western world. The Palestinians, when they are reduced to this duality—this boundary between these two great dimensions—are suppressed in the existence of their interiority, and this is why this film concerning Kashmir really has universality. For a philosopher like me, it is a film about the people of the boundaries—all people of boundaries—and so it's a film concerning what is the existence of the people, not the existence of the state, not purely the existence of a culture, not purely the existence of some outside dimension, but really the existence of the people as such. And you know this existence is something that learns to exist not in representations, not in strength, not in the form of a state, but to exist as Jews have existed for a very long time, in the form of a people with its proper weakness. And so, for all these reasons, there is a philosophical dimension in Udi Aloni's film.

And this film has images of this people, of its land, of its life; images of its culture: family life, hard work, images of occupation, Indian soldiers, bombs, destruction, but finally images of what this pure existence is and a discussion of the continuity and possible future of this weak existence that can be reduced to a strict boundary.

My second point is that the film of Udi Aloni is a film about different stages, steps, of the actions of the people against occupation.

First our idea of fighting with the same means as the occupation itself and then—the result of a long history of revolt, struggle, armed struggle—we finally have a nonviolent movement; which is a movement of what? The transformation of the pure existence of the people into a political form. The nonviolent movement is only to show the existence of the people, to give a collective form to the weak existence of the people. And the philosophical idea is that when you show the weakness there is strength. Showing weakness is a new strength, maybe something like an artistic idea, and this is why it's so appropriate to the movie of Udi Aloni. The great creations, the colors, the women, and so on are not only part of a classical demonstration—they are much more: they are the strength of the weakness without arms, without new and terrible organizations, but when everybody is here with himself or herself as the only arms, and we can show the weakness to the world itself. So Udi Aloni in that sense is really an activist of the Kashmiri people, because the movie shows the weakness of the Kashmiri people in relation to everybody, and this people, which was hidden in the corner of the world in a boundary between Pakistan and India, becomes something else: the strength of its pure existence.

And this is a lesson I think. I don't think the future for them is clear; there are terrible means against all that. It's possible to crash, to destroy that sort of showing of the weakness as a new strength, but it's really a great idea of relationship between existence and politics, the idea that we can find a new politics by showing existence. All people who are oppressed, negated, and so on, are often invisible. The invisibility of the poor, the invisibility of the weakness, the invisibility of the people is a great reason for oppression, but when you show the weakness, when you create a new visibility of the people, you have a new sequence of the politics of emancipation, the politics of freedom, and this point is very important in the film. It's really a philosophical point, because it's the relationship between being and happening, thinking and visibility, between, finally, existence and politics. Something appears as a new stage of its collective existence; the people of the boundary, the people of the weakness, the people who are reduced to nothing by the struggle between Pakistan and India, become visible. This visibility cannot be forgotten, and Udi Aloni's film is also the memory of this visibility.

My third point is that the film is about the interplay, the relationship between the soil of this people and the conflict and interest of big states, the history of the boundaries itself, the history of the conflict between India and Pakistan in the place where Kashmir exists, and I appreciate the film's involvement on this point, the relationship between the existence of the people and the existence of two big states. It simultaneously makes the film complex and simple. It is complex because it's a great question concerning the relationship between the people and the state. What is, after all, the relationship between the people and the state exactly? Naturally, it's a fundamental question concerning signification, for example, of the Israeli state, but it's also the signification of a question concerning every state. The state is always saying that it is a state of a people: Egypt is the state of the Egyptians, France is the state of the French, and so on. But it's unclear what the signification of this affirmation is—in what sense a state is a state of a people. You know that a very important point in Marxism—after all, we can peek into Marxism from time to time—is not the state of a people, but something separated from the people. The great dimension of the state is the separation and not the expression of the people. We have a conflict between two ideas concerning the relationship between the people and the state. The first idea is that the state expresses the people, the state is a representation of the people, the state is really the state of the people, and the second is that the state is the state of some interest, and this interest cannot be reduced to the interest of the people as such. There is a separation between the state and the people. In the case of Marxism, as we know perfectly well, the interests are the interests of the dominant class or, perhaps more generally, more philosophically, the interest of the state is not to constitute harmony with the existence of the people. And we can see that in the film of Udi Aloni: there is a people, there is a state, but between the state and the people there is a clear separation: so it's a lesson concerning the point of separation between the people and the state, and it is, in my conviction, a universal point. We are really to assume that we can't reduce a state to being an expression of the people. There is, for everybody everywhere, tension, and very often there is contradiction between the decisions and the interests of the state and the existence of the people. And it's a lesson of the movie and it is a lesson of the weak existence of Kashmir. And so the film of Udi Aloni is also for us a film concerning the way of thinking, the way of action when we assume this point as we do something, when we organize something, when we discuss something under the conviction that the state really is not our state; the state is a state, and we know that there is probably a need for the existence of the state, but we are not to assume that the state is our state if our state signifies a state as a correct expression of our collective existence. And the problem is complex, because not only is the state not ours by necessity but also the state is never the future of our existence, the state is always a state of the present; it is the state of the situation as such. The state is a state of the strength of the situation. In the weakness of the pure existence of the people there is representation of the future that is not inscribed in the state. So the state is not the expression of our existence—not only in the present but much more in the future—and so we have to affirm that the creation of the future is never a creation by the state. Only people decide of the future, by resistance, by existence, by new ideas, by new poems, by new films, by new activities—the people decide the future. But they cannot decide the future with freedom if they don't assume that their existence is not reducible to the actions of the state, and when we have situations where the people are without a state, like Kashmir, like Palestine, we can see precisely how the future is decided, good or bad. It's another problem that the future is decided by people and not the state. There is, you know, something nihilistic in the state, in the existence of the state. The state wants only its continuation, so the states prefer people's death to their proper death. The state is always a monstrous creation, and it is why the great idea of communism—we can speak of communism from time to time—was the idea of the hand of the state. Why this strange idea of the hand, the progressive hand of the state? It's because the state is not the representation of the real future of people, but a representation of its immediate strength, with destruction and with death. And so, more generally, life is not on the side of the state but on the side of the weakness of peoples.

Fourth point: the film is about the relationship between inside and outside. I have said something about this point before. It's a very important point. Kashmir is neither outside nor inside India. It's in a situation of boundary. In that sort of situation we must go from outside to inside. We have to create something that is purely inside and after that return to the outside. It's a movement. In the beginnings of the struggle of the Kashmiri people we see not this movement but the movement to go outside to fight. And it was the same for the first sequence of existence of Palestinian resistance. At the moment we go outside we shall see inside, and when you see the failure of this movement there is a real situation of disorganization, of disorientation—a very difficult moment. And so it's the same thing in Udi Aloni's film. We can understand that after we discover the true movement. And the true movement is to go from outside to inside first, to create a new subjectivity before the question of relationship to the outside, to first exist. To exist, the people must first exist inside themselves, to create a new movement from outside to inside. And we need the creation of a new form of freedom. We can say that collective freedom is always a result of a movement from outside to inside: not only contradiction and violence against what is outside, but first return to the inside. And we can say it's something like poetic movement. Poetic movement because we can say that poetry is always creation in language of a new form of interiority, of a new paradigm of *to be* inside yourself. And it is why Udi's film's description of the movement from outside to inside is also a poetic description and not only a political one. We are here in close relationship between politics and poetry, which is, in the history of a people, a very important moment—when the people finds its poet—and this moment is the moment in which something in the proper language of this people is said concerning the movement from outside to inside, and it's a creation of a new language, naturally. But of course the creation of a new language is the creation of a new subjectivity. And Udi's film is also about this universal lesson, because today I think, if I understand something of the situation here, the two peoples: the Israelis—Jews, and the Palestinians—are most doomed in this movement from outside to inside, because they are, for the moment, if I can tell you something like that, abandoned to outside—the Western world for Israelis, which is a terrible outside that cannot become your inside, and, on the other part, something like a religious fantasy, which is also a terrible outside. And so the problem is not a strictly tactical problem between military forces and so on. We have here a political problem that is a metaphysical one because we have to create new interiority—new interiority so certainly as to give a new sense, poetically and politically, to the word *Jew* and to the word *Palestinian*. And it's a long process. But the film of Udi Aloni is about this point. A part of the situation here—because my friend Udi Aloni, who is sometimes an extremist, is also cautious—is that he can speak of Kashmir to prepare for something else. We can see the universal lesson of all that. A universal question is when the people is in confrontation with the question of its existence, the question of the weakness of its pure existence. Apart from the strength of the state and not on the side of the death and not on the side of destruction. Never. The state yes, but the people—the life the people—no. And so when we are in that sort of situation we have to create a new feel for popular freedom, for collective existence, and this creation is always sort of interior—an occasion of interior from outside to inside. And we must create this kind of movement here, on both sides of the situation, and thus to be and to invent a part of the state, a part of the presence of the state, in your case, but a part of the absence of a state on the other side of the situation. Because two peoples can be together—peoples can always be together. The states cannot be together, but peoples can, and they must. And, with all that Udi, in his film, says to us, we must construct a new collective freedom. Maybe the situation is a situation of destruction, of death, of horrible conflict, of false ways, of the awful state, of the strength of the state; the situation is that we have a dictatorship of outside. But a dictatorship from outside is a moment to create a new interiority, and the construction of the film itself goes in this direction, because the construction of the film is in the multiplicity. You have seen that words image the past and the present, the personal life and the collective life, intimacy and collectivity, and so on. And this multiplicity is the element for the creation of a new interiority; it's the element for the movement from outside to inside. And so it's a complexity, but with harmony, with peace.

Another point is that the film is a film concerning peace in a situation that is a situation of war, with soldiers, certainly, checkpoints, and so on—maybe massacres too. We can see explosions, bombs, soldiers, and so on.

Finally, the film itself grasps the intimacy of the weakness of the existence of the people, and it is the rhythm of peace. The most important dimension of peace is not the end of the war—that is only a short and purely tactical definition of peace. Peace is something beyond war, something beyond the opposition between war and peace. The true peace is not the peace that is opposed to the war. The true peace is a creation—the creation of a new situation where we have the existence of the people, and the pure existence of the people is beyond the opposition between war and peace. It's something like peace beyond peace itself because it's a new form of existence.

I hope—this is my final word—you can create here the movement that is the movement of peace—peace that is beyond the common idea of peace.

THREE INTERVENTIONS

THE RELIGIOUS QUESTION AND QUESTION OF POWER

There are always contradictions when there is interplay between the religious question and question of power. Without this point we have many examples that different religious convictions can live together. But when the religious problem becomes also a problem of power in any situation, when religion becomes a part of the power of the definition of the state, there is, naturally, a war of religions. I think there is a necessity to understand the religious question from the point of view of the contradiction of religion and state: if we go directly to the contradiction between religions, we don't understand anything. Because it is always when a religious definition becomes a state religion that we have big problems, and so I think that it is from the point of view of people. They always say something like there's no problem if my neighbor has another religion than me—in concrete life there is no problem. The problem is when you say that "My religion should be the official religion of my country, of my state." But when we are inside the people we can always relate to many forms of religious activities, which is why the true question of religion is a political question. It's a question inside the relationship between people and state. And so we must affirm the complete difference between politics and religion, and when there is nothing like that sort of affirmation there is a problem. It is the reason why a problem can exist on both sides.

A NONVIOLENT MOVEMENT

I have said that we cannot completely have a prevision of the future concerning a nonviolent movement. I think that when a nonviolent movement is really a movement of the existence of the people—not only something like a political means, but showing the existence of the people for a long time, not only in one demonstration and so on—there is something that creates a new situation for the power itself. A truly new situation. We have some historic examples. The most characteristic nonviolent movement has been the movement in Poland against the Communist state. It was nonviolent, it was a movement of workers principally, and it was what I may define a complete movement, a movement that was really a movement of everybody, and, finally, the power was without power concerning that sort of movement. It's not something that goes by itself. For example, in the case of Kashmir, the movement continues, but Indian soldiers are there too.

THE PEOPLE WHICH ARE ON THE BOUNDARY

I think that the people who are on the boundary have to create the movement from outside to inside to show their existence absolutely. And it is because this existence is oppressed and negated that they have to show the special weakness. I think when you are on the boundary you are always suppressed, in a sense. We are reduced to two strengths, two states;

naturally, we can be obscured on the boundary or something like that. We can disappear on the boundary, but it's not popular existence. The popular existence on the boundary is a weak existence that is under two different strengths. And so you have to show your existence, absolutely. You know to show one's existence is a very important movement—not only here. For example, we had in France some years ago a big movement of undocumented workers, and undocumented workers were precisely the paradigm of invisibility: their name was clandestine and so on, they didn't exist, they were something for only the police, for jail. They had big demonstrations, and that was definite proof of their existence, and so, finally, everybody today says they exist, they are real, they are part of our people. It's a problem, perhaps, but they are part of our people. So this was a very clear example of the transformation of pure weakness, because the life of an undocumented worker in a suburb of Paris is not a strong existence—I can tell you, I know them. And so it's a very clear example of pure weakness in a country that has been transformed merely by showing their collective existence, and so it's really by showing weakness that we create strength. The problem after that is not solved—there are many problems today concerning undocumented workers. But it's not the problem of their existence—they are not in the invisibility.

There are some muffins there if you want. . . .

A Conversation on Queerness, Precariousness, Binationalism, and BDS

JUDITH BUTLER: There are some muffins there if you want them . . .

UDI ALONI: I want to start with the last film you were in, *Examined Life*, directed by Astra Taylor. A number of preeminent philosophers were there, each one explaining his own philosophy. You, instead of discussing your philosophy like the others, chose to speak with Sunny, the sister of the filmmaker. Why did you choose dialogue?

JUDITH BUTLER: Well, Sunny was my student, and I had come to know her fairly well. She moves in a wheelchair. She has had a series of disabilities from birth. She's a brilliant artist. She took a course of mine on Nietzsche. So I had an independent relationship to her.

Astra said to me that she wanted to make a film in which philosophers were in motion, walking, moving in some way. She asked me, "would you walk and talk?" and I thought, "surely I can walk and talk." It's a fine philosophical tradition, the peripatetic tradition, which dates back to Socrates. I love walking and talking. It is excellent to be in the world, to be of the world, to be interrupted by the sounds of the world. But the Socratic peripatesis requires a dialogue. And it also struck me as very odd that I was being asked to walk when Sunny was there, and I wondered: what is it for Sunny to take a walk? Why do we assume that

November 27, 2009.

everybody can take a walk? Or why do we assume that a walk requires two feet or being able to stand upwards or being able to balance on whatever feet one has? So I wanted to call into question the idea of taking a walk. When I asked Sunny, "do you take walks?" I wasn't sure if that would be the term she would use for going out for a stroll in her wheelchair. She said, "yes, I take walks everyday" and I replied, "perfect! Let's start with that." You can take a walk in a variety of ways: on wheels, through film, in your dreams. It doesn't necessarily mean that one has the mobility and balance that we associate with physical walking. I wanted to let "taking a walk" become a metaphor, or at least a transposable term that could describe any number of ways of being in motion.

UDI ALONI: That walk stayed with me for days, after the movie, after I left the theater and went home. You spoke of this kid, the one who always had a queer walk, and just because of that walk he was murdered by his friend. How movement can be everything. There was something amazing and yet simple in that. Some say that your writing is complicated, but there is a simplicity that is very deep at the same time.

I want to go back a bit. In Israel, people know you well. Your name was even in the popular film *Ha-Buah* (*The Bubble*). (*Laughs.*)

JUDITH BUTLER: (*Laughs.*) Although I disagreed with the use of my name in that context. I mean, it was very funny to say, "don't Judith Butler me," but "to Judith Butler someone" meant to say something very negative about men and to identify with a form of feminism that was against men. And I've never been identified with that form of feminism. That's not my mode. I'm not known for that. So it seems like it was confusing me with a radical feminist view that one would associate with Catharine MacKinnon or Andrea Dworkin, a completely different feminist modality. I'm not always calling into question who's a man and who's not, and am I a man? Maybe I'm a man. (*Laughs.*) Call me a man. I am much more open about categories of gender, and my feminism has been about women's safety from violence, increased literacy, decreased poverty, and more equality. I was never against the category of men.

UDI ALONI: A beautiful Israeli poem asks, "How does one become Avot Yeshurun?" Avot Yeshurun was a poet who caused turmoil in Israeli poetry. I want to ask, how does one become Judith Butler—especially with the issue of *Gender Trouble*, the book that so troubled the discourse on gender?

JUDITH BUTLER: You know, I'm not sure that I know how to give an account of it, and I think it troubles gender differently depending on how it is received and translated. For instance, one of the first receptions [of the book] was in Germany, and there it seemed very clear that young people wanted a politics that emphasized agency or something affirmative that they could create or produce. The idea of performativity—which involved bringing categories into being or bringing new social realities about—was very exciting, especially for younger people who were tired with old models of oppression—indeed, the very model men oppress women or straights oppress gays. If you're straight, you're in an oppressive position; if you're gay, you're in a subjugated position.

It seemed that if you were subjugated there were also forms of agency that were available to you, and you were not just a victim, or you were not only oppressed, but oppression could become the condition of your agency. Certain kinds of unexpected results can emerge from the situation of oppression if you have the resources and if you have collective support. It's not an automatic response; it's not a necessary response. But it's possible. So I was trying to hold out the possibility of agency. I think I also probably spoke to something that was already happening in the movement. In a way, theory only registers what is already happening in a social movement. I was part of a social movement. I put into theoretical language what was already being impressed upon me from elsewhere. So I didn't bring it into being single-handedly. I received it from several cultural resources and put it into another language.

There it seemed to me that both misogynists and feminists had very strong ideas about what it is to be a woman. The misogynists wanted women to be a certain way, but the feminists also had very strong ideas about what it was to be caring, what it was to have a woman's relation to nature, what it was to have sexual desire that was necessarily heterosexual, or what femininity was as a psychic or cultural reality. There were a lot of people who thought, No! My politics, my life, even my feminism is about calling into question whether those ideas of femininity are necessary, and if I don't fall into these categories, if I don't fall neatly into received ideas of masculinity or of femininity, what social place is there for me? Do I become a dead thing? A no-thing? Am I un-namable? Am I monstrous? Or am I indeed part of a new movement that is trying to articulate gender and sexual complexity, trying to find a new language for gender and sexual complexity that doesn't fit any longer into the binary categories of gender?

UDI ALONI: The text of *Gender Trouble* is not easy, trying to understand the relation of language and body and gender, which may even come

before sex. You were traveling with your writing into different and esoteric lands. Did it surprise you that people suddenly got it?

JUDITH BUTLER: When I was first writing *Gender Trouble,* I did not yet
have a secure academic position. I was in a nontenure track position,
temporarily teaching part-time, and making very little money. I spent
a lot of time on my own. I did receive a wonderful fellowship at the
Institute for Advanced Study, which put me in touch with some major
feminist thinkers who gave me moral support. They said, "yes, go write
your book." But I never thought anyone would read the book. It never
occurred to me that it would be a popular book, never occurred to me
that it would be translated into twenty-five languages, or whatever it
is. I was on my own. So I didn't know how to address an audience. I
didn't know how to write in a more open style. And, in a way, because I
didn't expect an audience, I didn't write for an audience. I didn't know
to whom I was writing or even for whom. Maybe I had a better sense
of for whom. But, sometimes, if you have a very fatalistic idea about
whether the words will be received, the fatalism gets spilled into the
prose. So I think that's part of the difficulty, quite frankly.

I think another reason for the difficulty is if you to try to call into
question commonsense assumptions about what it is to have a sex or
be a gender, you have to actually use a language that allows for ordinary language to be destabilized. You have to take people to another
perspective that's not one of common sense, that's not one of received
assumptions or even (sometimes) ordinary language. Now I actually
think that my language has become a little bit more ordinary, or a little more open, with time. I will never be a popular writer. But that's
because I'm now much more interested in persuading. At the time of
Gender Trouble, even though some people hadn't read the Freud or the
Lévi-Strauss or the Monique Wittig, they understood something was
happening and they were able to follow the train of thought. There was
a very strong criticism and an idea of performativity: the performativity of gender. And if those two points were understood, one could get
through the rest and see what was happening.

UDI ALONI: Before we go forward into the more political realm, I want to
take a step back to philosophy. You are a scholar of Hegel. So there's the
part of philosophy, and there's activism.

JUDITH BUTLER: I'm just now finishing my course on Hegel—on Kant,
Hegel, and Marx. I love reading Hegel. For me, he is one of the most
interesting theorists in the world. I'm never tired of him. If I were an

activist all the time, I would be very unhappy. I need my work in philosophy and literature, a work that is not always rationalized by an explicit political agenda. That is also true of my love of Kafka. I wrote a piece on Alfred North Whitehead; there's not a moment of politics in the entire essay. It's actually about feeling.

UDI ALONI: But it's important that there's a part that is not rationalized by politics.

JUDITH BUTLER: It's not trying to rationalize the politics. Surely there are connections, resonances. There are reasons why I care about Hegel and the problem of recognition, the problem of time, and the question of the unhappy consciousness. I do think that these issues resonate with cultural formations that are politically relevant, but I'm not always drawing those links. I think that the engagement with philosophical literary texts in a close way is an extremely important exercise of reading and criticism. It's an exercise that I hope to be able to teach to my students, and I don't really care whether they come out politically—or whatever they think politically is set aside at the moment we read that. Now, of course, some Althusserian may come in and have his argument against Hegel, and I may say, "fine, let's look at the text and see whether Hegel commits the sin that Althusser says he does." But I have no interest in guiding them to a political conclusion. That would ruin my day. (*Laughs*.)

UDI ALONI: That may be a detour later in our conversation, when we speak about cultural boycott. (*Laughs*.) Maybe we'll save it for the end.

After you became "Judith Butler," we started to hear more about Jews and Jewish texts. People came to hear you speak about gender and suddenly they were faced with Gaza, divine violence. It felt that you had moved on to places that hold more interest for you. It almost felt like you had some closure on the previous matter. Is there a connection, a continuum, or is this a new phase?

JUDITH BUTLER: All right, let's go back further. I'm sure I've told you that I began to be interested in philosophy when I was fourteen, and I was in trouble in the synagogue. The rabbi said, "you are too talkative in class. You talk back, you are not well behaved. You have to come and have a tutorial with me." I said "OK, great!" I was thrilled. He said, "What do you want to study in the tutorial? This is your punishment. Now you have to study something seriously." I think he thought of me as unserious. I explained that I wanted to read existential theology focusing on Martin Buber. (I've never left Martin Buber.) I wanted to read Paul Tillich. I wanted look at the question of whether German idealism could be linked with National Socialism. Was the tradition of Kant and Hegel responsible in some way for the origins of National Socialism? My third question was why Spinoza was excommunicated from the synagogue. I wanted to know what happened and whether the synagogue was justified.

So I entered philosophy through three very different and distinct Jewish preoccupations: A real interest in what could be left of god after 1945. Could you have a Jewish existential theology? An absolute horror about National Socialism and wanting to know whether intellectual positions that preceded it could be responsible for it—or, if not, how we would distinguish them. And also some suspicion that the synagogues maybe weren't always doing right by all the Jews. I wanted to know what the norms were by which you could stay in the synagogue and whether, by being philosophically critical, you ran the risk of being exiled from the synagogue. I suppose I identified with that question, because I was on probation.

UDI ALONI: Now I must be Jewish: what was your parents' relation to Judaism?

JUDITH BUTLER: My parents were practicing Jews. My mother grew up in an Orthodox synagogue and after my grandfather died, she went to a Conservative synagogue and a little later ended up in a Reform synagogue. My father was in reform synagogues from the beginning.

My mother's uncles and aunts were all killed in Hungary. My grandmother lost all of her relatives, except for the two nephews who came with them in the car when my grandmother went back in 1938 to see who she could rescue. It was important for me. I went to Hebrew school. But I also went after school to special classes on Jewish ethics because I was interested in the debates. So I didn't do just the minimum. Through high school, I suppose, I continued Jewish studies alongside my public school education.

UDI ALONI: And you showed me the photos of the bar mitzvah of your son as a good, proud Jewish mother. (*Laughs.*)

JUDITH BUTLER: (*Laughs.*) Yes, but he had leeway to come up with any interpretation he wanted of the story of Noah. He started his speech, his *parashah*, by saying that he didn't really believe in god, and there was a problem because he had to refer to god with a gendered pronoun. And he said that, if there were a god, he was quite sure that god didn't really have a gender, but he was going to use "he" just because it was easier.

So it's been there from the start, it's not as if I arrived at some place that I haven't always been in. I grew very skeptical of a certain kind of Jewish separatism in my youth. I mean, I saw the Jewish community was always with each other; they didn't trust anybody outside. You'd bring someone home, and the first question was "Are they Jewish, are they not Jewish?" Then I entered into a lesbian community in college—late college, graduate school—and the first thing they asked was, "Are you a feminist, are you not a feminist?" "Are you a lesbian, are you not a lesbian?" and I thought, "Enough with the separatism!"

It felt like the same kind of policing of the community. You only trust those who are absolutely like yourself, those who have signed a pledge of allegiance to this particular identity. Is that person really Jewish, maybe they're not so Jewish. I don't know if they're really Jewish. Maybe they're self-hating. Is that person lesbian? I think maybe they had a relationship with a man. What does that say about how true their identity was? I thought, I can't live in a world in which identity is being policed in this way.

But if I go back to your other question . . . In *Gender Trouble* there is a whole discussion of melancholy. What is the condition under which we fail to grieve for others? Or the condition under which we fail to be able to acknowledge a loss and to grieve a loss? I presumed, throughout my childhood, that this was a question the Jewish community was asking itself. It was also a question that I was interested in when I went to study in Germany. The famous Mitscherlich book on the incapacity to mourn, which was a criticism of German postwar culture, was very very interesting to me.

In the seventies and eighties, in the gay and lesbian community, it became clear to me that very often, when a relationship would break up, a gay person wouldn't be able to tell parents, his or her parents. There would be no public acknowledgment of the loss. It was as if there had never been a relationship and there had never been a loss. So here people were going through all kinds of emotional losses that were unacknowledged, and that became very acute during the AIDS crisis. I was most familiar with this in the U.S., where people were dying and there was no public acknowledgment of the death, and there was no public acknowledgment of what the relationships were that had been lost. In the earliest years of the AIDS crisis, there were many gay men who were unable to come out about the fact that their lovers were ill, A, and then dead, B.

They were unable to get access to the hospital to see their lovers, unable to call their parents and say, "I have just lost the love of my life" or "my lover has gone through a monstrous death and was denied medical support at the end, and now there is no public acknowledgment of this loss."

This was extremely important to my thinking throughout the eighties and nineties. But it also became important to me as I started to think about war. After 9/11 I was shocked by the fact that there was public mourning for many of the people who died in the attacks on the World Trade Center, less public mourning for those who died in the attack on the Pentagon, no public mourning for the illegal workers of the WTC, and, for a very long time, no public acknowledgment of the gay and lesbian families and relationships that had been destroyed by the loss of one of the partners in the bombings. Then we went to war very quickly, Bush having decided that the time for grieving was over. I think he said that, after ten days, the time for grieving was over and now was the time for action. At which point we started killing populations abroad with no clear rationale. And the populations we targeted for violence were ones that never appeared to us in pictures. We never got little obituaries for them. We never heard anything about what lives had been destroyed. And we still don't.

I then moved toward a different kind of theory, asking under what conditions certain lives are grievable and certain lives not grievable or ungrievable. It's clear to me that in Israel-Palestine, and in the violent conflicts that have taken place over the years, there is differential grieving. Certain lives become grievable within the Israeli press, for instance—highly grievable and highly valuable—and others are understood as ungrievable because they are understood as instruments of war or they are understood as outside the nation, outside religion, or outside that sense of belonging which makes for a grievable life. The question of grievability has linked my work on queer politics—especially the AIDS crisis—with my more contemporary work on war and violence, including the work on Israel-Palestine.

UDI ALONI: It's interesting because when the war on Gaza started I couldn't stay in Tel Aviv anymore. I visited the Galilee a lot. And suddenly I realized that many of the Palestinians who died in Gaza have families there, relatives who are citizens of Israel. What people didn't know is that there was a massed grief in Israel. Grief for families who died in Gaza, a grief within Israel, of citizens of Israel. And nobody in the country spoke about it, about the grief within Israel. It was shocking.

I want to say one thing about melancholy. When Gershom Scholem said that Shabtai Tzvi (who was considered to be a false messiah) had manic depression, Moshe Idel said, "what manic depression?" At that time there was no such thing as manic depression. Shabtai, in Hebrew, is Saturn; Saturn is melancholy. What he had was melancholy. And the Messiah is the one who tries to jump out of melancholy. It has nothing to do with manic depression. It's melancholy, and the Messiah tries to get out of it.

JUDITH BUTLER: Yes, although if you look at Klein on manic depression, you'll see that she is deriving it from Freud's analysis of melancholy.

UDI ALONI: That's true . . . Do you want to have a small break?

UDI ALONI: Where did we stop?

JUDITH BUTLER: Grieving.

UDI ALONI: Grieving . . . melancholy . . . Melanie Klein.

JUDITH BUTLER: I think at some point it would be interesting to talk about what it means to be cold or to practice coldness in relationship to the death of members of another population or an ostensible enemy population or something like that. You talked about people celebrating in Tel Aviv and being pleased that they were winning the war or triumphing over others or seeing massive destruction in Gaza. What does it mean to be elated or excited or happy seeing that? Also, what kind of coldness has been practiced? What kind of coldness is the precondition of that celebration?

UDI ALONI: Perhaps there are two kinds of celebrations. There is one of despair, people sitting in Tel Aviv drinking, getting drunk, but that's beyond decadence and they're not really happy. I don't judge those people. But during Gaza it felt different; it wasn't that way. It was a continued celebration. Something changed. You remember how, beforehand, I had been empathic for Israel. But something really changed with Gaza. It broke my heart. I felt I wasn't one of them. It felt like it wasn't even indifference; it was almost happiness. Maybe I'm exaggerating, but it was really hard to see. I was ready for BDS [the Boycott, Divestment, and Sanctions movement]. With the exception of those few holy people who go out and fight, the young "anarchists," the people who were in [the documentary film] Bil'in Habibti, those who feed the refugees and illegal immigrants at night and go to demonstrations during the day. I was always so optimistic, but . . .

JUDITH BUTLER: The Israeli government and the media started to say that everyone who was killed or injured in Gaza was a member of Hamas; or that they were all being used as part of the war effort; that even the children were instruments of the war effort; that the Palestinians put them out there, in the targets, to show that Israelis would kill children, and this was actually part of a war effort. At this point, every single living being who is Palestinian becomes a war instrument. They are all, in their being, or by virtue of being Palestinian, declaring war on Israel or seeking the destruction of Israel.

So any and all Palestinian lives that are killed or injured are no longer understood to be lives, no longer understood to be living, no longer understood even to be human in a recognizable sense, but they are artillery. The bodies themselves are artillery. And, of course, the extreme instance of that is the suicide bomber, who has become unpopular in recent years. That is the instance in which a body becomes artillery or becomes part of a violent act. If that figure gets extended to the entire Palestinian population, then there is no living human population anymore, and no one who is killed there can be grieved. Because everyone who is a living Palestinian is, in their being, a declaration of war or a threat to the existence of Israel or pure military artillery, materiel. They have been transformed, in the Israeli war imaginary, into pure war instruments.

So when a people who believes that another people is out to destroy them sees all the means of destruction killed, or some extraordinary number of the means of destruction destroyed, they are thrilled, because they think their safety and well-being and happiness are being purchased, are being achieved through this destruction. And what happened with the perspective from the outside, the outside media, was extremely interesting to me. The European press, the U.S. press, the South American press, the East Asian press all raised questions about the excessive violence of the Gaza assault. It was very strange to see how the Israeli media made the claim that people on the outside do not understand; that people on the outside are antisemitic; that people on the outside are blaming Israel for defending themselves when they themselves, if attacked, would do the exact same thing.

UDI ALONI: I have three different questions, but I think they are connected. I prefer to ask all of them at once, then let you answer as you wish. First: why Israel-Palestine? Is this directly connected to your Jewishness? Second: the way in which you describe the Palestinians under the gaze of the Israelis . . . it's not the *homo sacer* of Agamben?

JUDITH BUTLER: No, no.

UDI ALONI: OK, that's totally different. Third: when we were working on the Toronto Declaration, I felt that lively Tel Aviv functions precisely in order to present the native as the barbarian at the gate. This liberal, beautiful place is used to describe the Palestinians as savages whose lives are not of equal value. I'm curious as to whether you agree with this structure. It seems like the West uses its high culture to construct an image of a people with minor importance, such that it's easy to see them dying. So there are really two questions.

JUDITH BUTLER: There's the question of Jewishness and there's the question of Zionism. I grew up in a very strong Zionist community with very strong beliefs about Israel as a postwar sanctuary, Israel as a democratic state, Israel as under siege by forces of antisemitism. I certainly learned, as a very young person, that the legitimation of the state of Israel followed from the Nazi genocide against the Jews. And it took me a long time to understand that the basis of the state was discriminatory, that the Palestinian inhabitants had been forcibly removed, and that there had been substantial debates about how best to make a state and what form that state should have. Some of those debates happened within Zionism, and some of them were anti-Zionist debates. In my early twenties my mind started opening up to a critique of Zionism.

But let me just say this as a way of being succinct about it: as a Jew, I was taught that it was ethically imperative to speak up and to speak out against arbitrary state violence. That was part of what I learned when I learned about the Second World War and the concentration camps. There were those who would and could speak out against state racism and state violence, and it was imperative that we be able to speak out. Not just for Jews, but for any number of people. There was an entire idea of social justice that emerged for me from the consideration of the Nazi genocide.

I would also say that what became really hard for me is that if one wanted to criticize Israeli state violence—precisely because as a Jew one is under obligation to criticize excessive state violence and state racism—then one is in a bind, because one is told that one is either self-hating as a Jew or engaging antisemitism. And yet, for me, it comes out of a certain Jewish value of social justice. So how can I fulfill my obligation as a Jew to speak out against an injustice when, in speaking out against Israeli state and military injustice, I am accused of not being a good enough Jew or of being a self-hating Jew? This is the bind of my current situation.

Let me say one other thing about Jewish values. There are two things I took from Jewish philosophy and my Jewish formation that were really important for me . . . well there are many. There are many. Sitting *shiva*, for instance, explicit grieving. I thought it was one of the most beautiful rituals of my youth. There were several people who died in my youth, and there were several moments when whole communities gathered in order to make sure that those who had suffered terrible losses were taken up and brought back into the community and given a way to affirm life again. So that was really crucial to me. The other idea was that life is transient and, because of that, because there is no afterworld, because we don't have any hopes in a final redemption, we have to take *especially* good care of life in the here and now. That no one's death is going to be redeemed in a future world or in an afterworld; there is no redemption. Which means that life has to be protected. It is precarious. I would even go so far as to say that precarious life is, in a way, a Jewish value for me.

The third thing I would say is that I take Diaspora very seriously. The idea that the scattering of the Jews among the non-Jews produced a different kind of ethos; it meant that we always had to deal with the notion of how to live among those to whom we have obligations and from whom we need protection. In other words (*laughs*), there is the paranoid idea of Diaspora: be careful living with non-Jews, keep your door shut, arrive first with your rifle before they arrive with theirs. Yet there is another notion. You're living with the non-Jews, which means you have to figure out: what is the ethics of alterity? How do you live in a world that is truly mixed racially, mixed religiously? Where you live next to someone you never chose? Where you come up against people from various backgrounds? Where there is not necessarily a common background or common understanding? That struck me as the nonseparatist tradition in Judaism that I valued and that I sought to continue. So, in a way, my politics are profoundly diasporic. That also means that there are Jewish values and Jewish politics that are not necessarily framed within contemporary political Zionism. But it is still Jewish, and it is, in fact, an enormously important tradition to keep alive. That means that there's an enormously important set of debates about what it means to be Jewish or to allow Jewishness into your politics that cannot be preemptively decided by the Zionist framework.

UDI ALONI: May I challenge you here a little bit?

JUDITH BUTLER: Yes.

UDI ALONI: I realized something, through your way of thinking. A classic mistake that people made with *Gender Trouble* was the notion that body and language are static. But everything is in dynamic and constant movement; the original never exists. In a way I felt the same with the Diaspora and the emancipation. Neither are static. No one came before the other. The Diaspora, when it was static, became separatist, became the *shtetl*. And when the emancipation was realized, it became an ethnocratic state; it also became separatist, a reconstruction of the ghetto. So maybe the tension between the two, emancipation and Diaspora, without choosing one or the other, is the only way to keep us out of ethnocentrism. In the beginning of Zionism there was a huge group of binationalists there—people who were deeply interested in being open to the other. When they came to Israel, the Zionists tried to clear them out, to get rid of everyone different. I suppose my idea is not yet fully formulated. It relates to the way I felt that my grandfather was open to the language of exile while being connected to the land at the same time. By being open to both, emancipation and Diaspora, we might avoid falling into ethnocentrism.

JUDITH BUTLER: You have a tension between Diaspora and emancipation. But what I am thinking of is perhaps something a little different. I have to say, first of all, that I do not think that there can be emancipation with and through the establishment of a state that restricts citizenship, in the way that it does, on the basis of religion.

UDI ALONI: I absolutely agree.

JUDITH BUTLER: So, in my view, any effort to retain the idea of emancipation when you don't have a state that extends equal rights of citizenship to Jews and non-Jews alike is, for me, bankrupt. It's bankrupt.

UDI ALONI: Absolutely. That's why I would say that there should be binationalism from the beginning.

JUDITH BUTLER: Or even multinationalism. Maybe even a kind of citizenship without regard to religion, race, ethnicity, etc. In any case, the more important point here is that there are those who clearly believe that Jews who are not in Israel, who are in the *galut*, are actually either in need of return—they have not yet returned or they are not and cannot be representative of the Jewish people. So the question is: what does it mean to transform the idea of *galut* into Diaspora? In other words, Diaspora is another tradition, one that involves the scattering without return. A scattering of Jew among the non-Jew without return to purely Jewish or to the exclusively Jewish home. That's a very different idea. I am very critical of this idea of return, and I think *galut* very often demeans the diasporic traditions within Judaism.

UDI ALONI: In that regard, it's also interesting to think about the places from which we speak. As an Israeli, I feel that a Jew who is not in Israel has no reason to "return." As somebody who was born in Israel with Hebrew as my language, I fight against those who might force this "purity" upon me.

JUDITH BUTLER: But that's good. That's to bring a diasporic principle into the homeland. If we take the idea of mixity or the impure—which in some ways belongs to the Diaspora, but it doesn't have to—and we bring it back to the question of Palestine, then, I think, we're closer to [Edward] Said's formulation. That big question that, in some sense, he has bequeathed to us to take up in his place. Which is whether that idea of an ethics of alterity—an alterity that is built into the identity itself—can become a basis for a new political vision.

In a way it would not matter if one started from Israel-Palestine or another geographical location. What is at stake is the idea of giving up religious purity and political separatism as the ultimate or the only legitimate Jewish ideals. There are other traditions, both Jewish and non-Jewish—I would say necessarily Jewish and non-Jewish—that can be called upon to produce a different vision.

UDI ALONI: When I tried to explain to my brother, who's a Zionist, why I am not a Zionist, I argued that the issue is no longer ideological. At night, when he dreams, he hopes to wake up to a place where there are no Palestinians. When he wakes up and sees Palestinians, he fights for them as a liberal who believes in human rights. For me, if I dream that there are no Palestinians there, it's my worst nightmare. Today, it's no longer an ideological question, but rather: what is your dream about this land?

I thought that if we make a film about binationalism, the opening scene should be a meeting of the First Jewish Congress for Binationalism. It could be a secret meeting in which we all discuss who we would like to be our first president, and the others there send me to choose you . . .

JUDITH BUTLER: (*Laughs.*) That's very sweet.

UDI ALONI: because we need to have a woman, and she has to be queer. But not only queer, and not only woman. She has to be the most important Jewish philosopher today.

JUDITH BUTLER: But seriously, you know, it would be astonishing to think about what forms of political participation would still be possible on a model of federal government. Like a federated authority for Palestine-Israel that was actually governed by a strong constitution that guaranteed rights regardless of cultural background, religion, ethnicity, race, and the rest. In a way, binationalism goes part of the way toward explaining what has to happen. And I completely agree with you that there has to be a cultural movement that overcomes hatred and paranoia and that actually draws on questions of cohabitation. Living in mixity and in diversity, accepting your neighbor, finding modes of living together, ta'ayush. This is obviously absolutely crucial. And no political solution, at a purely procedural level, is going to be successful if there is no bilingual education, if there are no ways of reorganizing neighborhoods, if there are no ways of reorganizing territory, bringing down the wall, accepting the neighbors you have, and accepting that there are profound obligations that emerge from being adjacent to another people in this way . . . from being mixed in with another people in this way.

So I agree with you. But I think we have to get over the idea that a state has to express a nation. And if we have a binational state, it's expressing two nations. Only when binationalism deconstructs the idea of a nation can we hope to think about what a state, what a polity might look like that would actually extend equality. It is no longer the question of "two peoples," as Martin Buber put it. There is extraordinary complexity and intermixing among both the Jewish and the Palestinian populations. I think we need to give up the idea that a state expresses the cultural identity of its people. So there will be those who say "OK, well a state that expresses two cultural identities." No. State should not be in the business of expressing cultural identity.

UDI ALONI: Why do we use term *binationalism*? For me it is the beginning of a process, not the end. We could say "multinationalism" or "one-state solution." Why do we prefer to use the term *binationalism* rather than *one state* now?

JUDITH BUTLER: I believe that people have reasonable fears that a one-state solution would ratify the existing marginalization and impoverishment of the Palestinian people. That Palestine would be forced to accept a kind of Bantustan existence.

UDI ALONI: Or vice versa, for the Jews.

JUDITH BUTLER: Well, the Jews would be afraid of losing demographic majority if voting rights were extended to Palestinians. I do think that there is the fundamental question of "who is this we?" Who are we? The question of binationalism raises the question of who is the "we" who decides what kind of polity is best for this land. The "we" has to be heterogeneous; it has to be mixed. Everyone who is there and has a claim . . . and the claims are various. They come from traditional and legal grounds of belonging that are quite complicated. So one has to be open to that complication. One has to be open to the heterogeneity of the population. And one has to be committed to living beyond racism and beyond ethnocentrism. You live with others who come from other backgrounds, you are up against them, your children marry them, they go to school with you, they speak your language and you speak theirs, you are committed to translation as a societal and public practice. It's a whole commitment to a way of living in difference.

UDI ALONI: You gave an important speech in New York. It was very relevant for Israel, even though it was about the Netherlands. You spoke about the relationship between the lesbian and gay community and the Muslim immigrants there. In a way, it represented the relationship of the West to the Muslim world.

Israel-Palestine is a meeting point of East and West, of North and South, of many places. Binationalism is also a space that challenges the liberal refusal to live with those who don't respect feminism or gay rights. When I said that you, Judith Butler, should represent us in the Binational Congress, it was in this sense. How do you see the dialogue between the lesbian and gay community and Muslim immigrants in the Netherlands? This seems very relevant to the ways in which Israelis from Tel Aviv interact with Palestinians. Do you agree that there a connection?

JUDITH BUTLER: I do. I do agree that there is a connection. In general, I think that we have to be very wary of the way in which the United States used feminism to wage its war against Afghanistan. I think we have to be very wary of how the Dutch government uses its protection of the rights of homosexuals to close its borders to new immigrants from Turkey or North Africa. I think we have to be very careful of imagining that Israel is a democracy that will protect the rights of gays and lesbians against an incursion from Islam or from some sense of censorship or religious intolerance that will come from Palestine. I think that these are moves that, first of all, seek to export homophobia and misogyny as if they belong to the "other." Certainly, in the Netherlands, one could ask, for instance, about domestic violence, misogyny, homophobia, and racism within the traditional Dutch community, and there is still a lot of work to be done. One could certainly ask, in the United States, why Bush was suddenly worried about feminism in Afghanistan when he decimated aid to dependent families and made it much harder for single women to get state assistance or government funds to learn new skills. These are incredibly inconsistent policies.

My worry, of course, and what I said to the queer movement in Holland was that I think we have to remember that the queer movement, in particular, is a movement that is based on alliance. And it's not identitarian. It's not about representing only lesbian, gay people who are certified. (*Laughs.*) Or lesbian, gay, maybe bisexual people. Or lesbian, gay, maybe transgendered people, but maybe not transgendered people. It's not an identity-based movement. It's a movement that is actually about alliance. So, for instance, the queer movement began, I think very importantly, as a movement against homophobia. It said, "Hey, we don't really care who you sleep with, we don't really care what your fantasy life is like, we don't care who you're dreaming about. Come join us to fight homophobia. Come join us to fight the lack of funding for AIDS research, the lack of community support for those who are harassed by virtue of their sexual orientation or their gender presentation." It didn't really matter who you were or what your practices were. But that alliance also extended to questions of racism, to questions of disability. It was about forming community among subjugated people and objecting to legal and institutional restrictions that sought to disenfranchise minority populations. So no queer person should be in an alliance that is meant to produce a disenfranchised minority or to reproduce the status quo in which there is a disenfranchised minority, whether that minority is defined in terms of its sexual or its gender orientation, or presentation, or whether it is about race or religion or other notions of cultural or national belonging. The point is to engage a politics that is against strategies, especially state strategies, of minoritization that are unacceptable.

Of course, there are antagonisms in any alliance of that kind. Somebody who is fighting primarily against racism may not care so much about questions of sexual oppression or gender regulation, and somebody who is fighting for sexual liberation may not care so much about racism. But those people, if they are committed to a broader alliance politics, will have to come up against one another and will have to go through a set of antagonisms in order to figure out how to stay in alliance together.

So yes, there are antagonisms. There are clearly antagonisms. But if we start with the idea (if the state comes out with the idea or if an identity-based movement comes out with the idea) that, "oh, we have to be against Palestine because Palestine is homophobia," that is simply nonsense. Gays and lesbians have suffered sexual minoritization globally, as have Palestinians, who suffered minoritization and disenfranchisement. The real question is what does an alliance look like that can actually analyze those specific forms of disenfranchisement and produce a solidarity (which does not mean a unity), a solidarity with antagonism built in that can actually look at the way in which the state seeks to divide these populations and pit them against one another. An alliance that is against state violence and state strategies of minoritization is going to be wise about that strategy and resist the lure in favor of thinking about what interlocking minorities need to do together. Queer is about interlocking minorities; it has never been about an identity politics.

UDI ALONI: I must say, you should take a lot of credit for the fact that, in Israel, many of the people who follow you (who happen to be lesbians and not gay men) are lesbians against the Occupation.

JUDITH BUTLER: Listen, they're great! Black Laundry.

UDI ALONI: Black Laundry. And it's interesting that the gay men who support the idea march alongside them in the pride parade. "No pride in the Occupation." It is beautiful to see how philosophy becomes practice.

JUDITH BUTLER: No, no. It doesn't work this way, because the movement also produces the philosopher. I come out of the movement, I come out of these conversations, I come out of these struggles, and then I put it into some theoretical form. But I have not determined this. It is a back and forth.

UDI ALONI: It's a back and forth. In Israel, this was one of the few things that gave me hope. Because it was unbearable to see the pride parade with "I'm proud to be a soldier"—signs like that.

Now I want to move to the last part of the conversation. It was over three years ago, at the beginning of the second Lebanon war, that Slavoj Žižek came to Israel to give a speech on my film *Forgiveness*. The Campaign for the Academic and Cultural Boycott of Israel asked him not to come to the Jerusalem Film Festival. They said that I should show my film—as Israelis shouldn't boycott Israel—but they asked international figures to boycott the festival.

Žižek, who was the subject of one of the films in the festival, said he would not speak about that film. But he asked: why not support the opposition in Israel by speaking about *Forgiveness*? They answered that he could support the opposition, but not in an official venue. He did not know what to do.

Žižek chose to ask for your advice. Your position then, if I recall correctly, was that it was most important to exercise solidarity with colleagues who chose nonviolent means of resistance and that it was a mistake to take money from Israeli cultural institutions. Your suggestion to Žižek was that he speak about the film without being a guest of the festival. He gave back the money and announced that he was not a guest. There was no decision about endorsing or not endorsing a boycott. For me, at the time, the concept of cultural boycott was kind of shocking, a strange concept. The movement has grown a lot since, and I know that you've done a lot of thinking about it. I wonder what you think about this movement now, the full Boycott, Divestment, and Sanctions movement (BDS), three years after that confusing event?

JUDITH BUTLER: I think that the BDS movement has taken several forms, and it is probably important to distinguish among them. I would say that around six or seven years ago there was a real confusion about what was being boycotted, what goes under the name of *boycott*. There were some initiatives that seemed to be directed against Israeli academics, or Israeli filmmakers, cultural producers, or artists that did not distinguish between their citizenship and their participation, active or passive, in Occupation politics. We must keep in mind that the BDS movement has always been focused on the Occupation. It is not a referendum on Zionism, and it does not take an explicit position on the one-state or two-state solution. And then there were those who sought to distinguish boycotting individual Israelis from boycotting the Israeli institutions. But it is not always easy to know how to make the distinction between who is an individual and who is an institution. And I think a lot of people within the U.S. and Europe just backed away, thinking that it was potentially discriminatory to boycott individuals or, indeed, institutions on the basis of citizenship, even though many of those who were reluctant very much wanted to find a way to support a nonviolent resistence to the Occupation.

But now I feel that it has become more possible, more urgent to reconsider the politics of the BDS. It is not that the principles of the BDS have changed: they have not. But there are now ways to think about implementing the BDS that keep in mind the central focus: any event, practice, or institution that seeks to normalize the Occupation or presupposes that "ordinary" cultural life can continue without an explicit opposition to the Occupation is itself complicit with the Occupation. We can think of this as passive complicity, if you like. But the main point is to challenge those institutions that seek to separate the Occupation from other cultural activities. The idea is that we cannot participate in cultural institutions that act as if there is no occupation or that refuse to take a clear and strong stand against the Occupation and dedicate their activities to its undoing.

So, with this in mind, we can ask, what does it mean to engage in boycott? It means that, for those of us on the outside, we can only go to an Israeli institution, or an Israeli cultural event, in order to use the occasion to call attention to the brutality and injustice of the Occupation and to articulate an opposition to it. I think that's what Naomi Klein did, and I think it actually opened up another route for interpreting the BDS principles. It is no longer possible for me to come to Tel Aviv and talk about gender, Jewish philosophy, or Foucault, as interesting as that might be for me; it is certainly not possible to take money from an organization or university or a cultural organization that is not explicitly and actively anti-Occupation, acting as if the cultural event within Israeli borders was not happening against the background of Occupation. Against the background of the assault on, and continuing siege of, Gaza. It is this unspoken and violent background of "ordinary" cultural life that needs to become the explicit object of cultural and political production and criticism. Historically, I see no other choice, since affirming the status quo means affirming the Occupation. One cannot "set aside" the radical impoverishment, the malnutrition, the limits on mobility, the intimidation and harassment at the borders, and the exercise of state violence in both Gaza and the West Bank and talk about other matters in public. If one were to talk about other matters, then one would be actively engaged in producing a limited public sphere of discourse that has repression and hence the continuation of violence as its aim.

Let us remember that the politics of boycott are not just matters of "conscience" for left intellectuals within Israel or outside. The point of the boycott is to produce and enact an international consensus that calls for the state of Israel to comply with international law. The point is to insist on the rights of self-determination for Palestinians, to end the Occupation and colonization of Arab lands, to dismantle the wall that continues the illegal seizure of Palestinian lands, and to honor several UN resolutions that have been consistently defied by the Israeli state, including UN resolution 194, which insists upon the rights of refugees from 1948.

So an approach to the cultural boycott in particular would have to be one that opposes the normalization of the Occupation in order to bring into public discourse the basic principles of injustice at stake. There are many ways to articulate those principles, and this is where intellectuals are doubtless under a political obligation to become innovative, to use the cultural means at our disposal to make whatever interventions we can. The point is not simply to refuse contact and forms of cultural and monetary exchange—although sometimes these are most important—but rather, affirmatively, to lend one's support to the strongest antiviolent movement against the Occupation, which not only affirms international law, but establishing exchanges with Palestinian cultural and academic workers, cultivating international consensus on the rights of the Palestinian people, but also altering that hegemonic presumption within the global media that any critique of Israel is implicitly antidemocratic or antisemitic. Surely it has always been the best part of the Jewish intellectual tradition to insist upon the ethical relation to the non-Jew, the extension of equality and justice, and the refusal to keep silent in the face of egregious wrongs.

UDI ALONI: I want to share with you what Riham Barghouti, from BDS New York, told me. She said that, for her, BDS is a movement for everyone who supports the end of the Occupation, equal rights for the Palestinians of 1948, and the moral and legal demand of the Palestinians' right of return. She suggested that each person who is interested decide how much of the BDS spectrum she is ready to accept. In other words, endorsement of the boycott movement is a continuous decision, not a categorical one. Just don't tell us what our guidelines are. You can agree with our principles, join the movement, and decide on the details on your own.

JUDITH BUTLER: Yes, well, one can imagine a bumper sticker: "What part of 'justice' do you fail to understand?" It is surely important that many prominent Israelis have begun to accept part of the BDS principles, and this may well be an incremental way to make the boycott effort more understandable. But it may also be important to ask, why is it that so many left Israelis have trouble entering into collaborative politics with Palestinians on the issue of the boycott, and why is it that the Palestinian formulations of the boycott do not form the basis for that joint effort? After all, the BDS call has been in place since 2005; it is an established and growing movement, and the basic principles have been worked out. Any Israeli can join that movement, and they would doubtless find that they would immediately be in greater contact with Palestinians than they otherwise would be. The BDS provides the most powerful rubric for Israeli-Palestinian cooperative actions. This is doubtless surprising and paradoxical for some, but it strikes me as historically true.

It's interesting to me that very often Israelis I speak to say, "we cannot enter into collaboration with the Palestinians because they don't want to collaborate with us, and we don't blame them." Or: "we would put them in a bad position if we were to invite them to our conferences." Both of these positions presume the Occupation as background, but they do not address it directly. Indeed, these kinds of positions are biding time when there is no time but now to make one's opposition known. Very often such utterances take on a position of self-paralyzing guilt, which actually keeps them from taking active and productive responsibility for opposing the Occupation, making change even more remote. Sometimes it seems to me that they make boycott politics into a question of moral conscience, which is different from a political commitment. If it is a moral issue, then "I" as an Israeli have a responsibility to speak out for or against, to sink into self-berating or become self-flagellating in public and become a moral icon. But these kinds of moral solutions are, I think, besides the point. They continue to make "Israeli" identity into the basis of the political position, which is a kind of tacit nationalism. Perhaps the point is to oppose the manifest injustice in the name of broader principles of international law and the opposition to state violence, the disenfranchisement politically and economically of the Palestinian people. If you happen to be Israeli, then unwittingly your position shows that Israelis can and do take positions in favor of justice, and that should not be surprising. But it does not make it an "Israeli" position.

But let me return to the question of whether boycott politics undermines collaborative ventures or opens them up. My wager is that the minute you come out in favor of some boycott, divestment, or sanctions strategy, Udi, you will have many collaborators among Palestinians. I think many people fear that the boycott is against collaboration, but, in fact, Israelis have the power to produce enormous collaborative networks if they agree that they will use their public power, their cultural power, to oppose the Occupation through the most powerful nonviolent means available. Things change the minute you say, "we cannot continue to act as normal."

Of course, I myself really want to be able to talk about novels, film, and philosophy, sometimes quite apart from politics. Unfortunately, I cannot do that in Israel now. I cannot do it until the Occupation has been successfully and actively challenged. The fact is that there is no possibility of going to Israel without being used either as an example of boycott or as an example of antiboycott. So when I went, many years ago, and the rector of Tel Aviv University said, "Look how lucky we are. Judith Butler has come to Tel Aviv University, a sign that she does not accept the boycott," I was instrumentalized against my will. And I realized I cannot function in that public space without already being defined in the boycott debate. So there is no escape from it. One can stay quiet and accept the status quo or one can take a position that seeks to challenge the status quo.

I hope one day there will be a different political condition where I might go there and talk about Hegel, but that is not possible now. I am very much looking forward to teaching at Birzeit in February. It has a strong gender and women's studies faculty, and I understand that the students are interested in discussing questions of war and cultural analysis. I also clearly stand to learn. The boycott is not just about saying "no"—it is also a way to give shape to one's work, to make alliances, and to insist on international norms of justice. To work to the side of the problem of the Occupation is to participate in its normalization. And the way that normalization works is to efface or distort that reality within public discourse. As a result, neutrality is not an option.

UDI ALONI: So we're boycotting normalization.

JUDITH BUTLER: That's what we're boycotting. We are against normalization. And you know what? There are going to be many tactics for disrupting the normalization of the Occupation. Some of us will be well-equipped to intervene with images and words, and others will continue demonstrations and other forms of cultural and political statements. The question is not what your passport says (if you have a passport), but what you do. We are talking about what happens in the activity itself. Does it disrupt and contest the normalization of the Occupation?

UDI ALONI: You remember that in the Toronto Declararation against the spotlight on Tel Aviv at the film festival it was very clear that we do not boycott individuals, but the Israeli foreign minister tried to argue that we were boycotting individuals. Yet the question is about institutions.

On that note, I want to clarify: you will not speak in Tel Aviv University . . . forever? Well, not forever . . .

JUDITH BUTLER: When it's a fabulous binational university (*laughs*).

UDI ALONI: And it's a movement.

JUDITH BUTLER: It is a movement. And it will stay alive as a movement as long as there continue to be innovative ways of implementing and publicizing its principles and as long as many different tactics can work together. What it offers is a general set of principles to consult as we decide what to do, and it situates our decisions in the context of a growing nonviolent movement—it may well be the name for a future beyond disillusionment.

EPILOGUE

Oh, Weakness; or, Shylock with a Split *S*

... and what's his reason? I am a Jew. Hath
not a Jew eyes? Hath not a Jew hands, organs,
dimensions, senses, affections, passions; fed with
the same food, hurt with the same weapons, subject
to the same diseases, heal'd by the same means,
warm'd and cool'd by the same winter and summer
as a Christian is? If you prick us, do we not bleed?
If you tickle us, do we not laugh? If you poison us,
do we not die? And if you wrong us, shall we not revenge?
If we are like you in the rest, we will resemble you in that.
If a Jew wrong a Christian, what is his humility?
Revenge. If a Christian wrong a Jew, what should his
sufferance be by Christian example? Why, revenge.
The villainy you teach me, I will execute,
and it shall go hard but I will better the instruction.

—Shakespeare, *The Merchant of Venice*

BEFORE THE LAW

One morning, when the storm started shaking the treetops and the dogs howled in terror because of the thunder and flashes of lightning, fifty children of different ages went out to school in the city of Lydda in Israel. During the day most of them worked diligently, hoping the storm would abate so they could go back safely to the home where they were born and raised. At the sound of the bell announcing the end of the day, they were off and running back home. The tempest intensified, and with it the will to find oneself in the warmth of one's home, in the warmth of the seven homes of their extended family—the Abu Eid family.

But when they got home, the home was utterly destroyed. Fifty children stood shocked in front of their seven demolished homes, an uprooted palm tree and water bursting out of the broken pipe; they stood frozen in front of the haphazardly strewn furniture and the cries of their mothers facing the destructive power all by themselves. It was not the tempest that wrecked the homes of the fifty children, nor was it the conflagration of forest fires; the culprits were demolition contractors of the Judeo-democratic State of Israel, backed by the Judeo-democratic Supreme Court. The demolition was accompanied by the gloating looks on the faces of their Jewish neighbors.

Could it be that the Court did not consider the welfare of the children, citizens of the state, only because of their Palestinian ethnicity? Now that the slogan for the Jewishification of Lydda is back, may we suspect the Supreme Court of once again taking an active part in the crimes of racism and the renewing of the Nakba?

When the hip-hop group D.A.M.'s member Suhell Nafar and I arrived, everything was already in ruins: heaps of rubble in the heart of the neighborhood for all to see and beware. Suhell photographed the ruins. I wiped a tear. But rage is in order here, not pity. We must be strong and think of ways to struggle. Meanwhile, a protest tent and a shelter for the families were set up nearby. The demolishers did not leave a house or two for the families to take refuge in, nor did they wait for the spring in order to alleviate the suffering. It seems they wanted the destruction to be as painful and humiliating as possible.

HOW WOULD YOU SAY *NAKBA* IN THE PRESENT CONTINUOUS TENSE?

There are many forces in Israeli politics that hope the Palestinians in Israel will rebel, and so, in due course, it should be possible to expel them from the country. They say they do not seek a final solution since they oppose genocide; they are not barbarians. They only want to make sure the Arabs don't multiply like rabbits on Israel's holy land. That's why there are loyalty laws; that's why there is constant encroachment upon their living space; that's why more and more actions that distance the Arab citizens of Israel from the political, cultural, and physical arena are taking place.

Destroying a home is a cruel action in any context, but it's even crueler when it serves to emphasize who is allowed to stay in their home even without permission and who isn't. The Supreme Court is aware of the neighboring Jewish neighborhood, Ganei Aviv, which was approved retroactively.

The Supreme Court is aware of the fact that for the Jewish neighborhood a bridge was built over the railroad tracks so that Jewish children would not be run over, while for the Arabs the railroad was laid inside the neighborhood without a single bridge. The Supreme Court is aware of the neighborhoods that are being built for the religious settlers in Lydda instead of a luxurious neighborhood for those Arabs whose land the state covets.

The Supreme Court knows that in the mixed cities of Jaffa, Acre, and Lydda cruel creeping deprivation of Palestinian citizens of Israel is taking place.

The Court knows and collaborates. With my own eyes I saw Her Honor Dorit Beinisch de facto and retroactively approving a blatantly illegal new settler neighborhood situated on the robbed land of Bil'in. One cannot but wonder why she won't retroactively approve a neighborhood of Palestinians in Lydda, where they've been living for decades.

The Supreme Court of the State of Israel is a loyal servant of a racist ideology that does not differ much from the racism of the rabbis who signed the manifesto of the Israeli Nuremberg Laws. Like the court in Shakespeare's *The Merchant of Venice*, which bends the civil law in favor of the Christian ruler in order to harm Shylock the Jew, the Supreme Court in our reality has become a verbal whitewashing machine for occupation and plundering on a nationalist basis.

Do Beinisch and other liberal Israeli Jews really believe that there is a fundamental difference between expulsion under the guise of democracy and expulsion under the guise of theocracy? Is there a difference between the Jewish National Fund, which forbids leasing lands to Arabs on nationalist grounds, and the fascist Rabbi Eliyahu of Safed, who forbids it on religious grounds? For the Palestinians, they are both parts of the same well-oiled machine that advances their banishment from the public space and maintains them as strangers in their homeland.

THE NON-EUROPEAN SHYLOCK

Recently I saw Al Pacino playing the role of his life as Shylock on Broadway. Having deprived him of all his possessions, the enlightened people of Venice forced him to be baptized a Christian. The director added a shocking scene, which does not appear in Shakespeare's play. In the scene we see the people of Venice baptizing the defeated Shylock. Al Pacino comes out of his baptism wet and humiliated, bent and helpless before the "mighty and merciful" ruler who had spared his life having taken his home, his faith, and his dignity.

Despondently, Shylock picks up his fallen skullcap from the floor, puts it back on his head, and stares at the complacent people of Venice. The stare begins despondent and defeated, but it strengthens and sharpens and says: I, Shylock, adherent of the Mosaic faith, believe in a jealous and vengeful God; I shall return to take what's lawfully mine.

Edward Said could have seen the ultimate non-European in Shylock. Shylock refuses to speak for the God of grace. He, the weak who refuses to be a victim, knows that the virtue of grace is imposed upon him, in order not to act violently against the master, the master that never had mercy on him. Shylock, who understands the ruler's ruse, positions his own god as the god of justice against the Christian god of grace. He might too seek grace, but he soon identifies the grace as a part of the oppression mechanism to which he is subjected.

We can see Shylock as the Jew who was slaughtered in Europe and has come back to life as the contemporary European Muslim. It is possible that he has been resurrected only to take his revenge and be slaughtered anew. Tragically, the new Jew, as expected, does not recognize himself in the new European Muslim.

Whom does Shakespeare choose to send as the defender of the West from the non-European? Who might be the one who will save civilized, capitalist, law-abiding Venice, which believes in commerce and in an economic and political order? Shakespeare did not choose a fearless warrior for the mission, neither did he choose a fleet loaded with treasures. In fact, the ships in *The Merchant of Venice* are all lost at sea, in order to show the transience of the capitalist system and its inseparable vanity. Shakespeare chose a woman disguised as a man to come and save Venice from its own law—a law meant to protect the privileged, but suddenly being used against them. The woman appears as a male judge, presented as the law itself. Portia comes to save a member of the elite from Shylock's claws. He, on the other hand, demands equality before the law and revenge for the inequality and humiliation imposed on him merely for being a Jew.

The demand to be equal before the law is the revenge itself, because true equality is a death sentence to the privileged. Therefore, the privileged always equate the demand for equality with pure violence.

In her appearance as a male judge Portia injects divine law into state law. Ever since Antigone, and even before, women appear in Western culture as keepers of the divine law. Antigone is not only connected to the divine law but also acts as its extension and thus cannot act differently. As we remember, she is willing to die for it rather than submit to the political law of the father. Even Lacan, who claimed that the woman does not exist, in his seminar 20 attributes to her the direct connection to the real (the mystical), which is beyond the law of the father, beyond language itself. According to this line of thought, only the woman can touch and link us to the Real, which is beyond language, to the source of universal divine law. State law is the particular political law of the father. And here Portia, unlike Antigone, uses divine law not in order to sabotage state law but in order to obliterate its enemy. She chose not to follow Antigone but to collaborate with the law of the father. She will wipe out the villain who dares to show fidelity to the law only in order to destroy it and hence destroy the language of the privileged class. Portia would not die for justice with her beloved in a dark cave. At the expense of non-European Shylock, she will end up living forever with her metrosexual beloved. They will live the happy ending of a European ideal: love will win in the end, and the odd creatures with the beards, like Shylock and Ahmad, will return to where they came from, or shave their beards, and take the burka off their daughters so that coveting sons can have their way with them and teach them the nature of European love.

In a brilliant tortuous move, Portia as a judge shows that Shylock's mere will to shed the blood of a Christian justifies not only dropping his civil claim but also depriving him of his property, his life, and his faith. Demonstrating Christian grace, she spares his life. His daughter's conversion to the religion of the victors and her opting for progress also help to keep him alive. His tender daughter will not continue the covenant (of circumcision) manifest in the body of the Jew (or the Muslim). All he has to do to avoid execution is convert to Christianity, and thus he will live as one of us, in the universal body of progress—forever different.

As an antithesis of Portia, Antigone is willing to die to maintain the divine law of absolute equality among all human beings—equality that transcends the particular and the politics of difference. Thus she acts against the head sovereign, King Creon, who represents the state law—the sovereign who distinguishes between enemy and friend, between one brother and another. In contrast to her, Portia decides to present a model of an opportunistic or practical woman. As a woman, she knows that she is linked to the divine law and that she represents it, but instead of executing it against Creon and the state, she uses it to freeze the state law for the benefit of the rulers of the state itself. She executes the divine law only against the enemies of the state and applies grace when it comes to the class of the rulers, against the justice of those deprived of rights. In *The Merchant of Venice* the Christian divine law, which is supposed to be universal, cynically turns into the law of the state of emergency of secular democracy—a law that appears as divine intervention against everyone and everything non-European when needed.

Shakespeare realized that the woman had to meet three necessary conditions: 1. she had to be as much of a woman as possible; 2. she had to act and speak as a man, and thus by impersonating a man she would become a man; and 3. she had to act relentlessly against the non-European, that is she would not appear as a moderating force between the virtues of justice and grace, but rather as an intensifying force of the virtue of Christian grace, which would become the source of merciless cruelty toward the non-European. While in the Jewish Kabbalah of spheres it is believed that evil is a consequence of the excessive virtue of justice, in our model Christian grace materializes as merciless cruelty toward the non-European enemy.

Shylock identifies the root of the problem from the very beginning, and thus his two actions argue with the ruling European Christianity and of course with Pauline theology as well, even if unconsciously. Shylock demands the pound of flesh to be cut off nearest the heart. What does that act hint at? It hints against Paul, who contended that the bodily circumcision is a mere metaphor and that the real circumcision is in the heart: a spiritual practice, not a physical one. According to Paul, in spirit we are all equal before God, as written in the Epistle to the Galatians: "There is neither Jew nor Greek, there is neither bond nor free, there is neither male nor female."[1] Shylock's action is to bring the metaphor of the "circumcision which is in the heart" back to the concreteness of the body; he wants to circumcise the Christian's heart to remind him of the body that separates them. Shylock's well-known monologue, which supposedly presents itself as a repetition of the Pauline text stating that there is no difference between human beings, is in fact about the inability of the text about equality to subsist. The text sabotages itself, as Pauline universalism is impossible without profound understanding of identity politics. Shylock understands that the race of the masters and he himself do not feel pain in the same manner. They are not cold in the same manner, and they are not wounded in the same manner. As, during a symposium, a famous actor once told me, "all human beings urinate in the same manner,"

---

1. Galatians 3:28 (King James Bible).

and from the audience a man from Africa shouted, "you pee vitamins while I pee blood." Shylock understands that, and so, in order to save the text about equality from itself and enable it to have a space for subsistence, he chooses the way of terrorism and revenge, mainly in order to expose the structural lie of European equality.

And so I return to that shocking scene where Shylock picks up his skullcap from the floor and places it back on his head, a look of despair and revenge on his face. Shylock is no longer only a Jew. Having been baptized, he is a Christian, and so from now on the figure of Shylock is split. He demands revenge for the injustice imposed on him when he was baptized Christian. As a human being he demands universal justice, knowing his particular identity: "I am a Jew." And so he will fight for every outcast and against any injustice. But the very same act for which he takes his revenge on the Christian is the one that made him a Christian. Having been baptized, and good Christianity having penetrated his soul, he will imitate Portia, who has said, for the sake of her equal position, "I am a woman-man." Thus Shylock, for the sake of his equality, will say, "I am a European Jew." So stands Al Pacino and stares at the "decent people of Venice," and in my mind's eye I see the European and non-European Shylock directing his split gaze at me.

THE FREEDOM THEATRE IN THE JENIN REFUGEE CAMP

Facing Shylock's split gaze, I lower my eyes. The inability to contain the split makes me opt for purifying terrorism, but I realize that terrorism is in fact the representation of the weak pretending to be strong, the helpless fantasizing about gaining power. Terror attempts to ruin the figure of the collaborator, without contaminating the pure one that has split from him. But, in its quest for purity, terrorism, by not understanding that the split lies within itself, always ends up ruining itself.

Art can be another option. It fantasizes about the pure but almost-always-already ends up a collaborator.

Therefore, the artistic act as well should acknowledge the split gaze. For this reason I have been experimenting with militant art from a place of abandoning power, of abandoning victorious ideologies. One can choose to identify with weakness in an attempt to act from within the heart of weakness, not as a victim but as a warrior. Out of the presentation of the place, from the place, for the place, which is hardly a place, we might be able to create a revolutionary place.

What one needs to understand is that art—perhaps distinct from culture—is not supposed to be welcoming, and creating bridges that span nations and cultures is not its job. Militant art is the art of the weak, the person who barely exists in the public sphere. The person whose density is hardly noticed in the political world, the one whose opinion is taken into account by no one. Militant art is the artist's ability to act from a condition of near total disappearance and to create unrivaled power from that position of weakness.

It is important to say here that not every instance of establishment art is wrong—establishment art has created wonderful things throughout history. Nevertheless, the greatest artists always knew how to breach their agreement with the devil at the right moment. If artists do not bow to the state they will be defeated by it. But those willing to take risks for the sake of art will be those who create the beginnings of a new art. For this reason I have followed my friend Juliano Mer Khamis to Jenin. At the Freedom Theatre in the Jenin Refugee Camp, where I am now working, I could understand the real power of Shylock for the first time. While in a new production Juliano and the actors are penetrating the magical world of *Alice in Wonderland*, I am experiencing the power of weakness and art's ability to state something new. Or, as my friend Hezi Leskali once wrote in his horribly simple poem, "Oh, Weakness."

BACK TO LYDDA

On that cursed day of destruction, Nur—one of the fifty children who left home in the morning and went back to heaps of rubble—lost his dog; it was shot. The look on his parents' eyes, seeing their son kneeling on the doorstep of his destroyed home, holding the body of his slain dog in his arms, was like Shylock's despondent look, staring at the people of Venice. The parents' gaze defies us and says: I am here for all eternity; we are Palestinians.

EXCESS: THE RING

Antigone's dream as reported by my daughter, after viewing *The Merchant of Venice*, in which she was astonished by the seeming excess of act 5, scene 1:

PORTIA: If you had known the virtue of the ring,
Or half her worthiness that gave the ring,
Or your own honour to contain the ring,
You would not then have parted with the ring.
—Shakespeare, *The Merchant of Venice*, act 5, scene 1

"I am presenting a work of art which is really important to me. Instead of admiring it, people are mocking it, or fail to understand it. I am really hurt, and so I send a group of supermodels to rob prestigious malls and steal high-quality fashion items. Among the girls there is one who doesn't look like the others, and though she is pretty she is really not a supermodel. Everyone likes her for her supernatural powers. Her boyfriend has some superpowers as well, but his dad is a real sorcerer, and they are scared of him. Meanwhile the police are chasing the supermodels, but the girl manages to escape. Her boyfriend gives her a ring, and she must hide it so that neither his dad nor the police catch her. She decides to swallow it, and then she grows a penis and she is becoming her own boyfriend. In order to get the ring back she has to urinate it out, but that really hurts. She and I woke up in the tomb from the pain; the ring is already out, for Life."

EPILOGUE: *"ONLY WHEN IT IS DARK ENOUGH . . . "*

Our right for self-defense does not give us the right to oppress others; occupation leads to foreign rule, which brings resistance, resistance leads to oppression, which brings terror and counterterror. Terror victims are usually innocent people. Maintenance of the occupied territories will make us a nation of murderers and victims. Let us get out of the occupied territories immediately!
—Paid ad by Matzpen, *Haaretz*, September 22, 1967,
shortly after the Six Day War

Today what remains of the Israeli Jewish left is marching deliriously in demonstration trails, trying to collect their shards, which are spread on the streets of Tel Aviv. After years of an unsuccessful attempt to be both Jewish and democratic, socialist and greedy, enlightened and racist, fighting whole-heartedly against the occupation and serving in a brutal occupying army, the Jewish left understands it has reached a dead end. For decades the Israeli Jewish left perceived themselves as the lords of the land, only to find themselves losing ground, with awe and despair in their eyes.

However, for the Zionist left, it is time for repentance. Only by becoming accountable to their role in fostering this racist monster can the Zionist left experience *tikkun* (self-repair).

It would be a repetition of the same if the left tries to reconstruct itself as pure when its foundation is always already contaminated. The result will look as ridiculous and ugly as contemporary Jaffa, where leftist Jewish Israeli planners give reverence to Arabic architecture while dispossessing the Arabs themselves.

For the first time in history what remains of the left is sharing a bit of the same destiny as persecuted Palestinian citizens of Israel. Alas, this creates an opening for Palestinians and Jews to collaborate in reconstructing a determined, militant left. This left can structure itself as a nonviolent resistance movement, sabotaging the legitimacy of the theocratic democracy of Israel. This multicultural, binational front will act with conviction, fidelity, and a reasonable measure of self-irony.

Forty-four years have passed since the publication of the mythological prophetic analysis ad by Matzpen. The genuine ones in the Zionist left now understand that it was them, not necessarily the right, who planted the seeds of racism in public discourse.

The abandonment of democracy for ethnic superiority is woven through the entire Israeli Jewish left ideology. This includes the role of the Supreme Court in legitimizing the Occupation, Ben-Gurion instituting military rule over Palestinians (despite being citizens of Israel), and, cruelly enough, it was immediately following the experience of the collective trauma of Nakba. And even the prestate foundation of the Jewish left advocated Hebrew-only labor.

Why bother intellectualizing whether a Jewish and democratic state is oxymoron or axiom? Reality teaches us that today those two values stand as rivals at high noon, and only one can survive the duel.

For those who choose the proper model of a democratic and egalitarian state, it is time to prepare for battle. The weekly demonstrations in Tel Aviv are, and always were, insufficient to ward off the evil. Darkness is breaking out; there is no mercy. Indeed, we are a negligible minority, but perhaps if we break the ethnic, gender, and class barriers and stand as one, Palestinians and Jews, we can become a powerful minority alongside the forces of democracy and justice throughout the world.

Maybe, along with the Tunisians, we can be a new generation who seek justice and pleasure in the Middle East, inshallah.

Martin Luther King Jr. once said, " Only when it is dark enough can you see the stars." Let us pray that the stars we see will not be the missiles over Tel Aviv, Beirut, and Gaza announcing with their shining tails the apocalyptic war bequeathed to us by the Israeli government. Let us hope that the stars are of grace and justice. Stars that can open the gates to our mutual Middle East, for life.

Jenin in Wonderland

In Memory of Juliano Mer Khamis.

If I had any doubts left about joining the Freedom Theatre established by Juliano Mer Khamis with his friend Zakaria Zubeidi, the theatrical performance of *Alice in Wonderland*, directed by Juliano, made me understand that it was one of the best decisions of my life.

Having been part of the play's creative team, it would be inappropriate for me to write professionally about it, but I must say that I am truly proud to take part in such an exciting, subversive, vivacious, and dynamic project, orchestrated by Mer Khamis. The acting is superb, and the play includes texts that are simultaneously feminist, radical, and funny. The entire play is woven through with circus tricks and *comedia dell'arte*.

The audience included children from local schools alongside older Palestinians who wanted to enjoy a matinee. Journalist Gideon Levy was also in the audience, having come to test the mood in Jenin following the revolutions of Egypt and Tunisia.

April 5, 2011. Just before this book was sent to print, my dearest friend and true comrade, Juliano Mer Khamis, was murdered outside the Freedom Theatre in the Jenin refugee camp. Shortly before his tragic death, I wrote an optimistic text in adoration of his amazing work and his lust for life, art, and freedom. I would like to end this book with this text in memory of Juliano.

As soon as the curtain came up, the audience was enthralled by the play, which had the quality of a large-scale international production. Half-human creatures hanging from the rafters, a revolving stage, sensual music accompanying a strict tango, wonderful costumes, a world full of risk controlled by the iron hand of the Red Queen, played by the amazing Mariam Abu-Khalid.

Batul plays Alice most gracefully, hovering like Peter Pan between land and sky due to the somewhat malicious plot of the devious cat. Oh, wonderland is such a world of strangeness and danger! Yet Alice realizes that the other world, which purports to be real, is one where an attempt is being made to force her into marriage with the neighborhood nerd.

In order for her to be able to say "I don't" to her fiancé, she will have to go through all of the experiences—from the seductive cat to the Mad Hatter, who walks around with a swing of his hips while putting together his famous, rule-breaking tea party. Thus she challenges the tradition that robbed her of freedom of choice. This entire extravaganza takes place nowhere other than in the very heart of the Jenin refugee camp.

Right now this seems to me to be a symbolic preparation for Jenin's revolution because, just as Mustafa and some of the actors told me, the anticolonialist revolution in the Arab world must first go through the decolonization of the orientalist self-image of the Arabs themselves.

I asked one of the actors (who plays a particularly colorful and amusing role) which would be better: weapons or the theater? He smiled sadly and replied: "Five bullets were removed from my body; one is still in there. My sister was killed when the Occupation army came to catch me in my home, and the feelings of guilt and revenge are devouring my soul. Right now I believe in the theater, because it helps me learn to grieve and forgive perhaps even the soldiers who shot my sister, perhaps even myself, and to heal those wounds in my soul that are still open."

"Theater taught me that art could be part of the real struggle against the occupation," he told me. "But we don't have to be naive. If the cultural intifada does not work, if the Occupation won't shatter under its own evil . . . " He did not complete his sentence. He once told me, "I will always be a soldier in the liberation army, if necessary. But I will always prefer being an actor and liberation artist to being a liberation fighter."

Perhaps one of the most fascinating aspects of Juliano's story is that one can attend two plays that he directed, both in Arabic, just two days apart.

The first was *Alice* in Jenin, the second *Death and the Maiden* in Haifa. *Death and the Maiden* is political and realistic, and the cast includes some of the most preeminent Palestinian actors living in Israel. In the play, which deals with the posttraumatic Chilean society after fascism, Juliano directed performances of great power from Clara Khoury, Saleh Bakri, and Amer Hlehel.

At the same time, in Jenin, with novice actors from a refugee camp, he has created a celebration the likes of which the camp has never seen. These two plays position Juliano as a director who compromises nothing of his commitment to art. It is specifically by stretching the political and cultural boundaries of the Palestinian world, on both sides of the Wall, that he creates an artistic dialect that enriches Palestinian discourse. This may be a discourse with which we will smash the physical and mental wall that separates a Palestinian in Haifa from his brother in Jenin, a discourse that unites a culture so many wish to tear asunder.

When I asked Juliano what he had learned from the double experience inside the '48 borders and as a director of Palestinian theater, he replied, "the Palestinian audience is prepared to see, experience, and hear texts that are much more audacious than those which Palestinian creators are willing—or dare!—to put before it. But a new generation of creators has arisen; they don't self-censor, they don't reign themselves in, not with regard to the Occupation and not with regard to the internal, repressive tradition."

Perhaps the revolution is already here, only we haven't noticed that it has arrived. Long live the Freedom Theatre!

Translated by Dena Shunra

MY VERY SHORT BIBLIOGRAPHY

ONTOLOGY OF EXILE

Pledge to Our Language

Letter to Franz Rosenzweig

GERSHOM SCHOLEM

This country is a volcano! It harbors the language! One speaks here of many matters that may make us fail. More than of anything else we are concerned today about the Arab. But much more sinister than the Arab problem is another threat, a threat that the Zionist enterprise unavoidably has had to face: the "actualization" of Hebrew.

Must not the conundrum of a holy language break open again now, when the language is to be handed down to our children? Granted, one does not know how it will all turn out. Many believe that the language has been secularized, and the apocalyptic thorn has been pulled out. But this is not true at all. The secularization of the language is only a *façon de parler*, a phrase! It is impossible to empty out words that are filled to the breaking point with specific meanings lest it be done at the sacrifice of the language itself! The ghastly gibberish that we hear spoken in the streets is exactly the faceless lingo that "secularization" of the language will bring about; of this there cannot be any doubt! If we could transmit to our children that language which was transmitted to us, and if we could revitalize the language of the ancient books in this transitional generation, would it not then reveal itself to them? And then would not the religious power of this language perforce break open again one day? But which generation will bring this about? Is it not true that almost all of us live with this language over a volcano with the false security of the blind? Must not we or those who came after us stumble into the abyss when we fail to see again? And nobody can know whether the sacrifice of those who perish will suffice to close the hole and avoid the plunge into the abyss.

Those who initiated the rejuvenation of the language believed blindly and almost obstinately in its miraculous power. That was their good fortune! Nobody with clear foresight would have mustered the demonic courage to try to revitalize a language in a situation where only an Esperanto could have been created. They walked and still walk above this abyss, which remained hidden, and have transmitted this language to our youth together with all the ancient names and seals. Today it seems weird to us, and at times we are scared and frightened to hear a religious phrase quite out of place, in a totally unrelated context. Fraught with danger is the Hebrew language!

It cannot remain and will not remain in its present state! Since our children no longer have any other language, they and they alone will have to pay for this predicament, which we, none other, have imposed upon them without forethought and without question. If and when the language turns against its speakers, and this has occurred already on bitter and unforgettable occasions when the arrogance of this undertaking has become apparent, will we then have a youth that can exist and survive the revolution of a holy language?

Language is Name. In the name rests the power of language, its abyss is sealed with the name. We have no right to conjure up the old names day after day without calling forth their hidden power. They will appear, since we have called upon them, and undoubtedly they will appear with vehemence! We speak in rudiments, we speak a ghastly language: the names go in circles in our sentences, one plays with them in publications and newspapers. It is a lie that that is not important, even if a holy force may erupt suddenly out of the shame of our language! Names have their own life! If it were not so then woe to our children, who would be pushed into the void and emptiness without any hope!

Each word that is not newly created, but taken from the good old treasures, is ready to burst. A generation that accepts the most fruitful of our holy tradition, our language, cannot simply live without tradition, even if it might fervently wish to. The moment when the power stored in the language unfolds again, when the spoken word, the reality of our language, takes shape and reality again, that moment will place this holy tradition as a decisive token before our people. God will not remain silent in the language in which He has affirmed our life a thousand times and more.

Translated by Martin Goldner

We Lacked a Present

MAHMOUD DARWISH

let us go as we are:
a free lady
and a loyal friend
let us go together in two different paths
let us go as we are, united
and separated
nothing pains us
not the doves' divorce
nor the cold between the hands
or the wind around the church
all that bloomed of the almond trees was not enough
smile, then, so that the almonds would bloom more
between the butterflies of two dimples
soon we will have another present
If you look behind you will only see
an exile
behind you, you will see:
your bedroom
the yard's willows

Mahmoud Darwish, *Sarir al-Ghariba* (London: Riyad El-Rayyes, 1999).

the river behind the glass buildings
and the café of our trysts
all, all of them
preparing themselves to become an exile
let us be kind then
let us go as we are:
a free woman
and a friend who is loyal to her nays
our life was not enough to age together
to walk tired to the cinema
to witness the end of Athena's war with its neighbors
and see the peace banquet between Rome and Carthage
soon
for soon the birds will move from one epoch to another
as this path dust
which came in the form of meaning
and took us along in a passing trip
between two myths
so that it was inevitable
and we are inevitable
a stranger who sees himself
in the mirrors of his stranger?
"no, this is not my path to my body
there are no cultural solutions for existential worries
wherever you are
there, my sky is real
who am I to give you back the previous Sun and Moon
let us be kind . . .
let us go as we are:
a free lover
and her poet,
all that fell of December's snow
was not enough
smile, then, so that the snow may comb cotton on the Christian's
    prayers
soon we will return to our tomorrow, behind us
there, where we were young in the beginning of love
playing Romeo and Juliet
to learn Shakespear's lexicon . . .
the butterflies flew from sleep

like the phantom of a swift peace
crowning us two stars
and killing us in the struggle over the name
between two windows
lets us go, then
and let us be kind
let us go as we are:
a free woman
and a loyal friend
let us go as we are
we came with the wind from Babylon
and we march to Babylon . . .
my travel was not enough
so that, after me, the pine trees
would become an utterance for praising the southern place
here, we are kind
our wind is northern
and our songs southern
am I another you
and you another I?
"this is not my path to the land of my liberty
I will not be "I" twice
when a yesterday has replaced my tomorrow
and I have split into two women
I am neither eastern
nor am I western
nor am I an olive tree shading two Qur'anic verses
let us go, then
"there are no collective solutions for personal notions"
being together was not enough
for us to be together
we lacked a present to see
where we are
let us go as we are
a free woman
and an old friend
let us go together in two separate paths
let us go together
and let us be kind . . .

Translated by Sinan Antoon

An Opening for an Interview

AVOT YESHURUN

How does a man become Avot Yeshurun? The answer is—from the break-ings. I broke my mother and my father, I broke their home for them. I broke their good nights. I broke their holidays their shabbat days. I broke their self-worth. I broke their chance to speak. I broke their language. I despised their Yiddish, and their holy tongue I took for everyday use. I made them despise their life. I left the partnership. And when the dead-end moment descended upon them, I left them inside the dead end. So I'm here. In the land. I began to hear a voice coming out of me, being alone in the hut, on my iron bed, a voice calling me in my home-name, and the voice from me to me. My voice coming out of the brain and spreading all over the body, and the flesh shivers, a long while longer, then I began looking for a way to escape and to change the name and the last name. In time I succeeded in Hebraicizing the names.[1] It had the value of defense. In the presence of the voice, I awoke. I was afraid to fall asleep.

Translated by Lilach Lachman[2]

1. The original word (לשעבר) is made up and contains or is strikingly similar to words conveying at least four different meanings: "to break," "that, which was in the past," "to impregnate," and "to make Hebrew."
2. See Lilach Lachman, "'I manured the land with my mother's letters': Avot Yeshu-run and the Question of Avant-Garde," *Poetics Today* 21, no. 1 (Spring 2000): 61–93.

Who Is a Terrorist?

D.A.M.

Who is a terrorist? Am I a terrorist?
How can I be a terrorist when I'm living
in my own homeland?
Who is a terrorist? You are a terrorist!
You have taken everything I own
you have killed me and my ancestors
you want me to go to the law?
What for? You're the witness
the lawyer and the judge
you wish the worst for us
A minority to end up a majority
in the cemetery
Democracy? You remind me of the Nazis
because you've raped the Arab soul
and it became pregnant
giving birth to suicide bombers
and then you call us terrorists
you hit us and run
and complain when our children
throw stones
you ask: "Don't they have parents
to keep them at home?" Did you forget

that you've killed their parents?
And now that I'm hurting
you call me terrorist?
Who is a terrorist? Am I a terrorist? . . .
. . . Who is a terrorist? Am I a terrorist?
How can I be a terrorist when I'm living
in my own homeland?
Who is a terrorist? You are a terrorist!
You have taken everything I own
how do you stop being a terrorist?
You hit me on one cheek
and expect me to turn the other
so you can hit me again?
Tell me how you want me:
On my knees? With my hands tied?
On the ground smelling the rotting bodies?
Ruined houses? Lost families? Orphans?
Free with handcuffs on?
You kill and I dig the graves
you expect us to suffer quietly
so you can live in peace?
Our pain doesn't count
our blood is the blood of dogs
even less—because people care about dogs
our blood is cheaper
than the blood of dogs
No! My blood is not cheap
and I'll defend myself
even if you call me a terrorist
Who is a terrorist?
You are a terrorist!

A Man Goes

HAVIVA PEDAYA

To Subhi Hadidi

A man goes
from Damascus to Paris
whether he went through a tunnel
or cut through the air
I would not know
suddenly I saw the East in motion
quivering without a center
I covered the distance of years
from Jerusalem to Beer-sheva
and I did not prepare my things for an exile
like Ezekiel prostrate
in bed in Babylon
365 days
his beloved dead and Zion in exile
Abraham went up from Beer-sheva to Moriah
three days
binding and unbinding his son in his mind
three days butchering and weeping

Special thanks to Tzvi (Howard) Cohen for his inspiring suggestions for the English version.

we are still bound and unbound
who are they weeping and butchering
who are they laughing and butchering
how they all go
and there is already one who emerged
and came forward to the city of the dead
is that where we are headed
while I yearn to be dug out of the graves
for how long will there be nothing
but life racing backward
mask-face and my own face
if I were a man imprisoned in female form
if I were a prayer in tight pants
if the mountains of Jerusalem in the deserts of Beer-sheva
I have walked many a desert
without reaching the Moriah
now I feel in my homeland
for I suddenly perceive how fickle is this land
how disconcerting its tremor
and among my brothers I roam
some going from Iraq to America
some from Lebanon to Nicosia
some from Israel to Palestine
some from Israel to Israel to Israel to Israel
confronting absence for Israel is missing from Israel
you who wanted to be free in your land
prepare your things for an exile
there is no free man who has not been cast out
am I not a girl
am I not a woman
cast out from man
with no mother nor father
am I not a person
dispossessed of words
ousted but not in exile
yet in my own land my people
buried not in the desert
but in a redundancy become my coffin
exiled not in distance

but in this dust
conquering blood and tears
and choking
a man soars and soars
whether with weeping or with vodka
I wouldn't know
will it always be this way in the East
either spirit or soil
in the meantime I prefer to inhabit the word
another home does not yet exist
if it ever did
within my Hebrewness my blindness my arabesqueness
where it is merely music being played
my lips move
but my voice is not heard
the tongue in which the adults cursed and loved
from which I had been banished for salvation
"Hebrew speak Hebrew"
and still the East howls